AF576781

Critical Studies of the Asia-Pacific

Series Editor
Mark Beeson
University of Western Australia
Crawley, WA, Australia

Critical Studies of the Asia Pacific showcases new research and scholarship on what is arguably the most important region in the world in the twenty-first century. The rise of China and the continuing strategic importance of this dynamic economic area to the United States mean that the Asia-Pacific will remain crucially important to policymakers and scholars alike. The unifying theme of the series is a desire to publish the best theoretically-informed, original research on the region. Titles in the series cover the politics, economics and security of the region, as well as focusing on its institutional processes, individual countries, issues and leaders.

More information about this series at
http://www.palgrave.com/gp/series/14940

Obert Hodzi

The End of China's Non-Intervention Policy in Africa

palgrave
macmillan

Obert Hodzi
Department of World Cultures
University of Helsinki
Helsinki, Finland

Critical Studies of the Asia-Pacific
ISBN 978-3-319-97348-7 ISBN 978-3-319-97349-4 (eBook)
https://doi.org/10.1007/978-3-319-97349-4

Library of Congress Control Number: 2018954929

This Palgrave Macmillan imprint is published by the registered company Springer Nature Switzerland AG
The registered company address is: Gewerbestrasse 11, 6330 Cham, Switzerland

Contents

Abbreviations

AAA	Addis Ababa Agreement
ACD	Armed Conflict Dataset
AFISMA	The African-led International Support Mission to Mali
AQIM	Al-Qaida in the Islamic Maghreb
ATNM	*Alliance Touareg Niger-Mali* (Niger-Mali Tuareg Alliance)
AU	African Union
CCCC	China Communications Construction Company
CCTV	China Central Television
CMLN	*Comité Militaire de Libération Nationale* (Military Committee of National Liberation)
CNOOC	China National Offshore Oil Company
CNPC	China National Petroleum Company
CNRDR	*Comité national pour le redressement de la démocratie et la restauration de l'État* (National Committee for the Return of Democracy and the Restoration of the State)
COW	Correlates of War project
CPA	Comprehensive Peace Agreement
CPC	Communist Party of China
DPOC	Dar Petroleum Operating Company
ECOWAS	Economic Community of West African States
EIA	US Energy Information Administration
EU	European Union
FNLA	*Frente Nacional de Libertação de Angola* (National Front for the Liberation of Angola)
FOCAC	Forum on China-Africa Cooperation
FPLA	*Tuareg Front Populaire pour la Libération de l'Azaoud* (Tuareg Front for the Liberation of Azawad)

FRELIMO	*Frente de Libertação de Moçambique* (Mozambique Liberation Front)
GDP	Gross Domestic Product
GNI	Gross National Income
GNPOC	Greater Nile Petroleum Operating Company
ICJ	International Court of Justice
IGAD	Intergovernmental Authority on Development
IOs	International Organisations
MENA	Middle East and North Africa
MINUSMA	United Nations Multidimensional Integrated Stabilization Mission in Mali
MNLA	*Mouvement National pour la liberation de l'Azawad* (National Movement for the Liberation of Azawad)
MOFCOM	Ministry of Commerce (People's Republic of China)
MPA	*Mouvement Populaire de l'Azaouad* (Popular Movement of Azawad)
MPLA	*Movimento Popular de Libertação de Angola* (Popular Movement for the Liberation of Angola)
MUJAO	*Mouvement pour l'unicité et le jihad en Afrique de l'Ouest* (Movement for Oneness and Jihad in West Africa)
NAM	Non-Aligned Movement
NATO	North Atlantic Treaty Organisation
NCP	National Congress Party
NOC	Libyan National Oil Corporation
NOCs	National Oil Companies
NORINCO	China North Industries Corporation
NTC	National Transitional Council
ODI	Outward Foreign Investment
PDOC	Petrodar Operating Company
PLA	People's Liberation Army
PPP	Purchasing Power Parity
PRC	People's Republic of China
PRIO	Peace Research Institute Oslo
R2P	Responsibility to Protect
ROs	Regional Organisations
SAF	Sudan Armed Forces
SINOMACH	China National Machinery Industry Corporation
SPLA	Sudan People's Liberation Army
SPLM	Sudan People's Liberation Movement
SPLM/A	Sudan People's Liberation Movement/Army
SPLM/A-IO	Sudan People's Liberation Movement-in-Opposition
SPLMU	Sudan People's Liberation Movement United

TAZARA	Tanzania Zambia Railway Authority
UCDP	Uppsala Conflict Data Program
UDPM	*Union Démocratique du Peuple Malien* (Malian People's Democratic Union)
UN	United Nations
UNAMIS	United Nations Advance Mission in the Sudan
UNITA	*União Nacional para a Independência Total de Angola* (National Union for the Total Independence of Angola)
UNMISS	United Nations Mission in South Sudan
UNSC	United Nations Security Council
ZANLA	Zimbabwe African National Liberation Army
ZANU	Zimbabwe African National Union
ZAPU	Zimbabwe African People's Union
ZIPRA	Zimbabwe People's Revolutionary Army

List of Figures

List of Tables

CHAPTER 1

Rising Powers and Intervention in Foreign Intrastate Armed Conflicts

1.1 Introduction

How is China behaving as its relative economic power increases? Is it expanding its economic interests abroad? And is it increasing its intervention in foreign intrastate armed conflicts which threaten those interests? Conventional arguments in international relations (IR) suggest that generally as states' economic power rise they follow the same pattern of behaviour. "They expand. They send their soldiers, ships, and public and private agents abroad…, [and] they exert influence on foreigners in a variety of ways" (Mandelbaum 1988, p. 134). However, although in principle they follow the same pattern of behaviour, they express their expansionist projects in varied ways. "Some emerging powers in modern history have plundered other countries' resources through invasion, colonization, expansion, or even large-scale wars of aggression" (Zheng 2005, p. 20). Others are more covert, employing "non-threatening" strategies to take over sector by sector of another state without soldiers being involved until their economic and political interests prevail. China is a case in point. As put by Janice Gross Stein, "In America's backyard, in Africa, in the Gulf and on its southern and western peripheries, China is making deals for resources with no strings attached. Its overseas investments are growing as its trade surplus is mounting. And tens of thousands of Chinese aid workers and dam builders are found in virtually every corner of the globe—and all this without firing a shot" (2010, p. 12).

O. Hodzi, *The End of China's Non-Intervention Policy in Africa*,
Critical Studies of the Asia-Pacific,
https://doi.org/10.1007/978-3-319-97349-4_1

The overall common denominator between China and other non-Western rising powers such as Brazil and India is that expansion of their interests and foreign policy abroad is often preceded by high levels of domestic economic growth, which if sustained over a protracted period of time will result in rise of the state's relative economic power vis-à-vis other existing global powers. In turn, this enables increases in the rising powers' other material capabilities such as military, diplomatic and political, such that the combined growth of the economy and other material capabilities endows upon them "newly acquired power into greater authority in the global system to reshape the rules and institutions in accordance with their own interests"[1] and, more importantly, intervene in the internal affairs of other states in order to protect and safeguard their interests there. In March 2016, Wang Yi, China's minister of foreign affairs, captured the linkage between the rise in a state's relative economic power, expansion of its economic interests abroad and the need to protect those interests when he said:

> Like any major country that is growing, China's overseas interests are expanding. At present, there are 30,000 Chinese businesses all over the world and several million Chinese are working and living in all corners of the world…, China's non-financial outbound direct investment reached 118 billion dollars and the stock of China's overseas assets reached several trillion dollars. So, it has become a pressing task for China's diplomacy to better protect our ever-growing overseas interests.[2]

This is because "over the course of history, states that have experienced significant growth in their material resources have relatively soon redefined and expanded their political [economic and security] interests abroad" (Zakaria 1998, p. 3). And, in order to systematically give effect to their expansionist endeavours, they incrementally revise and expand their foreign policy within the constraints of their domestic and international capabilities.

It is therefore not automatic that once a state's relative material capabilities increase it can revise international rules and institutions to its taste—states do not rise and expand their interests abroad in a vacuum. Instead, they rise in an anarchic systemic order already dominated by other global powers; and how they express their emergent power is reliant not just on their relative capabilities but also on how other states, particularly existing global powers, perceive of, and respond to, their rise. For instance, "the growth of Athenian power led Sparta to conclude that there was no recourse but to fight,"[3] while the rise of expansionist Germany under the leadership of Adolf Hitler led to a global war. On the other hand, the rise of the United States at the twilight of Britain's imperial power was largely peaceful[4] because Britain, "while still enjoying preponderant strength, looked over the horizon..., [and] was able to successfully adapt its grand strategy to a changing distribution of power" (Kupchan 2012). But, in all this, the rising powers' upturn in the international system and their ability to withstand competition and pressure from existing global powers is dependent on their ability to sustain high levels of domestic economic growth; because upward mobility in the international system is not for states with low relative economic power.

An additional factor that determines how a rising power articulates its foreign behaviour as it expands abroad is political dynamics in countries that it expands into. By expanding its economic interests into a foreign country, a rising power effectively entangles itself with the political, social and economic dynamics of that particular country. Unlike the United States and West European powers, China and the other non-Western rising powers still do not give adequate consideration to internal dynamics in countries they expand into, particularly if those countries are considered to be of no global consequence, the majority of which are in Africa, where most lack essential elements of a state and can best be described as "quasi-states."[5] Typically, when rising powers expand their economic interests into such "quasi-states" their preoccupation is on warding off competition from other global and rising powers that have rival interests there, yet it is from the "quasi-states" themselves that major challenges to their foreign interests emanate from. The reason being that "since the end of the Cold War, weak and failing states have arguably become the single most important problem for international order" (Fukuyama 2004, p. 92).

Intrastate armed conflicts[6] are the dominant[7] challenge in some countries that rising powers expand their economic interests into. What makes the intrastate armed conflicts in those countries challenging for rising powers is that they pose "uncontemplated consequences." The consequences are uncontemplated because the conflicts are usually fought over issues local to the developing country and often have little to do with the rising power, or its interests in that country. Yet, the effects, albeit unintended by the warring parties, are indiscriminately felt by rising powers with interests there. Examples abound—in the armed conflict between the National Transitional Council (NTC) and Muammar Gaddafi's government in Libya, US$18–20 billion worth of investments owned by Chinese private and public enterprises were either destroyed or suspended. In Sudan, China invested approximately US$20 billion mostly in the oil industry before the country split after a protracted armed conflict. Two-thirds of its investments ended up in the new state of South Sudan, which in 2013 descended into a civil war resulting in major losses to Chinese companies.[8] Chinese nationals working abroad were also affected. For example, in 2011, the Chinese government evacuated more than 35,000 Chinese citizens working in Libya[9] due to the armed conflict. In Sudan,[10] Mali,[11] and the Central African Republic[12] Chinese workers were kidnapped or otherwise killed by rebels; and in 2014, Chinese companies had to evacuate Chinese nationals and scale down operations due to the armed conflict in South Sudan.[13]

The dilemma for rising powers, China in particular, is that the biggest concentration of energy and other strategic natural resources needed to sustain their domestic economic growth, which is critical to maintaining their relative economic power and global power status, lie in countries at risk of both political instability and intrastate armed conflicts. As noted by Michael Klare, the high concentration of energy resources in countries such as Iraq, Nigeria, South Sudan and Sudan means that access to such resources is "closely tied to political and socio-economic conditions within a relatively small group of countries"[14] at risk of instability and armed conflicts. Without the military power of the United States or socio-economic and political ties that Europe has with developing countries, especially in Africa due to their colonial heritage, non-Western rising powers are compelled to engage even more unstable countries like Libya and South Sudan for their raw material and energy needs, which plunges them into intrastate armed conflicts that they neither contemplated nor possess enough experience to handle.

What it means is that when the relative economic power of rising powers increases and they expand their economic interests abroad in search of markets and sources of raw materials to keep their economies growing, they become even more dependent on foreign sources of raw materials for their economic growth, thus compelling them to align access to such primary commodities with their national interest and security considerations.[15] How then do they respond to foreign intrastate armed conflicts that threaten those economic interests? In other words, do they increase their intervention in foreign intrastate armed conflicts as their interests expand abroad? What form do their interventions in those intrastate armed conflicts take, and are the methods of their intervention evolving?

1.2 Making Sense of the Intervention Behaviour of Rising Powers

Based on the above questions, and specifically focused on examining the intervention behaviour of China in intrastate armed conflicts in three African countries—Libya, Mali and South Sudan—the nature of this book's focus of enquiry is such that it requires both a theoretical and an empirical analysis of external interventions in intrastate armed conflicts. What makes the enquiry significant is that there is a simultaneous increase in intrastate armed conflicts in resource-rich countries in Africa, and an unprecedented expansion of rising powers such as China into Africa as they search for strategic primary commodities and markets to maintain their domestic economic growth and relative economic power. As discussed in Chap. 2 below, the current discourse on how these rising powers respond to intrastate armed conflicts in countries they expand their interests into is still limited. Part of the reason is that IR scholars and policymakers are predominantly fixated on geostrategic and geoeconomic competition among rising powers and/or dominant global powers rather than political and security dynamics in developing countries and how they affect the external behaviour of rising powers. In addition, dominant discourses in IR still portray intervention as a foreign policy instrument of major global powers, not rising powers. The result is a limited scope in understanding of the intervention behaviour of rising powers in intrastate armed conflicts in developing countries and how such a phenomenon is transforming the conceptual understanding of intervention in international politics.

Accordingly, focused on exploring the intervention behaviour of rising powers, particularly China's in foreign intrastate armed conflicts within the domain of foreign policy theory, this book explores the paradox highlighted above—that rising powers need primary commodities to sustain their domestic economic growth in order to maintain their relative economic power, but those primary commodities are concentrated in countries with high probabilities of intrastate armed conflicts; so, for rising powers such as China that have a stated general policy of non-intervention in the internal affairs of their trading partners, how do they balance observance to their non-intervention principle and protection of their interests in cases of intrastate armed conflicts in a foreign country, which under normal circumstances require some degree of intervention in that country's internal affairs?

In probing the linkage between a state's rise in relative economic power, expansion of economic interests abroad and consequent external intervention behaviour where those interests are threatened, the theoretical argument advanced here is that a state's foreign policy behaviour is not just determined by its position in the international system. Employing the neoclassical realist argument, the study explores whether rising powers increase their external intervention behaviour when their relative economic power increases, and when their perception of threat to their interests abroad evolves. Since the "change in threat perception" is a unit-level variable, the starting point is assessing the impact of the increase in China's relative economic power on its external intervention behaviour. To some extent, this is a complex, but not entirely novel, question—yet with the rise and decline of global powers it remains puzzling and relevant to understanding the evolutionary process of contemporary rising powers' external intervention behaviour in areas beyond their geographical regions and how that is challenging conventional understandings of intervention and global governance in the twenty-first century. Besides, although states may behave similarly in rising from obscurity to global significance, they rise in different domestic and international contexts[16] and therefore respond differently to both local and global issues—making their succeeding foreign behaviour peculiar.

The peculiarity of each rising power's foreign policy behaviour can by no means be fully understood from a theoretical perspective without concomitant empirical assessment of the behaviour in question. Departing from the tendency to focus on geopolitical and geoeconomic rivalry among rising powers and dominant global powers with "token" consideration to the colossal implications of intrastate armed conflicts in developing countries, this book empirically concentrates on China's intervention behaviour in intrastate armed conflicts that started between 2011 and 2013 in Libya (2011), Mali (2012) and South Sudan (2013). The main question that is explored is how and why increases in China's relative economic power, and changes in its perception of foreign intrastate armed conflicts as threats to its economic interests abroad, influenced its intervention in the intrastate armed conflicts in Libya, Mali and South Sudan over time. In pursuing that line of enquiry, this book seeks to empirically explain the temporal variance in China's intervention behaviour in the three intrastate armed conflicts, with the aim of deciphering emerging trends and patterns of China's intervention in intrastate armed conflicts in Africa.

1.3 Why China?

China is not the only rising power with expanding economic interests across the globe. South Africa, Brazil, India and Russia have also been classified as rising powers or more appropriately emerging economies due to their domestic economic growth and expanding global influence. This book, however, gives primary focus to China because it is undoubtedly the biggest rising power of the twenty-first century.[17] Powered by extraordinary economic growth and a demand for natural resources that outstrips its domestic supply capacity, China has been compelled to expand outward in search of new markets, primary commodities and energy resources to fuel its domestic economic growth. As an example, based on annual gross domestic product growth in 2007, China's economy grew by approximately 14%, India 10%, Russia 8%, Brazil 6% while South Africa managed 5%, compared to the United States and Germany which expanded by an average 3% and 4% respectively. With the global economic slowdown in 2014, India and China grew their GDP by 7.4%; Brazil 0.1%, South Africa 1.5%, Russia 0.6%, the United States 2.4% and Germany 1.6%.[18] The effect is that "economic power is shifting at a rapid pace and the next half-century will see major changes in the relative size and rankings of the world economies... [Notably] China will pass the USA in total gross domestic product (GDP) measured in terms of purchasing power parity (PPP) terms by 2016, and within a decade thereafter in dollar terms at market rates" (Armijo and Roberts 2014, p. 503, 505). Accordingly, there is a redistribution of economic power in the international system, which effectively can undermine the current liberal international order.[19]

Unlike in other rising powers, the extraordinary economic growth in China has been accompanied by an increase in high-technology exports,[20] and a global expansion of China's economic interests and activities. As shown in Fig. 1.1,[21] China overtook the United States and Germany to become the major exporter of high-technology products since 2004.

As a result, China dominates the global manufacturing sector, exporting its manufactured products across the world and at the same time consuming roughly a third of global supply of iron, steel and coal among other raw materials.[22] "In just over a decade, China has risen from relative insignificance to pole position in underwriting numerous resource-related transactions across the globe" (Moyo 2012, p. 1). Apart from being the largest consumer of primary commodities such as minerals, metal ore, fossil fuels and biomass, its domestic consumption levels are now four times

Fig. 1.1 China's high-technology exports, 2000–2012

larger than that of the United States.[23] Furthermore, in 2010, China overtook the United States to become Africa's largest trading partner, that is, besides being the largest trading partner of the majority of Asian and Latin America countries including India and Brazil. China is now also the European Union's second largest trading partner behind the United States, with trade between Europe and China exceeding €1 billion a day.[24]

Based on annual GDP growth, high-technology exports and consumption of primary commodities, it is projected that the "People's Republic of China will overtake the USA as the world's largest economic power" (Dadush 2014, p. 13). Although it does not yet possess military capabilities comparable to that of the United States,[25] the compounded effect of its high domestic economic growth and technological advances gives it extensive global influence in world politics global trade over other states, particularly in the Global South. As an example, China is now one of the major sources of development finance to other developing countries in the Global South, representing "a constellation of interests that are not only reconfiguring power relations between the North-South but also reflecting a level of South-South development engagements that are challenging the existing orthodoxy of the 'Washington Consensus'" (Naidu et al. 2009, p. 1). Furthermore, as China "accomplishes more in her domestic economic reform, the international community and many Third World countries share a common expectation that China should assume more international responsibilities for the world economy and security" (Yan 2006, p. 7). Indeed, the rapid rise in the economic power of China and the other rising powers is "causing a 'wind down' of *Pax-Americana*—the period of unrivalled US primacy since 1945" (Armijo and Roberts 2014, p. 503). Thus, "economic might has supplanted military strength as the primary currency of national power and prestige" (Schweller 1999, p. 47).

In addition, China's resultant global commodity campaign has been breath-taking. "In just over a decade China has risen from relative insignificance to pole position in underwriting numerous resource-related transactions across the globe" (Moyo 2012, p. 1). Combined with its official policy of non-intervention in the internal affairs of other countries, the implication of China's insatiable demand for natural resources meant that it engaged resource-rich countries such as Sudan, South Sudan, Mali and Libya that are susceptible to intrastate armed conflicts and political instability, effectively bringing to itself "high geopolitical risks, vulnerabilities and uncertainties" (Pang 2009, p. 247).

Although at first intrastate armed conflicts did not affect China's interests directly, over the past decade, Chinese workers have been targeted while Chinese-operated oil facilities in Sudan and South Sudan have been attacked by rebels, putting China's adherence to its principle of non-intervention in the internal affairs of other states to the test. With respect for state sovereignty and non-intervention in the domestic affairs of its African partners forming the core of China-Africa engagement, China is caught between the need to maintain access to strategic resources and protecting its economic interests abroad, both of which require some degree of intervention. This situation makes China a compelling study in assessing whether rising global powers expand and revise their intervention behaviour in developing countries when their economic interests there are threatened.

Notably, with the rise of its relative economic power leading to expansion of its economic interests overseas, China has begun to increasingly express interest in peace and security cooperation with the African Union, pledging to support efforts towards conflict resolution and management in Africa, particularly where intrastate state armed conflicts on the continent directly threaten its interests. There have, however, been some perceivable inconsistences in implementation of its non-intervention principle.[26] Its intervention in African intrastate armed conflicts seems to vary with each country. For example, in 2013, Beijing sent its special envoy for African Affairs, Ambassador Zhong Jianhua, to mediate between the warring parties in the South Sudanese civil war,[27] yet it did not do the same for the conflict in the Central African Republic despite the conflicts emerging at the same time. In the Libyan conflict, China vehemently argued that "there must be no attempt at regime change or involvement in civil war by any party under the guise of protecting civilians,"[28] but it was largely supportive of the French military intervention in Mali. These contradictory policies make a case for a systematic analysis of what really explains this variation in China's intervention behaviour regarding African intrastate armed conflicts.

On a broader scale, dominant IR theories presuppose that intervention is a preserve of great powers (Tillema 1989; Steiner 2004, p. 16). Accordingly, studies on intervention in foreign intrastate armed conflicts tend to exclude rising global powers such as China. Where China has been specifically included in such research, the focus has mainly been on its role in peacekeeping operations or in providing "no-strings" attached aid to states in conflict. By including China as a non-Western rising global power in the broader "intervention in foreign intrastate conflicts" discourse, this book deepens the current research agenda by expanding the discourse on China's evolving foreign policy and behaviour in Africa. It also extends the current research on China-Africa relations beyond trade and economics to security and intervention. Through a systematic analysis of China's economic, diplomatic, political and multilateral intervention strategies, the book probes peculiarities of China's intervention strategies in African conflicts, questioning whether the strategies are influenced first by an increase in its relative economic power, and then secondly by its changing perception of threats to its interests abroad. The study therefore contributes to the growing research on China's "non-intervention" practice by assessing its intervention strategies in African countries—an area that is still developing in scholarly and policy-oriented research.

More importantly, an analysis of China's intervention behaviour in African intrastate armed conflicts is critical to an understanding of its impact on global governance and that of other rising powers in general. Considering the combined shift in economic and political power from the West to the rest as noted by Fareed Zakaria, how China takes on the responsibility towards international peace and security commensurate with its rising global power status is of interest not just to the United States, but also to the African Union and African countries engaging with China. This analysis is particularly compelling for the African Union as it transitions from non-intervention in the internal affairs of its member states to a more proactive non-indifference approach that demands intervention in cases of war crimes, crimes against humanity, genocide and unconstitutional military takeover of governments in line with international norms leaning towards responsible sovereignty and the Responsibility to Protect (R2P). China's intervention in African intrastate armed conflicts is therefore critical to the emerging global peace and security order.

1.4 Methodology

As stated above, this study employs the neoclassical realist theoretical framework to explore how increases in China's relative economic power vis-à-vis other states and changes in perception of threat to its interests abroad combine to explain China's intervention behaviour in intrastate armed conflicts in Libya, Mali and South Sudan. What is distinct about neoclassical realism is that "it carries with it a distinct methodological preference for theoretically informed narratives ... that trace the ways different factors combine to yield particular foreign policies" (Rose 1998, p. 153). In this book, the theoretically based narrative is combined with historical analysis of China's rise in the international system, the evolving of its perception of threats to interests abroad and their consequential impact on its intervention behaviour.

Neoclassical realism seems to proffer a plausible explanatory framework. In general terms, it is a theory of foreign policy rather than international outcomes, which explains variations in foreign policies and external behaviour of states over time.[29] It incorporates "the complex model of state-society relations implicit in classical realism, while building upon neorealism's insights about constraints of anarchy and the relative distribution of material power" (Taliaferro 2006, p. 470). Systemic and unit-level variables are therefore combined to explain the foreign policy and behaviour of individual states. As put by Gideon Rose, for those that adhere to neoclassical realism,

> The scope and ambition of a country's foreign policy is driven first and foremost by its place in the international system and specifically by its relative material capabilities. This is why they are realist. They argue further, however, that the impact of such power capabilities on foreign policy is indirect and complex, because systemic pressures must be translated through intervening variables at unit level. This is why they are neoclassical. (Rose 1998, p. 146)

Based on Gideon Rose's explanation of neoclassical realism, there are three distinct propositions that neoclassical realists make. These are: (1) an increase in relative material power of a state will lead to a corresponding expansion of the scope and ambition of its foreign policy activity; the reverse is also true, a decrease in a state's relative material power will result in a corresponding contraction of its foreign policy activity; (2) the process in proposition 1 is not gradual or uniform because it does not solely depend "on objective material trends but also on how political decision-makers subjectively perceive them" and (3) countries with weak states take longer to translate the increase in their relative material power into expanded foreign policy activity (Rose 1998, p. 167).

Propositions 1 and 2 summarise the neoclassical realist causal logic which provides an alternative explanation of states' foreign policy based on interaction between systemic and domestic-level factors. This makes neoclassical realism distinct from structural realists who give primacy to structural factors as the main determiners of international outcomes. The neoclassical realist causal logic also places domestic-level factors as intervening variables between the relative distribution of power among states (independent variable) and foreign policy behaviour (dependent variable). The focus is on how systemic and domestic factors interact with one another to explain a state's foreign policy. To do that, neoclassical realists emphasise two domestic variables—decision-makers' perceptions of the distribution of power, and domestic state structure—suggesting that both individual decision-makers and domestic politics matter in understanding the foreign policy of a state.[30]

The resultant methodology is therefore a qualitative theoretically based narrative and historical analysis which supposes a dual-causal focus on both systemic and domestic-level factors and how they combine to explain China's intervention behaviour in African intrastate armed conflicts. Furthermore, the book entails an interpretation of critical historical events and processes relating to China's relative economic power in the international system and articulation and understanding of its non-intervention behaviour over time—this is principally done in Chap. 3. A historical analysis of China's relations with Libya, Mali and South Sudan since the countries' independence is also conducted in a way that leads to an understanding of various intervention methods employed by China in the three African countries' intrastate armed conflicts, further enabling an assessment of trends and patterns of China's intervention in African intrastate armed conflicts.

The use of the theoretically based historical narrative and analysis entails the use of case studies to effectively trace how an increase in relative economic power translated through perception of threat to interests abroad combines to explain China's intervention behaviour in Libya, Mali and South Sudan. Not only is the case study method suitable for a theoretically based historical narrative and historical analysis method, it is also suitable for studies that employ the neoclassical realist theoretical framework. For neoclassical realism often "employs the case-study method to test general theories, explain cases and generate hypothesis ... [In order to] address important questions about foreign policy and national behaviour, and ... produce a body of cumulative knowledge" (Elman and Elman 2003, p. 317). As this study is aimed at explaining China's intervention in African intrastate armed conflicts, case studies are the best suited method in order to adequately address the matter and assess the emerging trends and patterns of China's intervention behaviour in African armed conflicts.

With a large number of intrastate armed conflicts across the African continent, the main challenges that confront studies of external intervention in intrastate armed conflicts include the overwhelming need for an all-encompassing analysis of every possible conflict. The reasoning is often that the more the case studies, then the better it is to generalise the findings; hence, multiple cases can potentially enhance the scope of a study. Although it is plausible to use multiple case studies, taking into consideration time and resource constraints, a choice has to be made between scope and depth. Besides time and resource limitations, this study opted for only three cases in order to be able to analyse the cases in depth in a manner that would enable production of comprehensive "cumulative knowledge." The study therefore employs the method of structured, focused comparison. The method is structured in that a general set of questions are asked of each case study in order to standardise the collected data, making a systematic comparison and cumulation of the case study findings possible; it is also focused because it does not deal with every random aspect of the case study; instead, it centres on a specific aspect of the case being studied.[31] Overall, the method of structured, focused comparison employs "a well-defined set of theoretical questions or propositions to structure an empirical inquiry on a particular analytically defined aspect of a set of events" (Levy 2008, p. 2), a method which provides a systematic comparison conducive for generating empirical generalisation and testing hypotheses.[32]

Intervention in foreign intrastate armed conflicts can be attributed to multiple causalities, which place considerable pressure on data collection and selection of cases to be studied in order to come up with plausible explanations of why states intervene in some intrastate armed conflicts, and also to help explain temporal variation in external intervention behaviour. As observed by James Rosenau, single case studies or a collection of multiple case studies may be instructive, making interesting contributions to knowledge,[33] but without systematic comparison and "scientific consciousness" they do not add value to hypothesis testing and theory development.[34] This is where the use of the method of structured, focused comparison becomes compelling because it specifically "seeks to investigate causality and attempts to isolate those factors that cause (independent variable) a particular outcome or phenomenon (dependent variable)" (Smith-Hoehn 2010, p. 46). In addition, the comparative method also entails two predispositions. The first predisposition has a bias towards qualitative analysis and tends to look at cases as wholes, comparing one with the other. Secondly, premised on the assumption that history matters, the method values interpretation and context—showing "how historical processes and practices, as well as long-established institutional arrangements, impact and shape the contemporary environment in which decisions are made, events unfold, and struggles for power occur ... demonstrating a meaningful continuity between the past and the present" (Lim 2016, p. 14). This method therefore enables "stating lessons in a systematic and differentiated way from a broader range of experience that deliberately draws upon a variety of historical cases" (George 1979, pp. 42–43). Notably, there are four purposes of comparing cases. Cases can be compared in order to control, to understand, to explain or to predict. The focus of this study is to explain China's intervention behaviour in African intrastate armed conflicts; therefore, the purpose of the comparison of cases is to "build theoretical generalisations by collecting case-based knowledge ... [because] each case or each small-n comparison gives the comparatist another piece to work into a larger puzzle" (Smith-Hoehn 2010, p. 47). In this study, the larger puzzle is to explain why China's interventions in African intrastate armed conflicts vary over time.

While acknowledging that "African conflicts are widely varied ... [and that] case studies do not fit into tidy packages that present themselves for direct comparison" (Boulden 2013, p. 16), the study notes that the comparative method is "uniquely suited for analysing *complex causality*, i.e. the fact that a particular social phenomenon is probably affected by several economic, political, cultural and/or socio-economic factors" (Smith-Hoehn 2010, p. 43). The set of events that will be analysed are intrastate armed conflicts in Libya, Mali and South Sudan. Specifically, the study analyses the Libyan armed conflict between the armed opposition groups later organised under the NTC and Muammar Gaddafi's government. The period under study is February 2011, when the conflict began, until October 2011, when Muammar Gaddafi was captured and killed, signalling the end of the armed conflict between the two sides. For Mali, the study focuses on the 2012 Tuareg rebellion and the Malian army's 2012 coup d'état. The Tuareg rebellion began in January 2012, and the coup took place in March 2012 resulting in the establishment of a government of national unity in August 2012. Third, the study analyses the intrastate armed conflict between rebels led by Riek Machar and the government of President Salva Kiir that began in December 2013 in South Sudan.

By focusing on the above specific cases, the study seeks to explain China's varied intervention in these three different intrastate armed conflicts, making it possible to explore trends and patterns of China's intervention behaviour in African civil wars, thus enabling the yielding of "useful generic knowledge"[35] about China's intervention behaviour. The "systematic comparison and cumulating of the cases"[36] therefore make it possible to hypothesise, make theoretical generalisations and produce generic knowledge relating to external intervention in foreign intrastate armed conflicts. This is something that could be replicated and tested in other similar studies, particularly those relating to intervention in foreign intrastate armed conflicts by rising global powers.

1.4.1 Selection of Intrastate Armed Conflict Cases for Study

The Uppsala/PRIO conflict database categorises conflicts as minor or major wars depending on the number of battle-related deaths. A minor war is where there are "between 25 and 999 battle-related deaths in a given year" while "at least 1,000 battle-related deaths in a given year" are designated as major war (Themnér 2013, p. 8). According to the Uppsala/PRIO conflict database, 25 countries in Africa experienced minor and/or major war between the year 2000 and 2013. Out of the 25 countries, 12 experienced civil war. The table below shows the number of conflicts that were experienced in Africa between 2000 and 2013.

As shown in Fig. 1.2, the peak of internal armed conflicts in Africa was reached in the year 2001, when 16 minor wars and four intrastate armed

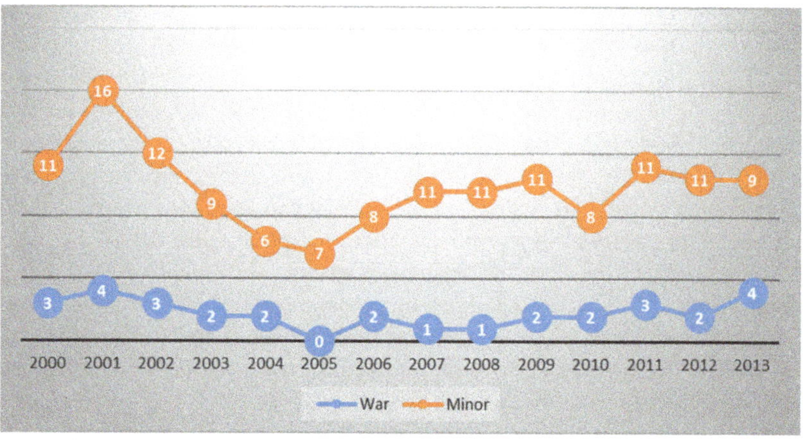

Fig. 1.2 Intrastate armed conflicts in Africa, 2000–2013

conflicts[37] were recorded. In 2005 there were no recorded civil wars, while conflicts surged in 2006 and reached the level of four intrastate armed conflicts in 2013. The highest number of civil wars were recorded in Sudan, Somalia and the Democratic Republic of Congo. Nevertheless, the armed conflicts in all three countries have been protracted; that is, they have occurred over extended periods of time, sometimes stretching over several decades and consist of "several crisis episodes of varying frequency and intensity."[38] Because of that fact, the profile, causes and actors involved in the conflicts vary over time, making it difficult to determine the duration of each episode of the conflict. This situation presents significant challenges to a study that seeks to analyse external intervention in intrastate armed conflicts over a specific period of time. The intrastate armed conflicts in Somalia, Sudan and the Democratic Republic of Congo have been ongoing for decades; hence they are excluded from this study because they fall outside of the period under study.

Furthermore, intrastate armed conflicts that occurred between 2000 and 2005 were not included in the study because prior to 2005, the R2P principle had not been adopted by the United Nations General Assembly as an international norm. The significance of R2P to this study is that it placed a general responsibility on states to protect their populations from genocide, war crimes and crimes against humanity, but were they fail to discharge that duty, it authorised the international community to take collective action through the

United Nations Security Council (UNSC). Since then the principle has been evoked in Cote d'Ivoire and Libya. As a member of the UNSC, China's intervention behaviour in foreign intrastate armed conflicts is therefore affected; hence it is a major factor in that it provided legitimation and justification for members of the international community to intervene in order to protect civilians in cases where their government cannot protect them from genocide, crimes against humanity or war crimes. Although China has maintained its non-interference principle, the adoption and implementation of R2P puts this principle to the test and has had an effect on its intervention behaviour. While this study does not focus on the impact of R2P on China's external intervention behaviour, it nevertheless recognises that R2P was a significant milestone in global perceptions of foreign intervention in other states' intrastate armed conflicts. Thus, the adoption of R2P at the 2005 United Nations World Summit marked the beginning of a new external intervention dispensation in global governance.

After excluding intrastate armed conflicts that occurred before adoption of R2P in 2005, Chad, Sudan, South Sudan and Libya were the only countries that had civil wars between 2005 and 2013. Of these four countries, Chad and Sudan are excluded from the study because, like the conflicts in the Democratic Republic of Congo and Somalia, they are protracted conflicts that have been ongoing since 1966 and 1971, respectively, and could potentially skew the results. Another reason for their exclusion is that the conflicts in Chad and Sudan tended to be state-sponsored massacres of civilians who were represented by militia groups fighting to protect minority rights rather than seize political power. In Sudan, the Sudan Liberation Movement and Justice and Equality Movement rebel groups fought against the government of Sudan and the Janjaweed, s government of Sudan-sponsored militia group. The main reason for the conflict was oppression of Darfur's non-Arab population. Hence, they sought recognition and equal rights for the Darfurians rather than to usurp political power from the Khartoum government. Meanwhile, the armed conflict in Chad lasted for only a month. In April 2006, rebels seeking to oust the government of President Idris Deby fought government forces. By May 2006, the conflict had subsided and President Deby was declared winner of a presidential election. The armed conflict in Chad was therefore too short to assess China's intervention.

In the end, two countries remained as suitable case studies, that is, Libya and South Sudan whose intrastate armed conflicts began in 2011 and 2013 respectively. However, selected cases should be able to provide "the kind of control and variation required by the research problem."[39] Three controlling variables are therefore critical to the selection of cases that would be able to explain why China's interventions in foreign intrastate armed conflicts vary over time. The three are: (1) severity of the conflict; (2) level of economic and diplomatic engagement with China; and (3) intervention. In terms of "severity of the conflict," South Sudan and Libya had at least 1000 battle-related deaths in one calendar year; hence they are designated as civil wars in terms of the Uppsala/PRIO database on armed conflict. Secondly, both had diplomatic relations with China before the outbreak of their respective intrastate armed conflicts and, in terms of economic engagement, Chinese private and state-owned enterprises had extensive investments in the two countries—oil in South Sudan, and telecommunication and infrastructure development in Libya. Thirdly, China's intervention in the two countries' intrastate armed conflicts varied; in the case of Libya it largely opposed foreign bilateral intervention but reluctantly supported limited multilateral intervention, while in South Sudan it actively engaged in both bilateral and multilateral intervention. Both cases are therefore relevant to discussing why China's intervention would vary in countries where it has comparably significant economic interests and diplomatic relations, and where the severity of the conflicts was also largely the same—at least 1000 deaths in one calendar year.

Yet, two cases that are largely similar are insufficient to determine the trend and pattern of external intervention. In addition, the two cases do not provide "the opportunity for finding novel theoretical relationships as well as confidence that a study has been conducted in a rigorous way … creating a robust set of findings that have relevance in a wide range of contexts" (Wicks 2010, p. 289, 290). There is need for a deviant case where China intervened either bilaterally or multilaterally even though it had no comparably major economic investments in that country, and where the severity of the conflict was less than 1000 battle-related deaths in one calendar year. The Uppsala/PRIO database on armed conflict defines such conflicts as minor wars because the battle-related deaths in one calendar year were at least 25. The purpose of the deviant case is to identify underlying influences[40] of China's varied intervention behaviour in African intrastate armed conflict and to dispel the obvious conclusion that can be drawn from the cases of South Sudan and Libya that China intervenes on the basis of severity of the conflict and/or economic investments. In that respect, a deviant case assists in probing "for new—but as yet unspecified—explanations"[41] of China's varying intervention in African intrastate armed conflicts over time and with each country.

Of all the countries that experienced minor wars between 2005 and 2013, China only multilaterally intervened in Mali, which makes it a suitable deviant case because China did not have significant investments there compared to Libya and South Sudan, and the conflict was minor in terms of battle-related deaths. Considering the above caveats, three cases are analysed in this study: (1) Libya, (2) Mali and (3) South Sudan. What distinguishes these three cases from other countries that experienced intrastate armed conflicts in Africa is that the armed conflicts in the three countries occurred within months of each other—the armed conflict in Libya started in February 2011 ending in October 2011; the Tuareg rebellion that culminated in a military coup in Mali took place in January and March 2012 respectively ceasing in August 2012 when a government of national unity was established; and lastly, the intrastate armed conflict in South Sudan began in December 2013 and is still ongoing. The utility of the intrastate armed conflicts happening within months of each other is that it becomes possible to examine the trend and pattern of China's external intervention behaviour and also to examine why the intervention varied within a three-year period. Furthermore, unlike single case studies which are common to studies on China's intervention in African conflicts, multiple case studies increase the methodological rigour of a study by "strengthening the precision, the validity and stability of the findings," (Miles and Huberman 1994, p. 29), suggesting that "evidence from multiple cases is often considered more compelling" (Yin 1994, p. 45).

In addition, what makes the selected cases comparable is that China's main interest in each of the three countries is a dominant single primary commodity. In the case of Libya and South Sudan it is crude oil while cotton dominates trade relations between China and Mali. From 2011 when South Sudan officially seceded from Sudan, China's imports from South Sudan are 100 per cent crude petroleum valued at US$446 million in 2012, US$2.25 billion in 2013 and US$3.96 billion in 2014.[42] During the same period, China's imports from Libya constituted of an average of 97% crude petroleum valued at US$3.58 billion (2010), US$1.81 billion (2011), US$5.55 billion (2012), US$1.81 billion (2013) and US$650 million (2014).[43] Although Mali has no crude petroleum for export yet, China's major economic interests in Mali are cotton and agriculture.

China imports an average of 80 percent of Malian cotton and related products such as oily seeds.[44] Mali is also among top African countries that China has agricultural projects in. In total, Chinese companies hold approximately 26,174 hectares of land under rice and sugarcane crops.[45]

The tables below show Chinese imports from, and exports to, Libya, Mali and South Sudan.

As shown in Figs. 1.3 and 1.4, China's imports from and exports to Libya and Sudan (North + South) are comparable in that there is a marked reduction in Chinese imports from Libya and South Sudan in the years that the countries had intrastate armed conflicts. For instance, China's imports from Libya fell from US$4.515 billion in 2010 to US$2.063 billion in 2011; although they peaked to US$6.375 billion in 2012 as Libya stabilised, renewed armed conflicts explain the downward spiral from 2013 to 2015. By 2015, Libya's total exports to China amounted to only US$949 million. Similarly, Libya's imports from China fell from US$2 billion in 2010 to a meagre US$720 million before they peaked again. A similar trend is also noticeable in South Sudan, whose trade statistics are combined with those of northern Sudan due to the intertwined nature of their economies. The outlier nature of the Malian case is reflected in the fact that trade relations between Mali and China are significantly lower than Libya and South Sudan. This makes a case for challenging the assumption that China intervenes only in countries that it has major economic and trade interests in.

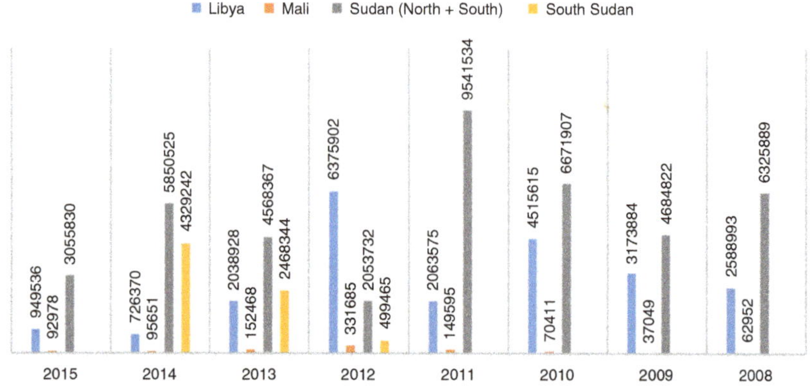

Fig. 1.3 China's imports from Libya, Mali, Sudan (North + South) and South Sudan (Unit: US$ thousand)

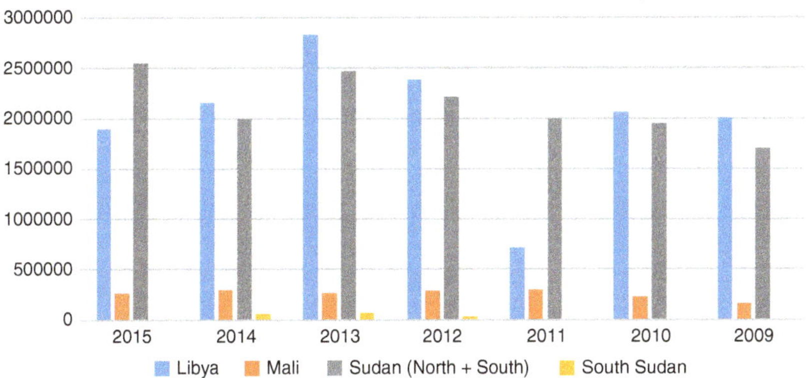

Fig. 1.4 China's exports to Libya, Mali, Sudan (North + South) and South Sudan (Unit: US$ thousand)

1.4.2 Data Collection and Analysis

Conducting research on China-Africa security engagements is difficult for two reasons: First there is lack of easily accessible data, and secondly, the subject is considered highly sensitive by both China and African countries, including organisations such as the African Union, so few are willing to talk about the subject. Thus, the research began with desk-top data gathering and analysis. This effort focused on the theoretical underpinnings of the study; China's engagement in Africa, in particular the selected cases; and also on the context and conflict assessment of the selected cases. During this stage, data was mainly obtained from official statements issued by international organisations such as the United Nations, and the African Union, and also statements of Chinese government ministries, in particular the Ministry of Foreign Affairs, and the Communist Party of China. In addition, information from the PRC's official state news agencies such as Xinhua, newspapers and publications of Chinese IR and security think tanks such as the State Council's China Centre for International Studies, the China Institute for Contemporary International Relations, Shanghai Institute of International Studies and the China Institute of International Studies were used. To avoid overreliance on Chinese and African sources of information, the research also utilised publications from Western and African think tanks such as the Chatham House and the South African Institute of International Affairs, as well as official statements from the

United States, France and the European Union on the topic. This constituted the background analysis upon which field research and interviews were based.

What became clear from the analysis of primary and secondary data is that Chinese internal policy discussions and documents are not easily accessible. Official data from governments of Libya, Mali and South Sudan was not available online and was hardly accessible. Also, the data from African governments, the African Union and China tended to be official and standardised in a manner that suggested it was mostly public relations-cum-propaganda information. Because of these difficulties there was need for extensive interviews with Chinese, African policymakers and other relevant stakeholders. Using semi-structured interviews to get opinions and views that are not so often contained in official statements, the researcher conducted a total of 12 interviews in Hong Kong, Ethiopia, the United States, Taiwan and Germany, and also by email with respondents in China, South Sudan, Mali and Libya. Selected interviews that were conducted include: interviews with a researcher and officials at institutions such as China's Ministry of Commerce, Shanghai Institute for International Studies, China Institute of International Studies, Chinese Communist Party School, the China Foreign Affairs University, the Institute for Peace and Security Studies at the University of Addis Ababa (Ethiopia), and the Center for Chinese Studies at Stellenbosch (South Africa), Renmin University, Tsinghua University, Ethiopian government, among others.[46]

From June to August 2015, the researcher was hosted at the Institute for Peace and Security Studies at the Addis Ababa University, Ethiopia, as a visiting researcher. The strategic importance of the Institute for Peace and Security Studies is that it jointly organises the Tana High-Level Forum on Security in Africa which is attended by former and current African presidents as well as high-level officials from major countries such as the United States, China and Britain; and it also jointly runs the Africa Peace and Security Programme with the African Union's Peace and Security Department. In the course of the three months, the researcher had access to the Institute's extensive library, and other African peace and security studies experts at the Institute. Affiliation to the Institute also enabled the researcher to conduct semi-structured interviews with three African Union high-level officials directly working on intrastate armed conflicts in Libya, Mali and South Sudan. Three other interviews were conducted with conflict analysts at the Intergovernmental Authority on Development (IGAD), a regional organisation for eight countries in the Horn of Africa and East

Africa. IGAD has been playing the mediatory role in the South Sudan conflict. Other ad hoc, unofficial discussions on the subject matter were held with a Chinese diplomat working at the Mission of the People's Republic of China to the African Union, as well as a Norwegian diplomat who had participated in South Sudan conflict mediation as part of the IGAD-PLUS initiative which includes the United States, Norway, the UK, Italy, the European Union and the United Nations. Discussions with academics in panels on China-Africa security relations at several academic conferences such as the International Studies Association conferences in Buenos Aires (2014), New Orleans (2015) and Atlanta (2016), as well as other academic conferences in Taiwan and Germany, helped in gathering insightful opinions that proved helpful to this study.

Due to the aforementioned data collection methods, the "high proportion of it [collected data] is text based, consisting of verbatim transcriptions of interviews or discussions, field notes or other written documents" (Ritchie and Spencer 2002, p. 309). To provide structure, meaning and coherence to the data, the researcher employed preliminary data analysis "in order to highlight emerging issues, to allow all relevant data to be identified and to provide directions for the seeking of further data" (Grbich 2007, p. 25); this was done during the data collection process. The preliminary data analysis allowed the researcher to identify and follow up on issues previously not considered as central to this research but that emerged from the preliminary data analysis as significant research issues. In order to reduce the data into meaningful categories, the conceptual mapping approach to thematic analysis was used to systematically identify, analyse and categorise patterns within data. Content analysis was useful in analysing trends in the three selected case studies, making it possible to develop hypotheses about China's intervention in African intrastate armed conflicts through the emergent "trends and patterns of words used, their frequency, their relationships and the structures and discourses of communication" (Grbich 2007, p. 112).

1.5 Definition of Key Terms

1.5.1 Intervention

Intervention is "one of the vaguest branches of international law ... at no time clear and even now in a fluid condition," stated Sir Percy Henry Winfield in 1922. A century later, intervention is still a concept laden with historical and political undertones that betray its origins in political rather than academic discourse. And, like everything political, Raymond John Vincent argues in his book *Nonintervention and International Order* that intervention describes "events in the real world, and [is] not a purely abstract concept." The challenge is for scholars to capture in a single concept those "events in the real world"—which can range from a speech by a statesman to a military takeover of another state. Several attempts have already been made and there are as many definitions of intervention as there are scholars. Some scholars tend to focus on its coerciveness. Hedley Bull falls into this category. He defines intervention as "dictatorial or coercive interference, by an outside party or parties, in the sphere of jurisdiction of a sovereign state, or more broadly of an independent political community" (Bull 1986, p. 1). Others focus on intervention's intended objective, arguing as Christian Reus-Smit does that "Interventions are always transformative; they are transgressions to reconfigure identities, institutions, and practices" (Reus-Smit 2013, p. 1058). Regardless, the implication is that as a concept, *intervention* is used reflexively but without a specific working definition.[47]

In this book, intervention shall be in reference to political, military, economic or diplomatic actions undertaken by a governmental or intergovernmental actor of the international system [with or without consent of the target state], the purpose of which is to affect the direction, duration or outcome of an intrastate armed conflict.[48] As put by Karen Feste, the definition of intervention can be extended "to include various forms of involvement and assistance by an external state in an ongoing civil war (e.g., U.S. commitments to Greece in the 1940s and covert aid to Afghan resistance fighters in the 1980s)" (2003, p. 178). Similarly, Earl Conteh-Morgan (2001) also broadly conceptualises intervention to include "both coercive/military forms of intervention, and non-military coercive forms of intervention." Specifically, this study is concerned with unilateral actions such as mediation, diplomatic, political, economic or military taken by the government of China or its appointed agents, or multilaterally taken through the UNSC with or without the consent of the appropriate authorities in Libya, Mali and South Sudan. Actions or inactions taken through the UNSC include abstaining, vetoing or voting for resolutions that lead to multilateral actions such as imposition of no-fly zones, sanctions and deployment of peacekeepers or other forces under the United Nations. The purpose of these unilateral and multilateral actions should be to affect the duration, direction or outcome of the intrastate armed conflicts in Libya, Mali and South Sudan.

1.5.2 *Intrastate Armed Conflicts*

In Africa, intrastate armed conflicts rather than interstate wars are more prevalent and "remain the dominant form of conflict."[49] The paucity of interstate wars is attributable to the de facto and *de jure* committal by founders of independent African states to non-interference, respect of national sovereignty and adherence to pre-independence territorial borders.[50] However, while there was "peace" among states, the majority of newly independent countries experienced a surge in civil wars and military takeover of governments. Part of the reason why there was a surge of civil wars is that a significant number of African countries gained independence at the height of "the Cold War politics of the 1950s, 60s and 70s. [Therefore] Independence converted Africa into a battleground for East-West Cold War rivalry" (Francis 2006, p. 46). Within that period, there was a steady increase in proxy wars in countries such as Somalia, Ethiopia, Guinea, Angola and Mozambique. "After the collapse of the Berlin Wall in 1989, some previously frozen conflicts in Africa reignited violently, including those in Liberia, Sierra Leone, Rwanda, and the Democratic Republic of Congo" (Cilliers and Schuenemann 2013, p. 3). Intrastate armed conflicts reached their peak in the early 1990s before subsiding. Although there has been a significant decline in civil wars compared to the 1990s, they still remain extensive; their nature and intensity as well as the complexity of actors involved have also evolved, making them more devastating and difficult to conceptualise.

Scholarly focus on causes and consequences adds to the complexity of reaching a common definition of intrastate armed conflicts, hence, it is "an imprecise and poorly observed phenomenon"[51] to which different conflict databases and studies apply varying methodological approaches to defining and analysing it. The resultant effect is that "scholars and analysts interested in intrastate conflict are defined and divided by their epistemological worldview and methodological approaches,"[52] which are usually the result of subjective and ad hoc variables such as, ethnicity, poverty, inequality, religion, regime type and resource scarcity that are employed to explain the causes and nature of civil wars.[53] Consequently, the definition of what is a civil war is not universally acknowledged.

Due to varying methodologies and emphasis on different variables, several definitions of civil war exist. In her book *Foreign Powers and Intervention in Armed Conflicts*, Aysegul Aydin defines civil war as "intrastate violence that crosses the threshold of 200 fatalities" (2012, p. 131).

The Correlates of War (COW) project conceptualises civil war as being a "sustained combat between/among organised armed forces taking place within the territorial boundaries of a state system member and leading to 1,000 battle-related deaths (of combatants) per year (or 12-month period starting from the war onset" (Sarkees 2014, p. 242). On the other hand, the Uppsala Conflict Data Program (UCDP)/International Peace Research Institute, Oslo (PRIO) describes civil war as an internal contested incompatibility between the government of a state and internal opposition group(s) that concerns government and/or territory where the use of armed force between two parties, of which at least one is the government of a state, results in at least 25 battle-related deaths. Unlike the others, Gersovitz and Kriger (2013) do not give a death threshold in their definition of civil war; rather, they define it as "a politically organised, large-scale, sustained, physically violent conflict that occurs within a country principally among large/numerically important groups of its inhabitants or citizens over the monopoly of physical force within the country" (Gersovitz and Kriger 2013, pp. 160–161). Although varying in emphasis, these definitions "converge around the same key dimensions of the phenomenon,"[54] that is, (1) a sustained armed resistance/combat, (2) within the boundaries of a recognised sovereign state, (3) between the government of the state and one or more internal organised armed opposition groups, and (4) reaching a certain numerical threshold of deaths.

The existence of a state, particularly for African countries such as Somalia whose statehood is questioned, is the starting point in determining whether an armed conflict constitutes a civil war. Max Weber envisaged a state as "the form of human community that (successfully) lays claim to the monopoly of legitimate physical violence within a particular territory—and this idea of 'territory' is an essential defining feature" (Weber, cited in Owen and Strong 2004, p. 33). An intrastate armed conflict is therefore a civil war, first, because it occurs within the territorial boundaries of a sovereign state. What further distinguishes civil wars from other equally large-scale internal violent conflicts, however, is the civil war belligerents' objective of capturing and possessing the monopoly of force within an international system state. Unlike "one-time events" such as political assassinations, a civil war entails "large-scale and sustained internal political violence that contests the monopoly of force" (Gersovitz and Kriger 2013, p. 161). A civil war is therefore distinct from other forms of internal violence because it is "political" in nature and purpose, meaning that the interest and purpose of the civil war actors must be to influence "the distribution or preservation of power, or a shift in power ... [Therefore, they strive] for power, either power as a means in the service of other goals, whether idealistic or selfish, or power 'for its own sake,' in other words, so as to enjoy the feeling of prestige that it confers" (Weber, Owen and Strong 2004, pp. 33–34). Thus, for as long as the purpose of the violence is not for political power, as is the case with organised criminal organisations, or terrorist insurgent groups like *Al Shabab* in Somalia and Kenya, it cannot be defined as civil war.

A third distinct component of the definition of civil war regards the involved actors, that is, the armed opposition groups(s) challenging the monopoly of violence within a state on one hand and an incumbent government that possesses such authority on the other. "The challengers may seek to replace the incumbents in control of the monopoly of force within the extant territory of the state, or they may seek the secession of part of the original territory" (Gersovitz and Kriger 2013, p. 161). The incumbent or national government is codified as those "forces that were at the start of the war in *de facto* control of the nation's institutions, regardless of the legality or illegality of their claim" (Sarkees 2014, p. 242), while national institutions are defined as "institutions of governance and whichever party begins the war in possession of the institutions of governance (parliament, the palace, etc.) may be termed the government. When each side in a civil war controls an institution (e.g. Chile's Congressionist rebellion that pitted President against Congress), then the executive or monarch's faction ought to be termed the government" (Dixon 2003, p. 4). "This excludes a number of internal wars from the civil war definition, most notably wars of liberation from colonialism..., [that] are instead listed as extra-systemic wars" (Collier and Hoeffler 2007, p. 714); or other internal armed conflicts between non-state armed groups, or one-sided violence perpetuated by either a government or an armed group. The involvement of an incumbent government in an armed combat with one or more organised armed opposition groups is therefore essential in distinguishing a civil war from other forms of internal violence.

Although conflict databases such as the COW project, Heidelberg Institute for International Conflict Research, the UCDP/PRIO and the Armed Conflict Dataset agree that a civil war is a sustained armed combat/resistance within a sovereign state between an incumbent government and internal armed opposition group(s), they differ on the numerical threshold of deaths. COW sets the threshold at "1,000 battle-related deaths (of combatants) per year (or 12-month period starting from the war onset)" (Sarkees 2014, p. 242). For the UCDP)/PRIO the internal armed conflict should result in at least 25 battle-related deaths.[55] In contrast, the Heidelberg Institute for International Conflict Research sets the threshold at more than 1080 battle-related combatant and civilian fatalities.[56]

Differences in the death threshold reflect the divergence of methodologies, data-gathering approaches and analysis of conflicts by the different databases. Depending on the database, death thresholds may relate to the cumulative monthly or annual number of battle-related deaths. In some cases, it can be combatant deaths only, as is the case with the COW database, or may include both combatant and civilian deaths as in the case of the Uppsala/PRIO database. While the death threshold may be used to either include or exclude a conflict from the database, both the Heidelberg Institute for International Conflict Research and the Uppsala/PRIO database use it to classify conflicts according to their intensity. However due to varying numerical death thresholds among conflict databases, the same conflict may not be classified in the same category. Thus, reliance on the numerical death threshold criterion alone makes the definition and classification of conflicts uncertain—making it problematic to comprehensively analyse the duration, pattern, trend, dynamics and recurrence of the conflict over time. So, although the databases agree on other elements constituting a civil war, they significantly differ on the operationalisation of the concept. In that case, when "databases are so different that they are not based on the same types of raw data, then they probably should not be used to test exactly the same theory" (Kauffmann 2008, p. 6), because it would lead "to different views of where and when conflict occurs" (UNCTAD 2004, p. 161).

Debate on the conceptualisation and operationalisation of "civil war" by various conflict databases is complex; the debate therefore falls beyond the scope of this study. For that reason, the study bases its conceptual and operational understanding of "civil war" or intrastate armed conflict on one international database, the Uppsala/PRIO database on armed conflict[57]; and focuses on civil wars that happened in Africa between 2005 and 2013. Uppsala/PRIO defines armed conflict as "a contested incompatibility that concerns government and/or territory where the use of armed force between two parties, of which at least one is the government of a state, results in at least 25 battle-related deaths in one calendar year."[58] The death threshold of a minimum of 25 battle-related deaths is less than the usual 1000 battle-related deaths used by databases such as the COW. However, Uppsala/PRIO categorises conflicts depending on their intensity—which is measured by the number of battle-related deaths. It codes the intensity variable in two categories: (1) minor—between 25 and 999 battle-related deaths in a given year, and (2) war—at least 1000 battle-related deaths in a given year.

This study is concerned with war, that is, intrastate armed conflicts (civil war) defined as a contested incompatibility that concerns government and/or territory where the use of armed force between the government of a state and one or more internal opposition group(s) with or without intervention from other states, of which at least one is the government of a state, results in at least 1000 battle-related deaths in one calendar year. Uppsala/PRIO defines these conflicts as internal armed conflict if there is no intervention from other states, and as internationalised internal armed conflict if there is intervention from other states. In this study, the terms "civil war" and "intrastate armed conflict" are used interchangeably to refer to both internal and internationalised armed conflicts as defined by Uppsala/PRIO.

1.6 Book Outline

This book contains seven chapters. The background and introduction of this study have been given in this first chapter. The chapter laid the general background of the research context. The theoretical and empirical significance of the study was discussed, and a brief introduction of the main arguments was made. In a nutshell, it mentions the main case studies—Sudan, South Sudan and Libya—as well as the minor cases that will be intermittently referred to in the study. It then shortly made reference to the neoclassical realist theory, which is the main theoretical framework applied in this study.

The second chapter discusses the global discourse on intervention in foreign intrastate armed conflicts by China and other non-Western rising powers. It assesses the prevailing discourse on the topic and the emerging gaps. The main argument advanced in the chapter is that the major gap in existing scholarship is the lack of systematic theoretical and empirical study of intervention in foreign conflicts by rising powers, particularly China. The chapter advances the argument that in external intervention studies, practice has preceded theory. The focus of IR theorists has remained on "states-that-matter" such that the theories do not explain the behaviour of small or rising states. It therefore makes an argument for the use of neoclassical realism as a theoretical framework able to explain the foreign policy behaviour of rising powers.

The third chapter explores the argument that a state's position in the international system determines its foreign policy and external intervention behaviour. It begins by giving a critical historical analysis of China's evolving understanding of foreign intervention, its foreign intervention policy and external intervention behaviour from imperial times to the establishment of the People's Republic of China in 1949, and until 2015. The aim is to trace the historical evolving nature of China's foreign policy regarding intervention in other states' internal affairs vis-à-vis changes in its relative economic power and position in the international system in order to understand current Chinese intervention behaviour.

Chapter 4 is the first of the three chapters that discusses China's intervention in specific intrastate armed conflicts in Africa. It explores Sino-Libya diplomatic, political and economic relations from a historical perspective, and then focuses on China's economic interests in Libya and how the outbreak of the intrastate armed conflict in 2011 affected those interests in a manner and scale never before experienced by China in Africa. The main argument advanced in the chapter is that China's response to the intrastate armed conflict in Libya changed from non-interventionism to ambivalent interventionism.

Following onto the previous chapter on Libya, the fifth chapter examines China's intervention in the Malian intrastate armed conflict. Through a historical analysis of Sino-Mali diplomatic, political and economic relations since diplomatic relations were established in 1960, the chapter discusses China's response to previous Tuareg rebellions and coup d'états in Mali. The argument pursued in this chapter is that in hindsight, based on its experience in Libya, China's intervention in Mali was, although indifferent, more alert to the threats imposed by the Malian armed conflict, enabling it to take more pragmatic strategies.

As the last in the three chapters assesses China's intervention in African intrastate armed conflicts, the sixth chapter examines China's intervention in South Sudan. The argument advanced in the chapter is that, unlike in Libya and Mali, China's intervention in South Sudan was proactive, purposeful and assertive, suggesting that its perception of African intrastate armed conflicts as threatening to its external economic interests is constantly evolving. Like the previous chapters, this argument culminated from a tracing of Sino-South Sudan relations.

Based on conclusions made in Chaps. 4–6, the overall argument advanced in the final chapter is that China's intervention behaviour in African intrastate armed conflicts is a result of the combined effect of an increase in its relative economic power, which compelled it to expand its interests into politically volatile countries in search for raw materials and markets to keep the engine of its economy on the trot, and changing perception that intrastate armed conflicts in Africa threatened its interests there. On the basis of this argument, this chapter assesses the trends and patterns of China's intervention in Africa drawing extensively from arguments made in the previous chapters. It then discusses how China's intervention behaviour in African intrastate armed conflicts challenges existing conventional understandings of intervention as a foreign policy tool used by Western great powers to safeguard their strategic interests abroad.

Notes

1. Ikenberry, GJ 2008, 'The rise of China and the future of the West: Can the liberal system survive?' *Foreign affairs*, vol. 87, no. 1, p. 26; Hoge Jr., JF 2004, 'Global power shift in the making: Is the United States ready?", *Foreign Affairs*, vol. 83, no. 1, pp. 2–7.
2. People's Republic of China Ministry of Foreign Affairs 2016, *Foreign Minister Wang Yi meets the press*, 9 March, viewed 22 May 2016, http://www.fmprc.gov.cn/mfa_eng/zxxx_662805/t1346238.shtml
3. Tritle, LA 2010, *A new history of the Peloponnesian war*, Wiley-Blackwell, p. 36.
4. Feng, Y 2006, "The Peaceful Transition of Power from the UK to the US", *The Chinese Journal of International Politics*, vol. 1, no. 1, pp. 83–108.
5. Jackson, RH 1993, *Quasi-states: sovereignty, international relations and the Third World*, Cambridge University Press.
6. In this study, the terms, civil war and intrastate armed conflicts are used interchangeably.
7. Cilliers, J & Schuenemann, J 2013, 'The future of intrastate conflict in Africa more violence or greater peace?' *Institute for Security Studies* Paper 246, p. 2, viewed 3 January 2014, https://www.issafrica.org/uploads/Paper246.pdf
8. Attree, L 2012, *China and conflict-affected states: Between principle and pragmatism*, Saferworld: London, viewed 3 January 2014, http://www.saferworld.org.uk/downloads/pubdocs/FAB%20Sudan%20and%20South%20Sudan.pdf
9. '35,860 Chinese evacuated from unrest-torn Libya' 2011, *Xinhua*, 3 March, viewed 10 January 2014, http://news.xinhuanet.com/english2010/china/2011-03/03/c_13759456.htm

10. 'Sudan rebels kill 5 Chinese hostages' 2008, *The Telegraph*, 27 October, viewed 10 January 2014, http://www.telegraph.co.uk/news/worldnews/africaandindianocean/sudan/3270057/Sudan-rebels-kill-5-Chinese-hostages.html
11. 'China strongly condemns Mali hotel attack, confirms 3 nationals killed' 2015, *Xinhua*, 21 November, viewed 21 November 2015, http://news.xinhuanet.com/english/2015-11/21/c_134839619.htm
12. 'Two Chinese kidnapped on Cameroon-C.Africa border' 2012, *AsiaOne,* 15 October, viewed 12 March 2014, http://news.asiaone.com/print/News/AsiaOne%2BNews/Crime/Story/A1Story20121015-377828.html
13. '97 Chinese workers evacuated from South Sudan to Khartoum' 2013, *People Daily*, 25 December, viewed 3 January 2014, http://english.peopledaily.com.cn/90883/8495532.html
14. Klare, M 2001, *Resource wars: the new landscape of global conflict,* Henry Holt, New York, p. 44.
15. Ibid., p. xii, 14.
16. Zheng, B 2005, 'China's "peaceful rise" to great-power status', *Foreign Affairs,* vol. 84, no. 5, p. 24.
17. Kristof, ND 1993, "The rise of China", *Foreign Affairs,* vol. 72, no. 5, p. 59.
18. The World Bank. 2015. GDP Growth (Annual %). Available at: http://databank.worldbank.org/data/reports.aspx?Code=NY.GDP.MKTP.KD.ZG&id=af3ce82b&report_name=Popular_indicators&populartype=series&ispopular=y
19. Schweller, RL 1999, 'Realism and the present great power system: Growth and positional conflict over scarce resources', in EB Kapstein & M Mastanduno (eds.), *Unipolar politics: Realism and state strategies after the Cold War*, Columbia University Press, New York, p. 31.
20. The World Bank World Development Indicator Database conceptualises high-technology exports as products with high R&D intensity, such as in aerospace, computers, pharmaceuticals, scientific instruments and electrical machinery. Data are in current US$ (billion).
21. Source: World Bank World Development Indicator Database.
22. Ikenberry, GJ 2008, "The rise of China and the future of the west: can the liberal system survive?" *Foreign affairs,* vol. 87, no. 1, p. 26.
23. West, J, Schandl, H, Heyenga, S & Chen, S 2013, *Resource Efficiency: Economics and Outlook for China*, United Nations Environment Programme (UNEP), Bangkok, p. 1.
24. European Commission, *Trade: China*, European Commission, viewed 10 August 2014, http://ec.europa.eu/trade/policy/countries-and-regions/countries/china/

25. Armijo, LE & Roberts, C 2014, 'The emerging powers and global governance: Why the BRICS matter, in RE Looney (Ed.), *Handbook of Emerging Economies*, Routledge, New York, p. 506.
26. Gonzalez-Vicente, R 2011, 'China's engagement in South America and Africa's extractive sectors: New perspectives for resource curse theories', *The Pacific Review*, vol. 24, no. 1, pp. 65–87.
27. 'China sends envoy to South Sudan to push peace talks' 2013, *Reuters*, 27 December, viewed 10 February 2014, http://www.voanews.com/content/reu-china-sends-envoy-south-sudan-push-peace-talks/1818388.html
28. UN Security Council 2011, *6531st meeting, S/PV.6531*, 10 May, p. 20, viewed 13 May 2014, http://www.securitycouncilreport.org/atf/cf/%7B65BFCF9B-6D27-4E9C-8CD3-CF6E4FF96FF9%7D/POC%20S%20PV%206531.pdf
29. Taliaferro, JW 2006, 'State building for future wars: Neoclassical realism and the resource-extractive state', *Security Studies*, vol. 15, no. 3, p. 480.
30. Cox, M & Stokes, D 2012, *US foreign policy*, Oxford University Press, Oxford, p. 13.
31. George, AL & Bennett, A 2005, *Case studies and theory development in the social sciences*, MIT Press, Cambridge, p. 67.
32. Smith-Hoehn, J 2010, *Rebuilding the security sector in post-conflict societies: Perceptions from urban Liberia and Sierra Leone*, LIT Verlag, Muenster, p. 46.
33. George, AL & Bennett, A 2005, *Case studies and theory development in the social sciences*, MIT Press, Cambridge, p. 68.
34. Rosenau, JN 1968, 'Moral fervor, systematic analysis, and scientific consciousness in foreign policy research', in A Ranney (ed.), *Political science and public policy*, Markham, Chicago, pp. 197–238.
35. George, AL & Bennett, A 2005, *Case studies and theory development in the social sciences*, MIT Press, Cambridge, p. 67.
36. Ibid.
37. 'Intrastate armed conflict' is used interchangeably with 'civil war' in this section.
38. Carment, D, Samy, Y & El Achkar, S 2009, 'Protracted conflict and crisis mediation: A contingency approach', in J Bercovitch & S Gartner (eds.), *International conflict mediation: New approaches and findings*, Routledge: New York, p. 216.
39. George, AL & Bennett, A 2005, *Case studies and theory development in the social sciences*, MIT Press, Cambridge, p. 83.
40. Kazancigil, A 1994, "The deviant case in comparative analysis: High stateness in comparative analysis', in M Dogan & A Kazancigil (eds.), *Comparing nations: Concepts, strategies, substance*, Blackwell, Cambridge, p. 214.

41. Seawright, J & Gerring, J 2008, 'Case selection techniques in case study research a menu of qualitative and quantitative options', *Political Research Quarterly*, vol. 61, no. 2, p. 302.
42. The Observatory of Economic Complexity n.d., *What does China import from South Sudan*, viewed 13 July 2016, http://atlas.media.mit.edu/en/visualize/tree_map/hs92/import/chn/ssd/show/2010/
43. The Observatory of Economic Complexity n.d., *What does China import from Libya*, viewed 13 July 2016, http://atlas.media.mit.edu/en/visualize/tree_map/hs92/import/chn/lby/show/2010/
44. The Observatory of Economic Complexity n.d., *What does China import from Mali*, viewed 13 July 2016, http://atlas.media.mit.edu/en/visualize/tree_map/hs92/import/chn/mli/show/2010/
45. Brautigam, D. 2015, *Will Africa Feed China?* Oxford University Press, Oxford.
46. All the six think tanks are part of the Think Tank 10 + 10 Partnership Plan supported by the Chinese Ministry of Foreign Affairs and organised under the Chinese Follow-up Committee of the Forum on China-Africa Cooperation. The Plan links 16 think tanks in Africa and China together.
47. There are many other definitions (Lyons and Mastanduno 2005, p. 12; Weiss 2007, p. 18; Lu 2006, p. 1; Ramsbotham and Woodhouse 1996, p. 40; Rosenau 1968, p. 167).
48. Rioux, JS & Bucher, JC 2003, 'Third party intervention as conflict management: The case of Africa', *Paper presented at 16th Nordic and Baltic peace research conference*, St. Petersburg, Russia, p. 7, viewed on 16 June 2014, http://www.institutidrp.org/contributionsidrp/Rioux_7octobre2003.pdf
49. Cilliers, J & Schuenemann, J 2013, 'The future of intrastate conflict in Africa more violence or greater peace?' *Institute for Security Studies* Paper 246, p. 2, viewed 3 January 2014, https://www.issafrica.org/uploads/Paper246.pdf
50. The Organisation of African Unity 1964, 'Resolutions Adopted by the First Ordinary Session of the Assembly of Heads of State and Government held in Cairo, UAR, from 17 to 21 July 1964' OAU: Addis Ababa. At that conference the Heads of State and Government "SOLEMNLY DECLARES that all Member States pledge themselves to respect the borders existing on their achievement of national independence" (AHG/Res. 16(1)), viewed 17 August 2014, http://www.au.int/en/sites/default/files/ASSEMBLY_EN_17_21_JULY_1964_ASSEMBLY_HEADS_STATE_GOVERNMENT_FIRST_ORDINARY_SESSION.pdf
51. Collier, P & Hoeffler, A 2007, 'Civil war', in T Sandler & K Hartley (eds.), *Handbook of defense economics: Defense in a globalized world, Volume 2*, North-Holland Publications, Amsterdam, p. 713.
52. Newman, E 2014, *Understanding civil wars: Continuity and change in intrastate conflict*, Routledge, London, p. 2.

53. Ibid.
54. Kalyvas, NS 2007, 'Civil wars', in C Boix & SC Stokes (Eds.), *The Oxford handbook of comparative politics*, Oxford University Press, Oxford, p. 417.
55. Themnér, L 2013, *UCDP/PRIO armed conflict dataset codebook*, Uppsala Conflict Data Program, viewed 3 September 2013, http://www.pcr.uu.se/digitalAssets/124/124920_1codebook_ucdp_prio-armed conflict-dataset-v4_2013.pdf
56. Heidelberg Institute for International Conflict Research 2014, *Conflict barometer 2013*, HIIK, Heidelberg, p. 10, viewed 3 September 2013, http://www.frsh.de/fileadmin/beiboot/BB9/BB-9-15-Anlage.pdf
57. The dataset is a joint project of the Department of Peace and Conflict Studies, Uppsala University, and the Centre for the Study of Civil War at the International Peace Research Institute, Oslo (PRIO).
58. Themnér, L 2013, *UCDP/PRIO armed conflict dataset codebook*, Uppsala Conflict Data Program, viewed 3 September 2013, http://www.pcr.uu.se/digitalAssets/124/124920_1codebook_ucdp_prio-armed-conflict-dataset-v4_2013.pdf

Bibliography

Armijo, L. E., & Roberts, C. (2014). The emerging powers and global governance: Why the BRICS matter. In R. E. Looney (Ed.), *Handbook of emerging economies* (pp. 503–524). New York: Routledge.

Aydin, A. (2012). *Foreign powers and intervention in armed conflicts*. Stanford: Stanford University.

Boulden, J. (2013). The United Nations Security Council and conflict in Africa. In J. Boulden (Ed.), *Responding to conflict in Africa: The United Nations and regional organizations* (pp. 13–32). New York: Palgrave Macmillan.

Bull, H. (1986). *Intervention in world politics*. Oxfordshire: Clarendon.

Cilliers, J., & Schuenemann, J. (2013). *The future of intrastate conflict in Africa more violence or greater peace?* Institute for Security Studies Paper 246, p. 2. Retrieved January 3, 2014, from https://www.issafrica.org/uploads/Paper246.pdf

Collier, P., & Hoeffler, A. (2007). Civil war. In T. Sandler & K. Hartley (Eds.), *Handbook of defense economics: Defense in a globalized world* (Vol. 2, pp. 711–739). Amsterdam: North-Holland Publications.

Conteh-Morgan, E. (2001). International intervention: Conflict, economic dislocation, and the hegemonic role of dominant actors. *International Journal of Peace Studies, 6*(2), 33–52.

Dadush, U. (2014). Key trends in the world economy. In R. E. Looney (Ed.), *Handbook of emerging economies* (pp. 13–29). New York: Routledge.

Dixon, J. (2003). *Suggested changes to the COW civil war dataset 3.0*. Paper presented at the annual meeting of the International Studies Association, Portland, Oregon, February 25–March 1.

Elman, C., & Elman, M. F. (2003). *Progress in international relations theory: Appraising the field*. Cambridge: MIT Press.

Feste, K. A. (2003). *Intervention: Shaping the global order*. Westport, CT: Praeger.

Francis, D. J. (2006). *Uniting Africa: Building regional peace and security systems*. Hampshire: Ashgate Publishing.

Fukuyama, F. (2004). *State-building: Governance and world order in the 21st century*. Ithaca, NY: Cornell University Press.

George, A. L. (1979). Case studies and theory development: The method of structured focused comparison. In P. G. Lauren (Ed.), *Diplomacy: New approaches in history, theory and policy* (pp. 43–68). New York: Free Press.

Gersovitz, M., & Kriger, N. (2013). What is a civil war? A critical review of its definition and (econometric) consequences. *The World Bank Research Observer, 28*(2), 159–190.

Grbich, C. (2007). *Qualitative data analysis: An introduction*. Thousand Oaks, CA: Sage.

Kauffmann, M. (2008). *Building and using datasets on armed conflicts*. Amsterdam: IOS Press.

Kupchan, C. A. (2012). The decline of the West: Why America must prepare for the end of dominance. *The Atlantic*, 20 March. Retrieved May 24, 2016, from http://www.theatlantic.com/international/archive/2012/03/the-decline-of-the-west-why-america-must-prepare-for-the-end-of-dominance/254779/

Levy, J. S. (2008). Case studies: Types, designs, and logics of inference. *Conflict Management and Peace Science, 25*(1), 1–18.

Lim, C. L. (2016). *Doing comparative politics: An introduction to approaches and issues*. Boulder: Lynne Rienner.

Mandelbaum, M. (1988). *The fate of nations: The search for national security in the nineteenth and twentieth centuries*. Cambridge: Cambridge University Press.

Miles, M. B., & Huberman, A. M. (1994). *Qualitative data analysis: An expanded sourcebook*. Thousand Oaks, CA: Sage.

Moyo, D. (2012). *Winner take all: China's race for resources and what it means for the world*. New York: Basic Books.

Naidu, S., Corkin, L., & Herman, H. (2009). Introduction. *Politikon, 36*(1), 1–4.

Owen, D. S., & Strong, T. B. (2004). *The vocation lectures*. Cambridge: Hackett Publishing.

Pang, Z. (2009). China's non-intervention question. *Global Responsibility to Protect, 1*, 237–252.

Reus-Smit, C. (2013). The concept of intervention. *Review of International Studies, 39*(5), 1057–1076.

Ritchie, J., & Spencer, L. (2002). Qualitative data analysis for applied policy research. In M. Huberman & M. B. Miles (Eds.), *The qualitative researcher's companion* (pp. 305–330). Thousand Oaks, CA: Sage.

Rose, G. (1998). Neoclassical realism and theories of foreign policy. *World Politics, 51*(1), 144–172.

Sarkees, M. R. (2014). Patterns of civil wars in the twenty-first century: The decline of civil war? In E. Newman & K. DeRouen Jr. (Eds.), *Routledge handbook of civil wars* (pp. 236–256). London: Routledge.

Schweller, R. L. (1999). Realism and the present great power system: Growth and positional conflict over scarce resources. In E. B. Kapstein & M. Mastanduno (Eds.), *Unipolar politics: Realism and state strategies after the Cold War* (pp. 28–68). New York: Columbia University Press.

Smith-Hoehn, J. (2010). *Rebuilding the security sector in post-conflict societies: Perceptions from urban Liberia and Sierra Leone.* Muenster: LIT Verlag.

Stein, J. G. (2010). From bipolar to unipolar order: System structure and conflict resolution. In U. Rabi (Ed.), *International intervention in local conflicts: Crisis management and conflict resolution since the Cold War* (pp. 3–18). London: IB Tauris.

Steiner, B. H. (2004). *Collective preventive diplomacy: A study in international conflict management.* New York: State University of New York Press.

Taliaferro, J. W. (2006). State building for future wars: Neoclassical realism and the resource-extractive state. *Security Studies, 15*(3), 464–495.

Themnér, L. (2013). *UCDP/PRIO armed conflict dataset codebook.* Uppsala Conflict Data Program. Retrieved September 3, 2013, from http://www.pcr.uu.se/digitalAssets/124/124920_1codebook_ucdp_prio-armed-conflict-dataset-v4_2013.pdf

Tillema, H. K. (1989). Foreign overt military intervention in the nuclear age. *Journal of Peace Research, 26*(2), 179–196.

UNCTAD. (2004). *The least developed countries report 2004.* Geneva: United Nations.

Wicks, D. (2010). Deviant case analysis. In A. J. Mills, G. Durepos, & E. Wiebe (Eds.), *Encyclopedia of case study research* (pp. 289–291). California: Sage Publications.

Yan, X. (2006). The rise of China and its power status. *The Chinese journal of international politics, 1*(1), 5–33.

Yin, R. K. (1994). *Case study research: Design and methods.* London: Sage Publication.

Zakaria, F. (1998). *From wealth to power: The unusual origins of America's world role.* New Jersey: Princeton University Press.

Zheng, B. (2005). China's "peaceful rise" to great-power status. *Foreign Affairs,* Vol. 84, No. 5, pp. 18–24.

CHAPTER 2

Bringing China into the Foreign Intervention Discourse

2.1 Introduction

The global discourse on intervention in external conflicts is largely Western-centric, focusing on the intervention methods and strategies of Western global powers. This is partly because China, until recently, was together with other states in Africa largely in "the limbo of the international system ... passively absorb[ing] the shock of having been made dependent on other parts of the world" (Bayart 2000, p. 217). Apart from reliance on Western global powers, China had no global import of its own, the nature and stability of its statehood was questioned, and it hardly constituted the focus of IR studies.[1] While China due to its massive economic capabilities is increasingly becoming noticeable in IR studies, still, together with the rest of the African countries, "even when they are made the focal point of IR, they are not treated as the referent object."[2] In fact, they are confined to the fringes of IR—frequently portrayed as inert spectators in the gallery of global power politics. Their actions and strategies in global politics, and in particular how they ought to respond to external conflicts, are interpreted through Western-centric lenses.

For China, this might be beginning to change—"the transfer of global wealth and power now under way—roughly from West to East"[3] is turning the tide. China, once the "Sick Man of the East,"[4] is now the second largest global economy, and it has achieved that in less than half a century. Together with other non-Western rising powers such as Brazil and India,[5]

O. Hodzi, *The End of China's Non-Intervention Policy in Africa*,
Critical Studies of the Asia-Pacific,
https://doi.org/10.1007/978-3-319-97349-4_2

China on an "upward trajectory of power and influence,"[6] a global phenomenon that Fareed Zakaria has described as the "the birth of a truly global order"[7] and the "third great power shift of the modern era."[8] This "modern era" global shift in economic power is coinciding with a "shift in relative interstate capabilities (power shifts)..., providing exceptional opportunities for rising powers to assert themselves both geopolitically and in the global governance arena" (Armijo and Roberts 2014, p. 503; Armijo and Katada 2014, p. 5). The result is that the emergence of China and its expanding role in global governance are challenging the United States' pre-eminence.[9]

In addition, the shifts are happening in the context of widespread dissatisfaction among countries in Africa with the global governance and unilateral military intervention strategies of the United States and its allies.[10] Hence, there are far-reaching transformations in the nature of the existing "posthegemonic" global order, which John G. Ikenberry defines "as an evolving order marked by increasingly far-reaching and complex forms of international cooperation that erode state sovereignty and reallocate on a global scale the sites and sources of political authority" (Ikenberry 2010, p. 18). The US National Intelligence Council warned that the diffusion of power referred to by Ikenberry can significantly reverse "the historic rise of the West since 1750 and restore Asia's weight in the global economy and world politics."[11] That reversal, if successful, could mean a return to the Westphalian order which was characterised by state independence, state sovereignty and non-intervention—values that have already endeared China to leaders of developing countries, especially in Africa. However, a review of current IR theory, in particular the realist and constructivist approaches, suggests a disconnect between theory and practice, indicating that there has been no significant shift in the global discourse on intervention in foreign conflicts.

2.2 Intervention in IR: Marginality of Non-Western Rising Powers

International Relations scholars generally agree that the twenty-first century has been so far characterised by "the rise of the rest ... [and by] the creation of an international system in which countries in all parts of the world are no longer objects or observers but players in their own right" (Zakaria 2008, p. 2, 3). As put by Christopher Layne, the US unipolar moment was just a geopolitical interlude that carried within it seeds of its own demise, and ultimately gave way to multipolarity.[12] However, theoretical developments in IR have not kept abreast with this unfolding empirical phenomenon. Hans Morgenthau's argument is that intervention is a foreign policy instrument used by great powers on behalf of their interests. To others such as Tillema (1989) and Steiner (2004, p. 16), intervention is a preserve of great powers. Such statements as Morgenthau's are instructive to the theoretical and empirical study of intervention and world politics such that a mention of intervention invokes the idea of a Western great power intruding into the domestic affairs of a small state in the Global South. Part of the reason why intervention is conceived of in that way is because realism is still the dominant paradigm in the study of international politics[13] and intervention (Morgenthau 1967; Bull 1984; Feste 1992). At the core of the realist thinking is that although theoretically all states exist within an interstate system that supposedly guarantees their sovereign equality, "the strong do to others what others cannot do to them" (Mandelbaum 1988, p. 135). The implication as argued by Pinar Bilgin is that the primacy of Western-centric IR compels both students and scholars to focus on great powers in the West while relegating Global South powers to the peripheries of their thinking.[14]

This relegation of non-Western powers is evidently more ubiquitous in the global discourse on intervention in external conflicts. Immanuel Wallerstein, architect of the World Systems Theory, put it that "strong states find it far easier to 'intervene' in the internal affairs of weaker states than vice versa,"[15] the major factor being that strong states possess military and economic capabilities that other states do not have. The reasoning about intervention has always been influenced by dominant global powers, which define and delimit its parameters. Andrew Keene illustrates this point when he explains that in the nineteenth and twentieth centuries Europeans adopted "one kind of relationship, equality and mutual interdependence, as the norm of their dealings with each other, and another, imperial paramountcy, as normal in their relations with non-Europeans" (2002, p. 6). For that reason, a distinction is made "between states of general interests (system-wide interests) and states with limited interests" (Handel 1990, p. 22). Since great powers are states of system-wide influence (due to a combination of their colonial heritage and superior material capabilities), their interests, which they ought to protect, extend beyond their borders and regions; hence, their "basic foreign policy consists of protecting and safeguarding [their] sphere of interest" (Reczei 1971, p. 74).

This distinction falls into Morgenthau's assertion that great powers intervene where their national interest requires it and where their power enables them to succeed.[16] It also follows that in order to explain intervention, realists emphasise national interest (Morgenthau 1967; Bull 1984; Feste 1992) and power (relative material capabilities) as the causal explanatory variables of why global powers intervene in foreign intrastate conflicts and why other states do not. The focus on interests and power as factors compelling states to intervene in other sovereignties demands further but brief explanation. First, national interests, whether domestic or foreign, are not exclusive to Western great powers. Principally, every state, great or small, from the North or the Global South, has interests that may extend beyond its territorial boundaries. What, however, differs among them is the scope of those interests and the methods of intervention they employ on their behalf. More so, the scope of a state's interests is not static or "cast in stone" so to speak. Neoclassical realists understand this better because their main proposition is that states expand their interests abroad when their relative material capabilities increase (Taliaferro 2004, p. 3; Mandelbaum 1988, pp. 134–135; Kennedy 1987, p. xxii; Zakaria 1998, p. 3). Because of their concern with interests and power, classical and neorealists do not explain the intervention behaviour of states like China whose relative material capabilities are increasing and whose interests are expanding abroad. Instead, they ridicule them as "states whose ambitions run ahead of their material capabilities"[17]—that is, rising powers whose expanding foreign interests are not commensurate with their military capabilities.

Secondly, power is a central concept to IR theory. Generally, the concept of power can be defined as either relational or material. However, "by far the majority prefers a material definition of 'power' as the capabilities or resources, mainly military, with which states influence one another. Power in this view is the actual capacity to raise armies, deploy navies, occupy territory, and exert various forms of pressure against other states."[18] Power is therefore usually defined as capabilities "that may or may not be translated into influence over many issues"[19] rather than control, as argued by those who define power from a relational perspective. In his conceptualisation of great powers, Kenneth Waltz defines power in terms of material capabilities. He notes that "states, because they are in a self-help system, have to use their combined capabilities in order to serve their interests. The economic, military, and other capabilities of nations cannot be sectored and separately weighed because state power is multidimensional. States are not placed in the top rank because they excel in one way or another. Their rank depends on how they score on all of the following items: size of population and territory; resource endowment; military strength; political stability; and competence" (Waltz 1979, p. 131).

It can be argued that because great powers, mostly in the West, possess comprehensive capabilities, they tend to have interests that other states do not have, and, in turn, their intervention behaviour is broader. Although Kenneth Waltz advocates an aggregate understanding of states' overall capabilities in deciding their global power status, scholars such as Christopher Layne (1993) give pre-eminence to military capabilities to determine whether a state is a great power or not. They are preoccupied with the "utility and fungibility of military power" (Mastanduno 1997, p. 49). As a result, according to Jack Levy there are four characteristics that distinguish great powers from other states; that is, they possess immense military capabilities which guarantee their security from other states; they are able to project their power abroad; they have a system-wide concept of security and they are able to protect their interests abroad more effectively than other states.[20]

While acknowledging the propensity of great powers to intervene in the internal affairs of small states, Richard Little notes that even small states also have a tendency to interfere in each other's domestic affairs on behalf of their interests.[21] For instance, Zimbabwe, Uganda and Rwanda are small states in the construct of most IR theory, yet they have militarily intervened on several occasions in the Democratic Republic of Congo's (DRC) intrastate armed conflicts. Although it might be rare for a small state to intervene in states beyond its region, that alone does not mean small states and, more so, rising powers should be in the periphery of the intervention discourse as they presently are. In that regard, the demarcation of states into ones with limited interests and others with system-wide interests only serves to show the scope of the reach of their interests and does not explain their intervention behaviour. Accordingly, the pervasive argument that the world's weakest states are the targets of intervention, with the world's most powerful states being the executors[22] which is propagated by realists and widely accepted in IR, does not hold in elucidating the intervention behaviour of states, great, small or rising in foreign intrastate conflicts.

In an anarchic system as envisioned by neorealists' interpretation of IR, "the distribution of power among these units [states] will be the most important variable conditioning their behaviour and the outcome of their interactions over the long run" (Wohlforth 1993, p. 2). Steve Chan challenges this neorealist perspective that state behaviour is determined by the systemic structure. He maintains that "structure is not everything or even the most important thing"[23] because it is not always the case that states in the same systemic structure behave in a similar manner[24]; neither do they share the same interests. One of the major effects of focusing on the systemic structure is that it perpetuates stereotyping and profiling of state behaviour, which has an effect on how intervention is analysed. Pearson fell into the "stereotyping trap" when he concluded that "major powers seem inclined to undertake economic or diplomatic-military protective, ideological, or regional power balance interventions in distant targets, while middle and small powers are likely to undertake territorial and social-protective interventions, as well as regional power balance interventions in nearby targets" (1974, pp. 262–263). To the contrary, history is awash with states that attempt to punch above their weight. Therefore, narratives that confine state behaviour to structure of the system disregard those "ambitious" states and expressions of their capabilities in foreign interactions.

Accordingly, the focus on the distribution of power in the interstate system and a bias towards military power has significant implications on the study of intervention. First, by explaining state behaviour as a function of a state's international attributes, particularly its relative military power,[25] the focus of intervention is transfixed on military intervention by great powers, disregarding the economic power and geoeconomic influence that China and other emerging economies have. Even though "markets can have as much influence as militaries"[26] realists would still argue that rising powers simply are not great powers; hence they cannot do what great powers do—"great powers intervene in the periphery because they enjoy a favourable international power position" (Taliaferro 2004, p. 3). Second, third-party intervention in foreign conflicts is understood from the perspective of great powers,[27] particularly the United States and is predominantly focused on intervention strategies used by such great powers. This suggests that intervention is a foreign policy tool[28] used by major powers to extend their influence and establish hegemony beyond their regions at the exclusion of other competing powers.

This prevalent focus on military capabilities of great powers also promotes the erroneous conception of intervention as coercive military action taken by states with higher relative capabilities against weaker states.[29] The implication is that it effectively inhibits critical investigation and analysis of other forms of intervention employed by different states that have material capabilities other than military capabilities. As a result, "the foreign policy choices of second-tier states [rising global powers] are arrived at deductively, irrespective of whether or not they correspond particularly closely either to policy options that have actually been adopted or to understandings of those choices within second-tier states themselves" (Hurrell 2006, p. 6). This is apparent in existing literature. For instance, Stephen Walt asks two questions: "How do the great powers choose which states to protect, and how do weaker states decide whose protection to accept?" (1987, p. 1). He completely ignores rising global powers and does not ask what they do. The disregard of rising global powers in current theoretical analyses is therefore distinct; hence the realist narrative fails to explain intervention by non-Western global powers in foreign intrastate armed conflicts.

Contrary to realists' perspectives, "constructivists focus on identity and ideas through enlightened agency" (Snyder 2005, p. 56). They dispute that interests and identities "follow either logically or causally from anarchy," arguing that they are "due to process, not structure … structure has no existence or causal powers apart from process" (Wendt 1992, pp. 394–395). In her book *The Purpose of Intervention*, Martha Finnemore posits that state interests are indeterminate because "in any case of intervention, one could impute a very reasonable set of interests that would explain intervention and another equally plausible set that would explain non-intervention" (2003, p. 5). So, instead of focusing on interests, she argues that focus should be on changing perceptions of interests and the utility of intervention as a tool of policy (Finnemore 2003, p. 5). She therefore proposed a theory of "strategic social construction" to explain how powerful states determine the values and perceptions regarding intervention depending on their current geostrategic and security interests. Nicholas Wheeler concurs, but he notes that those values and perceptions have to be accepted by other states in the international system as being legitimate and justifiable (Wheeler 2000; Finnemore 2003, p. 73). Thus, "intervention is not just a fig leaf for powerful states to cover their geopolitical pursuits but also a result of shifting views within societies about acceptable behaviour" (Ikenberry 2001). Yet still, like the realists, constructivists acknowledge that "rules about intervention are strongly if not entirely shaped by the actions of powerful states that actually have the capacity to intervene" (Finnemore 2003, p. 5). This consolidates the realist argument that the international system and the status of a state within that system play a crucial role in determining a state's foreign policy and behaviour.

A follow-on question to the constructivist's perspective on intervention is whether states intervene on the basis of objective national interests or on interests that are constructed over time based on existing and constructed values. Alexander Wendt argues that how a state acts is dependent on its identity and related interests. He maintains that "each identity has associated needs or objective interests, and actors' understanding of these in turn constitute the subjective interests that motivate their action" (Wendt 1999, p. 198). What Alexander Wendt supposes is that a state's identity shapes its interests upon which its foreign policy actions are based. Since he defines "national interest as the objective interests of state-society complexes, consisting of four needs: physical survival, autonomy, economic well-being, and collective self-esteem" (Wendt 1999, p. 198) states' foreign policy behaviour is foundationally based on their objective national interests. The interpretation of those interests, however, varies depending on how a state identifies itself. A state that identifies itself as a global power will act differently from a state that identifies itself as a rising power or a small state in the Global South.

The underlying factor among constructivists is that "the political and cultural context in which national interests are forged" matters (Burchill 2005, p. 205). Although states have the same objective national interests, their self-identity compels them to re-interpret those objective interests which explains why a state may behave differently at different times. How a state identifies itself determines how it acts in order to protect its interests abroad. National interests are therefore subjective interests because states interpret their identity and needs based on their different political, economic and cultural contexts. While constructivists assist in understanding identity and interest formation among states, their assumption, particularly Alexander Wendt's proposition that there are objective national interests (physical survival, autonomy, economic well-being and collective self-esteem) upon which a state's subjective interests are based, suggests that a state's relative position among other states determines its foreign policy actions. When a state expands its interests abroad and increases its material capabilities enabling it to have system-wide interests, then it will act differently than a state experiencing economic depression and shrinking material capabilities. The implication is that as a state interprets its interests broadly, it tends to behave differently. Thus, as put by Alexander Wendt "states' interpretation of these needs tends to be biased in a self-interested direction, which predisposes them to competitive, 'Realist' politics but that this does *not* mean that states are inherently self-interested" (Wendt 1999, p. 198).

There are several limitations within the classical realist, neorealist and constructivist explanations of external intervention in foreign intrastate armed conflicts. To begin with, realists and constructivists overly focus on material and structural factors in the international system to explain foreign intervention in both intrastate and interstate conflicts. By narrowly focusing on systemic variables as the key sources of foreign intervention behaviour, their analysis does not explain variations in the intervention behaviour of states within the same systemic rank or variations in the intervention behaviour of a particular state over time. Secondly, the liberal strand of IR literature on intervention emphasises economic interdependence among states and domestic processes and actors such as business interest groups to explain why states intervene in foreign intrastate conflicts. Although fundamental, on its own, this approach does not adequately explain whether or not the rise in a state's relative power has an influence on its intervention behaviour. The implication is that the focus is overly on states of global significance, which are normally the United States, Britain and France such that current understandings of the nature, methods and purpose of intervention are from these powers' perspectives. By only considering major global powers as interveners and the rest as targets of intervention, it disregards the intervention behaviour of states in transition from small powers to great powers, that is, rising powers. This encourages the "tendency to overstate the causal power of structural-global variables" (Regilme 2014, p. 1392), which in turn limits their explanatory power and scope of analysis.

How then can theories of foreign policy and IR explain the external intervention behaviour of rising powers? Broadly, there has to be an acknowledgement that the emergence of non-Western rising powers such as China, Brazil, South Africa and India "is transforming the geopolitical landscape and testing the institutional foundations of the post-World War II liberal order … they are intent on altering rules, not adopting them hook, line and sinker. These countries do not grant the United States the sole authority to define the limits of responsible sovereignty. They believe they are entitled to reshape international arrangements to suit themselves" (Patrick 2010). Indeed, the rise of these powers, particularly China, is causing a re-calibration of the global order. Inevitably, their rise has led to a "relative decline of the United States' position in the world—and with this relative decline in power an absolute decline in influence and independence, [hence] today's world is increasingly one of distributed, rather than concentrated power" (Haass 2008, p. 46). Where once the United States could unilaterally intervene or influence the international community to support its interventionist policies, it is now beginning to face resistance not just from China and Russia, but also from democracies like South Africa and Brazil. Libya and Syria present good examples of the diminished dominance of major powers' influence as far as intervention in foreign intrastate armed conflicts is concerned.

On the other side, the rise in power by these states has had an impact on their domestic political processes and subsequently their foreign policies. No longer are they confined to their regions or neighbourhoods; instead they are venturing further afield—challenging assumptions that geographical proximity is a factor in their intervention in foreign intrastate armed conflicts. In the process, new domestic actors are emerging that are beginning to influence domestic political processes and seeking to influence their countries' foreign policy and behaviour. There is therefore need for a theory such as neoclassical realism that examines both sides, starting from the effect of the international system on the foreign policy (intervention) behaviour of rising powers, and then moving further to also consider the influence of domestic politics and national interests on a state's foreign policy behaviour. Neoclassical realism combines those two essential elements and provides a basis for explaining the intervention behaviour of rising powers in foreign intrastate armed conflicts. But, how is intervention by non-Western rising powers accounted for in empirical studies?

2.3 Bringing China In

The focus of IR theorists remains largely hinged on explaining the intervention behaviour of Western global powers, and, where references are made to non-Western rising powers, they usually are from a Western-centric perspective. John Mearsheimer suggested a "theory of international politics that explains how rising great powers are likely to act and how the other states in the system will react to them. That theory must be logically sound and it must account for the past behaviour of rising great powers" (2004, p. 1). Others have argued that such a theory should note that the relationships they "hypothesise about might not apply across all regions of the world."[30] Steve Chan further argues that "theories based primarily on Europe's or America's experiences cannot be automatically assumed to be generalizable to Asia or China but at the same time, Asia's or China's experiences are also not necessarily unique" (2012, p. 3). As noted above, what is therefore needed is a theory that explains how non-Western rising powers are likely to act within the international system, and that can be achieved only by focusing on the rising powers themselves as "referent objects" rather than focusing on "perceptions and interests calculation of the West" regarding them (Bilgin 2008, p. 11). Developing a theory that explains how China and other non-Western rising powers act within the liberal international order is, however, beyond the scope of this book.

What is within the scope of this book is a discussion of how the rise of China is forcing a reimagining of intervention, its nature, methods, strategies and purposes—in other words, how is China influencing changes in the method, practice and purpose of external intervention. As it stands, the intervention behaviour of Western global powers—particularly the United States, Britain and France—also dominates empirical studies focused on interventions in foreign internal conflicts.[31] For instance, Patrick Regan analysed 196 cases of intervention in 138 intrastate conflicts that occurred over a period of 50 years, from 1944 to 1994. Of those conflicts, he observed that "nearly 40% (76 cases) of all interventions were carried out by major powers, 5% (10 cases) of the interventions were under UN auspices, and the remainder were attributed to minor powers" (1996, p. 345). During the Cold War era, the Soviet Union and the United States were the major interveners in foreign conflicts, albeit using proxies. In the post-Cold War period, the United States became the leading consistent unilateral intervener followed by France, which has maintained influence as well as economic and political interests in most of its former African colonies.

Few studies have therefore analysed intervention in foreign civil wars by neighbouring countries as well as Third World countries.[32] The main reason is obviously that there have only been a handful of states that consistently and unilaterally intervene in foreign intrastate conflicts. From 1944 to 1994, as observed by Patrick Regan, China only intervened in six intrastate conflicts, an average of once every decade, and all the six interventions were in Asian conflicts. The United States, Russia, France and Britain are by far the major interveners. Having made that observation, Regan concluded that success of an intervention strategy is not based entirely on features of the conflict but on characteristics of the intervention strategy and on the status of the intervener. The deduction was that interventions by major powers are more successful and common because they, the major powers, possess "larger and projectable military forces… [And] a wider range of economic resources that can be brought to bear in a foreign policy role" (Regan 1996, p. 348). Subsequently, the question of "who intervenes" has not been popular among intervention scholars, because it seemed obvious that only major powers intervene in other states' internal conflicts. Accordingly, having been explained at different levels of analysis using various methods and approaches, intervention is still portrayed as a foreign policy tool employed by Western global powers to protect their national interests and expand their foreign influence.

As a result, the discourse on intervention is fixated on non-consensual intervention by powerful Western states such as the United States, Britain and France, which possess extensive military power and global influence. The effect is that intervention is generally regarded as consisting of "various forms of non-consensual action that directly challenge state sovereignty" (Weiss 2007, p. 18). Meanwhile, intervention by China is either neglected or at best relegated to the peripheries of third-party intervention, international politics and foreign policy discourse. But that may not remain the same for too long—the emergence of China in global security governance and conflict management and resolution is beginning to challenge the dominance of the United States, France and Britain in external intervention. What makes China more imperative is that it does not entirely subscribe to the Western-centric order[33] or Western norms of intervention, R2P,[34] human rights, good governance and democracy,[35] upon which the global discourse on intervention is premised.

Since China does not fully subscribe to the liberal international order values, attempts to bring it in have predominantly focused on the need for the socialisation of China. For instance, in 2005, Robert Zoellick, the then US Deputy Secretary of State, sparked a debate on what it would take to make China a "responsible stakeholder," able to resolve global challenges alongside other Western global powers. In a speech titled *Whither China: From Membership to Responsibility*, he said:

> China's involvement with troublesome states indicates at best a blindness to consequences and at worst something more ominous… On my early morning runs in Khartoum, I saw Chinese doing *tai chi* exercises. I suspect they were in Sudan for the oil business. But China should take more than oil from Sudan—it should take some responsibility for resolving Sudan's human crisis. It could work with the United States, the UN, and others to support

> the African Union's peacekeeping mission, to provide humanitarian relief to Darfur, and to promote a solution to Sudan's conflicts. (Zoellick 2005)

In his view, China was acting as an irresponsible global stakeholder, concerned only with economic and strategic gains, and failing to intervene where it was supposed to.

Zoellick's speech acknowledged that of the current rising powers, China was the most significantly able to impose challenges on the systemic order. Second, it gave an impression that China should and has the capacity to take more responsibility in resolving internal conflicts in countries it trades with[36] alongside the United States, the United Nations and other actors that presumably hold the same view of global governance as the United States; and thirdly, that China should go beyond its own economic and strategic interests. Of more significance however, is that Zoellick's speech portrayed China as a power that needed to be tamed and socialised into a responsible stakeholder within the prevailing liberal world order. That thought reflects the dominant opinion in IR—"why can China, as an illiberal, authoritarian state, make rules for the world regarding humanitarian intervention? Why is it not the other way around in which international institutions socialise China into accepting the liberal humanitarian norms?" (Lee et al. 2012, p. 437).

In terms of the discourse on China's foreign policy, Zoellick's speech represents the prevailing view that China is an irresponsible power that constitutes a threat to the present-day global governance order. It is therefore not surprising that literature on whether China is a *status quo* or revisionist state and how the United States should respond to the "China threat" flourished. But, nowhere has the impact of China's rise in global power and influence been seen more than in Africa. What is more interesting is that both China and Africa "relate to the global system with a mutually reinforcing sense of historical grievances ... they share a neo-Westphalian commitment to state sovereignty and non-intervention"[37] much to the chagrin of Western global powers. On one hand, China's official view of the global system provokes "a flurry of criticisms aimed at Beijing's perceived amoralism" (Taylor 2007, p. 139), and, on the other, it made China popular among African leaders (Pang 2009, p. 238). Against this backdrop, research on China-Africa engagement has progressed from the human rights and good governance discourse of the late 1990s to the specificities of bilateral trade relations between China and individual African countries, particularly countries that possess strategic natural resources such as oil. Be that as it may, research on China's intervention behaviour in intrastate armed conflicts, particularly in Africa, is beginning to emerge[38] although it is primarily focused on China's evolving foreign official policy principle of non-interference in other states' internal affairs, and China's peacekeeping operations.

Research on the above two issues—China's non-intervention principle, and peacekeeping operations—often tends to be based on single case studies and is overly descriptive without systematically connecting theoretical thought with empirical analysis. For instance, much focus has been on China's engagement with Sudan, particularly in relation to the Darfur crisis.[39] As observed by Ian Taylor, researchers focusing on China-Sudan relations were mainly concerned with "Beijing's weapons-exporting policy and its involvement in Sudan's long running civil war" (Taylor 2007, p. 143), and they sought to prove the transformation of China's foreign policy from non-intervention in the domestic affairs of other states to conditional interference (Pang 2009). Although they provide detailed empirical analyses, the analyses are based on diverse explanatory variables that differ with each case study such that it is difficult to generalise the findings and establish patterns and trends in China's intervention behaviour. In the end, "most of these studies seem to lack a 'good theory' that presents 'the big picture' of what is happening in myriad realms of activity" (Regilme 2014, p. 1395). The bringing in of China into the global discourse on intervention in foreign conflicts is therefore characterised by the traditional complexities of a global order dominated by liberal values that is hesitant of acknowledging diversities in *modus operandi*. The attitude is that China, as an authoritarian and illiberal rising power, should be socialised to intervene in foreign conflicts in a manner and method consistent with those of Western global powers.

2.4 Reimagining Intervention

The nature and method of China's intervention, particularly in African intrastate armed conflicts, do not squarely fit into the dominant IR understanding of intervention as a non-consensual action, usually military in nature taken by a great power against another state. Part of the reason is that the dominant understanding of intervention is consistent with the dictionary definition of intervention as a "noun of action" that explains "the action of intervening, 'stepping in', or interfering in any affair, so as to affect its course or issue,"[40] which suits realists' arguments.

This conceptualisation of intervention as a non-consensual concrete action by a sovereign state is also attributable to the behaviourist approach which is concerned with an operational definition of intervention. As a result, literature on intervention is "pervaded with discussions of military interventions, propaganda interventions, economic interventions, diplomatic interventions, and ideological interventions, not to mention customs interventions and other highly specific actions through which one state experiences the impact of another" (Rosenau 1969, pp. 344–345). Since the "width of activities this term can cover"[41] is inexhaustible, understanding intervention in that sense makes it imprecise and "extremely ambiguous"[42]—conveying diverse meanings to different actors and scholars.

In practice, especially among state leaders and diplomats, what intervention is is a question of "whose ox is gored." This is partly because the thinking about intervention is structured by the contemporary distribution and differentiation of global power combined with politico-spatial assumptions[43] within an existing global order. The rise of China as an assertive global power, self-identifying as non-interventionary, is therefore challenging conceptualisations of key concepts in intervention such as state sovereignty in relation to both state-state relations and state-society relations.

It goes without saying that sovereignty is a key concept to determining what intervention is and it is at the centre of the global discourse on intervention. What makes it even more imperative is that there seems to be a difference in the conceptualisation of sovereignty between the West on the one side and China together with other countries in the Global South on the other. Historically, interpretations of what constitutes intervention correspond with shifts in the ideas and practice of state sovereignty vis-à-vis state-state relations. However, there is enough evidence to suggest that state-state relations have constantly been reconfigured. Scholars that take a historical approach to studying intervention argue that the concept takes on different meanings, or, at the very least, its boundaries are either shrunk or expanded depending on the existent global balance of power and dominant discourse regarding state-state relations and state-society relations. What constitutes intervention is therefore a factor of global power distributions, such that the perimeters of sovereignty and intervention shift depending on the prevailing global power distribution configurations. In the twenty-first century, state-society relations have been reconfigured and new parameters for intervention in the internal affairs of other states set.

Anne Marie Slaughter, a professor of politics and international affairs at Princeton University, points out that "'intervention' assumes that sovereignty is a closed sphere, when in fact it is an increasingly, and legitimately, permeable one." The assumed closed sphere of sovereignty vis-à-vis intervention emanates from the wording of Article 2(7) of the UN Charter, which states that "Nothing contained in the present Charter shall authorize the United Nations to intervene in matters which are essentially within the domestic jurisdiction of any state." But, the reality is that state sovereignty within the Westphalian system of international order is no longer sacrosanct and inviolable. The principle of R2P adopted at the World Summit in 2003 is an example of global attempts to set those new parameters by reconceptualising state sovereignty, the basis being that where a state is not able to protect its citizens from crimes against humanity, war crimes and genocide, members of the international community have an obligation to intervene. Actions previously regarded as intervention in the sense that they transgressed another state's sovereignty are no longer regarded as such because R2P expands the boundaries of state sovereignty. If state sovereignty delineated the private from the public, R2P has blurred that divide, making Lu's argument that intervention "assumes some distinction between the private and public domains" redundant.

Although principles such as R2P attempt to limit claims to state sovereignty, the reality is that the current global system is still essentially a sovereign order in which sovereign states constitute the core units that at times mandate or delegate their individual and collective right to act to multilateral institutions. The case of Libya and Syria shows that the reconceptualisation of state sovereignty even through R2P is facing resistance from non-Western rising powers that are seeking to restore the primacy of state sovereignty and non-intervention in the internal affairs of other states. China is at the forefront of that resistance because it self-identifies as a non-interventionary power whose foreign policy is premised on the Five Principles of Peaceful Coexistence: **mutual respect for sovereignty and territorial integrity**, mutual non-aggression, **non-interference in each other's internal affairs**, equality and mutual benefit, and peaceful coexistence. China's insistence on the traditional understanding of state sovereignty finds resonance with other countries in the Global South that regard the erosion of the principle of state sovereignty as a ploy by Western powers to intervene in their internal affairs with a veneer of legitimacy that principles like R2P give to the most powerful states.

Nonetheless, the implication is that what intervention is in practice and theory is still determined by contemporary Western conceptualisations of state sovereignty. However, since multilateral organisations, be they regional organisations (ROs) or international organisations (IOs), are also part of the sovereign order, intervention can no longer be limited to acts by sovereign states. ROs and IOs such as the North Atlantic Treaty Organisation (NATO), Economic Community of West African States and the United Nations are known to have intervened in several intrastate and interstate armed conflicts on behalf of their sovereign member states. This means either states that are opposed to intervention in the internal affairs of other states, or those that lack the material capabilities to unilaterally intervene in foreign conflicts, can do so through multilateral institutions.[44] What this suggests is that a contemporary definition of intervention ought to take into consideration the linkage between sovereign states and multilateral institutions. This is particularly important when analysing interventions by China and other rising powers which in most cases do not yet possess the capabilities or the political will to conduct unilateral interventions, but that instead use regional and international organisations to achieve their intervention objectives in foreign conflicts, while maintaining their identity as non-interventionary powers.

Secondly, contrary to the notion that intervention only consists of action rather than inaction, it can be argued that by not taking action in cases where if action had been taken a different outcome would have been reached, states actually intervene. Peter Schraeder explains this view in a hypothetical situation: "if Israel were attacked simultaneously by and subjected to an extended military conflict with all its Arab neighbors, complete U.S. neutrality most likely would ensure Israeli defeat" (Schraeder 1989, p. 2). So, even if the United States would not have directly intervened, by withholding its support for Israel, it would have intervened because its inaction would have affected the direction, duration and outcome of the conflict. Another notable example is China's tacit support for an imposition of a no-fly zone in Libya which significantly tilted the balance of power in the Libyan armed conflict against the Gaddafi regime leading to its downfall. If China had used its veto in the UNSC, the no-fly zone that incapacitated Gaddafi's air force would not have imposed and a different outcome might have been obtained. By abstaining, China effectively determined the duration and possible outcome of the conflict. Using abstention from voting in the UNSC Resolution 1978 (2011) that imposed a no-fly zone against Libya paving the way for military intervention by

NATO was part of China's strategy of intervention in foreign intrastate armed conflicts through inaction. As put by Wu Zhengyu and Ian Taylor, "abstention is an expedient strategy for China, since it precludes both criticism from the West regarding obstructionist opposition to contentious peace operations *and* criticism from the developing world, allowing China either to disassociate itself from controversial operations or to remain in accordance with its doctrine of non-interference even with respect to popular peace operations" (2011, p. 11). Thus, intervention is not confined to actions by sovereign states and IOs such as the United Nations; it also includes the strategy use of "inaction" to affect conflict dynamics in targeted states.

Thirdly, intervention can be defined as an action or inaction undertaken by a sovereign state or an intergovernmental actor of the international system, the purpose of which is to affect the duration, direction or outcome of an intrastate armed conflict. Implicit within this definition is the non-consensual nature of the action or inaction taken by the intervening actor. The widely held view is that where there is consent, there is legitimacy; therefore, the act is not considered as amounting to intervention. As a result, intervening actors strive to get the consent of the target of the intervention to avoid the controversies of non-consensual intervention. The challenge with consent is that it is difficult to determine whether it has even been given voluntarily by the appropriate authority or whether it has even been given in the first place. In the *Armed Activities on the Territory of the Congo (Democratic Republic of Congo* versus *Uganda)* case, the International Court of Justice considered arguments by Uganda that its armed forces were in the DRC at the invitation of the latter even though it was clear that the DRC government did not have effective control of major parts of the country. Similarly, states whose foreign policy is against intervention use consent to justify their intervention in other states. For instance, China argues that it is mediating the conflict in South Sudan at the invitation of the parties involved, and therefore, its actions are not intervention. Susan D. Wing describes it as intervention by invitation (2016, p. 71). But even when interventions are consensual or by invitation they also "subvert the managerial capacity of the state vis-a-vis the welfare of its citizens" (Conteh-Morgan 2001). Accordingly, the challenge with making consent or its absence central to the conceptualisation of intervention is that the same act or inaction taken with the objective of affecting the direction, duration or outcome of an intrastate conflict may be an act of intervention or not by merely determining whether consent was given by the target state.

The issue of whether or not there was consent potentially leads to inconsistency and lack of precision in the meanings attached to intervention—the understanding of intervention will be "structured by pre-existing vocabularies" and dependent on what states say intervention is and is not. As observed by Christian Reus-Smit, "just as meanings attached to words can change over time, actors can use different words to refer to the same thing,"[45] making the conceptualisation of intervention subjective and dependent on state interests. For example, the US support for rebel movements in Nicaragua was considered as intervention whereas China's support of liberation movements in Africa was seen as "friendly" support. Some may argue that the purpose of intervention and the relationship between the intervening actor and the target of intervention determine whether an action is considered to be an act of intervention or not. As an example, the government of South Sudan welcomed China's mediation efforts in the country's civil war, saying: "we welcome the Chinese role which we believe is constructive and seeks to resolve the conflict in South Sudan"[46]; but when the United States attempted to aid the process by imposing sanctions on those forces that could threaten the stability in South Sudan, the South Sudanese government accused the United States of meddling in its internal affairs,[47] yet the objective of the sanctions was to compel unwilling opposition and government leaders to respect the peace agreement signed in Addis Ababa. It cannot be argued that the United States had an ill-motive in forcing parties to abide by a peace agreement they had agreed upon. As shown in these two examples, if the conceptualisation of intervention is left to the whims of states to decide, then anything can be either intervention or not depending on the actors involved. It would simply make the concept more subjective and unscientific, giving it a "perplexing vagueness of meaning" (Winfield 1932, p. 236).

In an attempt to suit different circumstances, but in no way different from the above, Martha Finnemore suggests that "to qualify as intervention states had to use the term to describe the activity. Those involved had to understand that they were engaging in something called 'intervention' and had to use the term when writing to and talking with one another at the time" (Finnemore 2003, pp. 11–12). As previously argued, rather than avoiding vagueness and subjectivity in defining "intervention," Martha Finnemore adds to the confusion and amplifies the term's vagueness. Intervening states always justify their actions and do not usually refer to their actions as interventions. President Hollande framed his country's

2013 military intervention in Mali "as repayment of the country's historical debt toward Mali and this as a more acceptable framework of gift and counter gift between states and peoples" (Wing 2016, p. 72). Even more, states such as China that claim strict adherence to the principle of non-intervention never describe their actions as intervention even in cases where they are. In cases when it does intervene, along the same lines as President Hollande, China describes the intervention as mutually beneficial for the country it would have intervened in. Accordingly, the conceptualisation of intervention should go beyond the "telltale terminology … [because states] often engage in practices, and make justificatory claims, without describing what they are doing, or arguing their cases, with recognizable signature terms ('intervention', 'sovereignty', 'rights', 'responsibilities', 'democracy', etc.)" (Reus-Smit 2013, p. 1059). Therefore, there is need for a conceptualisation that "form the basis for a general theory of intervention"[48] by analytically distinguishing "acts of intervention" from states' intentions, interests and justifications.

Based on the above discussion, it is apparent that unlike the United States, China does not openly regard itself as a global power that intervenes in foreign intrastate armed conflicts. In addition, China has not undertaken unilateral military intervention in decades. As it is, Chinese soldiers are still largely confined within Chinese boundaries except those deployed at its military base in Djibouti and troops under the United Nations Peacekeeping operations in Mali and South Sudan; and, above all, Beijing still portrays its foreign policy as non-interventionary, and does not regard its behaviour as intervening in the internal affairs of other states. The common understanding of intervention as an intrusion by a sovereign state into the domestic affairs of another sovereign state is based on three assumptions: (1) intervening actors and the targets of intervention are sovereign states[49]; (2) intervention consists of action rather than inaction and (3) intervention is non-consensual, meaning the target of intervention is opposed to it[50]; therefore, the term does not explain China's activities in Africa and across the globe. Based on that understanding of intervention, it would be difficult to describe China's "actions" in the intrastate armed conflicts in Libya, Mali, South Sudan or any other country as intervention, yet China would have taken steps and measures that strategically affect the affect the duration, direction or outcome of an intrastate armed conflict in another country. Traditional and conventional conceptualisations of intervention as a non-consensual intrusion by a sovereign state into the domestic affairs of another sovereign state therefore do not articulate China's emerging behaviour in African intrastate armed conflicts.

Unlike the United States and France that have a propensity to unilaterally intervene militarily or impose sanctions against African countries, China tends to prefer using multilateral institutions to effect pressure on warring parties to either protect its interests or affect outcomes of the intrastate armed conflicts. As discussed above, this policy has enabled China to avoid being perceived as "interventionist" when in actual effect it uses its position in multilateral institutions such as the UNSC to intervene through action or inaction (votes of abstention, giving tacit approval for interventions) in African intrastate armed conflicts. As noted by Courtney J. Fung, in cases such as Sudan where "host states can block peacekeeping missions from actually deploying by refusing consent or rejecting potential troop contributions, China's perceived reputation as an 'anti-intervention' state can [and has] been a competitive advantage to getting the host state to accept China's troop contribution" (2015, p. 2). Hence troops deployed by China are not considered as intervention forces, while troops from the United States or France are considered intervention forces—the same action with the same impact but perceived differently. What this means is that conventional Western-centric and realist-oriented conceptualisations of intervention in foreign conflicts as being a foreign policy tool used by great powers that possess immense military capabilities to unilaterally intervene in foreign countries do not assist in analysing the evolving nature of China's intervention behaviour in Africa.

In addition, China is subtly but creatively employing its economic, political and diplomatic influence on African states and critical stakeholders to determine the duration, direction and outcomes of their intrastate armed conflicts. Using its dominance in the South Sudan oil sector, and South Sudan's reliance on China for revenue, China was able to compel the warring parties in South Sudan to guarantee protection of its assets and oil facilities. In Libya, it used the strategy of abstention to affect the direction and outcome of the conflict; and in Mali as well as in South Sudan it employed "non-threatening" UN peacekeeping to create a conducive environment in which its economic interests and nationals' safety are guaranteed. In all cases, China's actions and inactions, whether multilateral or unilateral, consensual or non-consensual, affected the duration, direction and outcome of the respective intrastate armed conflicts. And, this is peculiar not just to China, but also to other non-Western rising powers such as India, Brazil and South Africa that frown upon military and "non-consensual" intervention in other states' intrastate armed conflicts.

In order to capture Chinese external intervention behaviour, the focus should not be on its actions in foreign intrastate armed conflicts, but on the impact of such actions. Cognizant of the impact of China's actions and engagement in intrastate armed conflicts in Libya, Mali and South Sudan, it can be argued that intervention ought to be understood as being political, military, economic or diplomatic actions or inactions undertaken by a governmental or intergovernmental actor of the international system (with or without consent of the target state), *the purpose of which is to affect the direction, duration or outcome of an intrastate armed conflict.* The ultimate test for whether an action or inaction taken by one state regarding a conflict in another is intervention or not should be whether that action or inaction, taken unilaterally or multilaterally, with or without consent, affects the duration, direction and outcome of the conflict. This is a test that can be replicated in other cases involving rising powers, or even existing great powers that seek to maintain legitimacy and avoid criticisms that they are intervening in another state's internal armed conflicts. As put by Karen Feste, the definition of intervention can be extended "to include various forms of involvement and assistance by an external state in an ongoing civil war (e.g., U.S. commitments to Greece in the 1940s and covert aid to Afghan resistance fighters in the 1980s)" (2003, p. 178). Similarly, Earl Conteh-Morgan (2001) also broadly conceptualises intervention to include "both coercive/military forms of intervention, and non-military coercive forms of intervention." Accordingly, in determining whether an action or inaction amounts to intervention or not, for China, the most important factor is to determine whether it affected the duration, direction or outcome of the intrastate armed conflicts in Libya, Mali and South Sudan.

Notes

1. Jones, BG 2006, *Decolonizing international relations,* Rowman & Littlefield, Lanham; Tickner, AB & Wæver, O 2009, *International relations scholarship around the world,* Routledge, London; Bilgin, P 2008, 'Thinking past "Western" IR?', *Third World Quarterly,* vol. 29, no. 1, pp. 5–23; Cornelissen, S, Cheru, F & Shaw, TM 2011, *Africa and international relations in the 21st century,* Palgrave Macmillan, London; Dunn, KC & Shaw, TM 2001, *Africa's challenge to international relations theory,* Palgrave Macmillan, London.

2. Bilgin, P 2008, 'Thinking past 'Western' IR?' *Third World Quarterly,* vol. 29, no. 1, p. 11.
3. National Intelligence Council (US) 2008, *Global Trends 2025: A Transformed World,* Central Intelligence Agency, Washington D.C., pp. iv–vii.
4. Scott, D 2008, *China and the international system, 1840–1949: Power, presence, and perceptions in a century of humiliation,* State University of New York Press, New York, p. xi.
5. Alexandroff, AS & Cooper, AF 2010, *Rising states, rising institutions: Challenges for global governance,* Brookings Institution Press, Washington D.C., p. 1.
6. Hart, AF & Jones, BD 2010, 'How do rising powers rise?' *Survival,* vol. 52, no. 6, p. 67.
7. Zakaria, F 2008, *The Post-American World*, W.W. Norton, New York, p. 3.
8. Ibid., p. 2.
9. Layne, C 1993, 'The unipolar illusion: Why new great powers will rise', *International Security*, vol. 17, no. 4, p. 7.
10. In a leaked diplomatic cable, former US Ambassador to the United Nations Zalmay Khalilzad opined that "on the most important issues of the day—sanctions, human rights, the Middle East, etc.—Brazil, India, and most African states are currently far less sympathetic to our views than our European allies" (29 December 2007). Available at: http://www.wikileaks.org/plusd/cables/07USUNNEWYORK1225_a.html
11. National Intelligence Council (US) 2013, *Global Trends 2030: Alternative Worlds,* Central Intelligence Agency, Washington D.C., p. 15.
12. Layne, C 1993, 'The unipolar illusion: Why new great powers will rise', *International Security*, vol. 17, no. 4, p. 7.
13. Mastanduno, M 1997, 'Preserving the unipolar moment: Realist theories and U.S. grand strategy after the Cold War', *International Security,* vol. 21, no. 4, p. 49.
14. Bilgin, P 2008, 'Thinking past 'Western' IR?' *Third World Quarterly,* vol. 29, no. 1, p. 10.
15. Wallerstein, IM 2004, *World-systems analysis: An introduction,* Duke University Press, Durham and London, p. 55.
16. Morgenthau, HJ 1967, 'To intervene or not to intervene', *Foreign Affairs,* vol. 45, no. 3, p. 436.
17. Hurrell, A 2006, 'Hegemony, liberalism and global order: What space for would-be great powers?' *International Affairs,* vol. 82, no. 1, p. 2.
18. Wohlforth, WC 1993, *The elusive balance: power and perceptions during the Cold War,* Cornell University Press, Ithaca, N.Y., p. 5.
19. Ibid.
20. Levy, J 1983, *War in the modern great power system, 1495–1975,* University Press of Kentucky, Lexington, pp. 11–19.

21. Little, R 1987, 'Revisiting intervention: A survey of recent developments', *Review of International Studies*, vol. 13, p. 49.
22. Yoshihara, S 2010, *Waging war to make peace: U.S. intervention in global conflicts*, Praeger: California, p. 3.
23. Chan, S 2012, *Looking for balance: China, the United States, and power balancing in East Asia*, Stanford University Press, Stanford, p. 9.
24. Rose, G 1998, 'Neoclassical realism and theories of foreign policy', *World Politics*, vol. 51, no. 1, p. 150.
25. Mastanduno, M, Lake, DA & Ikenberry, G.J 1989, 'Toward a realist theory of state action', *International Studies Quarterly*, vol. 33, no. 4, p. 458.
26. Froman, MB 2014, 'The Strategic logic of trade: New rules of the road for the global market', *Foreign Affairs*, vol. 93, no. 6, viewed 16 July 2014, https://www.foreignaffairs.com/articles/americas/strategic-logic-trade
27. Hurrell, A 2006, 'Hegemony, liberalism and global order: what space for would-be great powers?', *International Affairs*, vol. 82, no. 1, p. 6.
28. Aubone, A 2013, 'Explaining US unilateral military intervention in civil conflicts: A review of the literature', *International Politics*, vol. 50, no. 2, p. 278.
29. Gent, SE 2007, 'The strategic dynamics of major power military interventions', *The Journal of Politics*, vol. 69, no. 4, p. 1089.
30. Lemke, D 2003, 'African lessons for international relations research', *World Politics*, vol. 56, no. 01, p. 115.
31. Feste, KA 2003, *Intervention: Shaping the global order*, Praeger, Westport, CT., p. 178.
32. Khosla, D 1999, 'Third world states as interveners in ethnic conflicts: Implications for regional and international security', *Third World Quarterly*, vol. 20, no. 6, pp. 1143–1156.
33. Alexandroff, AS & Cooper, AF 2010, *Rising states, rising institutions: Challenges for global governance*, Brookings Institution Press, Washington D.C., p. 1; Buzan, B 2010, 'China in international society: Is 'peaceful rise' possible?', *The Chinese Journal of International Politics*, vol. 3, no. 1, p. 14.
34. Pang, Z 2009, 'China's non-intervention question', *Global Responsibility to Protect*, vol., 1, p. 238.
35. Buzan, B 2010, 'China in international society: Is "peaceful rise" possible?', *The Chinese Journal of International Politics*, vol. 3, no. 1, p. 13, 15.
36. Zhengyu, W & Taylor, I 2011, 'From refusal to engagement: Chinese contributions to peacekeeping in Africa', *Journal of Contemporary African Studies*, vol. 29, no. 2, p. 147.
37. Cooper, AF & Flemes, D 2013, 'Foreign policy strategies of emerging powers in a multipolar world: An introductory review', *Third World Quarterly*, vol. 34, no. 6, p. 952.
38. Osondu, A 2013, 'Off and on: China's principle of non-interference in Africa', *Mediterranean Journal of Social Sciences*, vol. 4, no. 3, pp. 225–234.

39. Lee, PK, Chan, G & Chan, L 2012, 'China in Darfur: Humanitarian rule-maker or rule-taker?' *Review of International Studies,* vol. 38, no. 2, pp. 423–444; Large, D 2008, 'China and the contradictions of 'non-interference' in Sudan', *Review of African Political Economy,* vol. 35, no. 115, pp. 93–106; Macfarlane, R 2012, 'Why has China been vilified by the west for its engagement in Darfur and to what extent is this justified?' *Journal of Politics & International Studies,* vol. 8, Winter 2012/13, pp. 161–202.
40. Oxford English Dictionary (online), viewed 10 September 2013, http://www.oed.com/view/Entry/98431?redirectedFrom=intervention#eid
41. International Commission on Intervention and State Sovereignty 2001, *The responsibility to protect,* International Development Research Centre, Ottawa, p. 8.
42. Little, R 1975, *Intervention: external involvement in civil wars,* Rowman & Littlefield Publishers, Lanham, p. 2; Little, R 1987, 'Revisiting intervention: A survey of recent developments', *Review of International Studies,* vol. 13, no. 01, p. 49.
43. Reus-Smit 2013, p. 1059.
44. MacMillan, J 2013, 'Intervention and the ordering of the modern world', *Review of International Studies,* vol. 39, no. 05, p. 1039.
45. Reus-Smit, C 2013, 'The concept of intervention', *Review of International Studies,* vol. 39, no. 05, p. 1059.
46. 'China-supported consultations reactivate peace process in S. Sudan' 2015, *China Daily,* 13 January, viewed 13 January 2015, http://africa.chinadaily.com.cn/world/2015-01/13/content_19304552_2.htm
47. 'Obama signs executive order as South Sudan accuses US of meddling' 2015, *Voice of America,* 4 April, viewed 6 April 2015, http://www.voanews.com/content/obama-signs-executive-order-south-sudan-accuses-us-of-meddling/1886103.html
48. Little, R 1975, *Intervention: external involvement in civil wars,* Rowman & Littlefield Publishers, Lanham, p. 1.
49. Reus-Smit, C 2013, 'The concept of intervention', *Review of International Studies,* vol. 39, no. 05, p. 1058.
50. Weiss, TG 2012, *Humanitarian intervention,* Polity Press, Cambridge, p. 18.

Bibliography

Armijo, L. E., & Katada, S. N. (2014). New kids on the block: Rising multipolarity, more financial statecraft. In L. E. Armijo & S. N. Katada (Eds.), *The financial statecraft of emerging powers: Shield and sword in Asia and Latin America* (pp. 1–20). Basingstoke: Palgrave Macmillan.

Armijo, L. E., & Roberts, C. (2014). The emerging powers and global governance: Why the BRICS matter. In R. E. Looney (Ed.), *Handbook of emerging economies* (pp. 503–524). New York: Routledge.

Bayart, J. (2000). Africa in the world: A history of extraversion. *African Affairs, 99*(395), 217–267.

Bilgin, P. (2008). Thinking past 'western' IR? *Third World Quarterly, 29*(1), 5–23.

Bull, H. (1984). *Intervention in world politics.* Oxford: Oxford University Press.

Burchill, S. (2005). *The national interest in international relations theory.* New York: Springer.

Chan, S. (2012). *Looking for balance: China, the United States, and power balancing in East Asia.* Stanford: Stanford University Press.

Conteh-Morgan, E. (2001). International intervention: Conflict, economic dislocation, and the hegemonic role of dominant actors. *International Journal of Peace Studies, 6*(2), 33–52.

Feste, K. A. (1992). *Expanding the Frontiers: Superpower intervention in the cold war.* Westport, CT: Praeger.

Feste, K. A. (2003). *Intervention: Shaping the global order.* Westport, CT: Praeger.

Finnemore, M. (2003). *The purpose of intervention: Changing beliefs about the use of force.* Ithaca, NY: Cornell University Press.

Fung, C. J. (2015). What explains China's deployment to UN peacekeeping operations? *International Relations of the Asia-Pacific.* Retrieved May 16, 2016, from http://irap.oxfordjournals.org/content/early/2015/11/27/irap.lcv020.full.pdf+html

Haass, R. N. (2008). The age of nonpolarity: What will follow US dominance. *Foreign Affairs,* Vol. 87, No. 3, pp. 44–56.

Handel, M. I. (1990). *Weak states in the international system.* London: Frank Cass.

Hurrell, A. (2006). Hegemony, liberalism and global order: What space for would-be great powers? *International Affairs, 82*(1), 1–19.

Ikenberry, G. J. (2001). Review of saving strangers: Humanitarian intervention in international society, Wheeler, N.J. *Foreign Affairs,* Vol. 80, No. 6. Retrieved June 5, 2014, from http://www.foreignaffairs.com/articles/57287/g-john-ikenberry/saving-strangers-humanitarian-intervention-in-international-soci

Ikenberry, G. J. (2010). The three faces of liberal internationalism. In A. S. Alexandroff & A. F. Cooper (Eds.), *Rising states, rising institutions: Challenges for global governance* (pp. 17–47). Washington, DC: Brookings Institution Press.

Keene, E. (2002). *Beyond the anarchical society: Grotius, colonialism and order in world politics.* Cambridge: Cambridge University Press.

Kennedy, P. (1987). *The rise and fall of the great powers: Economic change and military power from 1500 to 2000.* New York: Random House.

Layne, C. (1993). The unipolar illusion: Why new great powers will rise. *International Security, 17*(4), 5–51.

Lee, P. K., Chan, G., & Chan, L. (2012). China in Darfur: Humanitarian rule-maker or rule-taker? *Review of International Studies, 38*(2), 423–444.

Mandelbaum, M. (1988). *The fate of nations: The search for national security in the nineteenth and twentieth centuries*. Cambridge: Cambridge University Press.

Mastanduno, M. (1997). Preserving the unipolar moment: Realist theories and U.S. grand strategy after the Cold War. *International Security, 21*(4), 49–88.

Mearsheimer, J. (2004). Why China's rise will not be peaceful. Retrieved September 1, 2018, from http://mearsheimer.uchicago.edu/pdfs/A0034b.pdf

Morgenthau, H. J. (1967). To intervene or not to intervene. *Foreign Affairs*, Vol. 45, No. 3, pp. 425–436.

Pang, Z. (2009). China's non-intervention question. *Global Responsibility to Protect, 1*, 237–252.

Patrick, S. (2010). Irresponsible stakeholders? The difficulty of integrating rising powers. *Foreign Affairs*, Vol. 89, No. 6, pp. 44–53.

Pearson, F. S. (1974). Foreign military interventions and domestic disputes. *International Studies Quarterly, 18*(3), 259–290.

Reczei, L. (1971). The political aims and experiences of the small socialist states. In A. Schou & A. O. Brundtland (Eds.), *Small states in international relations* (pp. 71–86). New York: Wiley-Interscience Division.

Regan, P. M. (1996). Conditions of successful third-party intervention in intrastate conflicts. *Journal of Conflict Resolution, 40*(2), 336–359.

Regilme Jr., S. S. F. (2014). The social science of human rights: The need for a 'second image reversed'? *Third World Quarterly, 35*(8), 1390–1405.

Reus-Smit, C. (2013). The concept of intervention. *Review of International Studies, 39*(5), 1057–1076.

Rosenau, J. N. (1969). Intervention as a scientific concept. *Journal of Conflict Resolution, 13*(2), 149–171.

Schraeder, P. J. (1989). *Intervention in the 1980s: U.S. foreign policy in the third world*. Boulder: Lynne Rienner.

Snyder, R. S. (2005). Bridging the realist/constructivist divide: The case of the counterrevolution in Soviet foreign policy at the end of the Cold War. *Foreign Policy Analysis, 1*(1), 55–71.

Steiner, B. H. (2004). *Collective preventive diplomacy: A study in international conflict management*. New York: State University of New York Press.

Taliaferro, J. W. (2004). *Balancing risks: Great power intervention in the periphery*. Ithaca, NY: Cornell University Press.

Taylor, I. (2007). Governance in Africa and Sino-African relations: Contradictions or confluence? *Politics, 27*(3), 139–146.

Tillema, H. K. (1989). Foreign overt military intervention in the nuclear age. *Journal of Peace Research, 26*(2), 179–196.

Walt, S. M. (1987). *The origins of alliance*. Ithaca, NY: Cornell University Press.

Waltz, K. N. (1979). *Theory of international politics*. New York: McGraw-Hill.

Weiss, T. G. (2007). *Humanitarian intervention: Ideas in action*. Cambridge: Polity Press.

Wendt, A. (1992). Anarchy is what states make of it: The social construction of power politics. *International Organization, 46*(2), 391–425.
Wendt, A. (1999). *Social theory of international politics.* Cambridge: Cambridge University Press.
Wheeler, N. J. (2000). *Saving strangers: Humanitarian intervention in international society: Humanitarian intervention in international society.* Oxford: Oxford University Press.
Winfield, P. H. (1932). Intervention. In *Encyclopedia of the social sciences* (Vol. 8, pp. 236–238). New York: Macmillan.
Wing, S. D. (2016). French intervention in Mali: Strategic alliances, long-term regional presence? *Small Wars & Insurgencies, 27*(1), 59–80.
Wohlforth, W. C. (1993). *The elusive balance: Power and perceptions during the Cold War.* Ithaca, NY: Cornell University Press.
Zakaria, F. (1998). *From wealth to power: The unusual origins of America's world role.* New Jersey: Princeton University Press.
Zakaria, F. (2008). *The post-American world.* New York: W.W. Norton.
Zhengyu, W., & Taylor, I. (2011). From refusal to engagement: Chinese contributions to peacekeeping in Africa. *Journal of Contemporary African Studies, 29*(2), 137–154.
Zoellick, R. B. (2005). Whither China: From membership to responsibility? *NBR Analysis, 16*(4), 5.

CHAPTER 3

Cyclical Patterns of China's Intervention Policy

3.1 Introduction

Has China's foreign intervention behaviour historically evolved with shifts in its relative economic power? Implicit within this question is an assumption that the relative distribution of economic power in the international system determines a state's foreign intervention behaviour. Of course, some would argue that the nature of the state and its foreign policy orientation matters more than its position in the international system. The simple empirical argument is that states with a colonial and imperial past such as Britain, France and Portugal are more inclined to intervening in foreign intrastate armed conflicts because of their colonial heritage. Indeed so, France has intervened in its former African colonies' intrastate armed conflicts on multiple occasions in the past 50 years,[1] more than China, which apart from control of "nations" such as Tibet and Xinjiang does not have an elaborate colonial history. But, however plausible this argument may be, it does not explain whether a state's intervention behaviour is determined by increases in its relative economic power.

In exploring the argument that a state's position in the international system determines its foreign policy and external intervention behaviour, this chapter begins by giving a critical historical analysis of China's evolving understanding of foreign intervention, its foreign intervention policy

O. Hodzi, *The End of China's Non-Intervention Policy in Africa*,
Critical Studies of the Asia-Pacific,
https://doi.org/10.1007/978-3-319-97349-4_3

and external intervention behaviour from imperial times to the establishment of the People's Republic of China (PRC) in 1949, and until 2015. The aim of the historical analysis is to give a concrete background of the evolving nature of China's foreign policy regarding intervention in other states' internal affairs vis-à-vis changes in its relative economic power and position in the international system. As put by Suisheng Zhao, being an ancient civilisation, "history is inscribed in China's mental terrain" and Chinese intellectuals and politicians have at times "reconstructed history to advance the current political agenda of the Chinese government and justify their concept of justice and their view of China's rightful place in the world" (2015, p. 981). Appreciating China's past understandings of intervention is therefore critical to analysing its current intervention policy and behaviour in Africa. Based on that background, the chapter then discusses the implication of China's increasing economic power and explores whether it has indeed resulted in an increase in its external intervention behaviour.

3.2 Intervention in Imperial China

China's foreign policy on intervention in the internal affairs of other states is an embodiment of its historical trajectory as a nation that considered itself the Middle Kingdom, and the epicentre of global civilisation surrounded by barbaric nations.[2] As put by Julia Ching, "through most of its history, China saw itself as the global order, surrounded on its borders by subordinate neighbors" (2004, p. 246). In John G. Ikenberry's conception of what powers with a preponderance of material capabilities do, imperial China transformed "its favorable power position into a durable order that commands the allegiance of other states within the order" (Ikenberry 2001, p. 4). It is therefore not surprising that the surrounding nations of Vietnam, Burma and Korea paid tribute to the Chinese emperors confirming the superiority of the Chinese civilisation. Yet, even as they paid tribute to China,

> Relations between China and Korea or China and Vietnam were not analogous to relations between sovereign nations in an anarchic international system or even between the colonizing power and its colony; rather, the nations surrounding China were considered inferior… Only through adoption of Chinese civilization, which the neighboring elites would be exposed to during their voyages to pay tribute to the Chinese emperor, would the nations of China's borders be accepted as anything but barbarians. (Kornberg and Faust 2005, p. 10)

But, for as long as the surrounding "barbaric" nations acknowledged the supremacy of its emperors, paid tribute and did not threaten its territorial integrity, China left them to determine their own internal affairs. Zhang Yongjin and Barry Buzan concur: "Participants and aspiring participants in *Pax Sinica*…, remained sovereign entities, to the extent that they retained their autonomy and independence in conducting their domestic and 'foreign' affairs'" (Zhang and Buzan 2012, p. 15). As further put by Brantly Womack, "in contrast to the colonialism of Western imperialism, China acted as the passive guarantor of a matrix of unequal but autonomous relationships rather than as an active metropolitan power" (2006, p. 135). Hence, even in the prime of its economic, technological and military power, imperial China "apparently never plundered nor murdered—unlike the Portuguese, Dutch, and other European invaders of the Indian Ocean" (Kennedy 1988, p. 7). It considered itself the centre of the global order, and a benevolent civilised superpower dominating its neighbours by cultural and economic superiority rather than by military force (Perdue 2015, p. 1003; Suzuki 1968, p. 183).

Intervention into the internal affairs of its tributary nations was however not uncommon. Since "it was normal for the Chinese to consider the barbarians subjects of the emperor, they thought it legitimate to protect these barbarians and their ruler from rebellious elements" (Lam 1968, p. 169). In other words, as the "Son of Heaven" there was an underlying reasoning that China could "intervene whenever and wherever she judged it necessary because the Chinese emperor was responsible for all the peoples under Heaven and because their rulers were viewed as his appointed representatives."[3] Therefore, "China, as the paramount leader, maintained order in the system and reserved the right to intervene in the internal affairs of its vassals" (Wang 2011, p. 145). In Jerome Alan Cohen's description, imperial China had the latent right of intervention that Chinese emperors activated on occasional basis, especially in cases where their direct interests were at risk (Cohen 1973, p. 475).

China's intervention in the domestic affairs of vassal states like Korea began as early as the Sui dynasty (581–618 CE), and the Liao dynasty, also known as the Khitan Empire (907–1125).[4] But, the most elaborate case of intervention by imperial China happened in October 1788, when the Qing emperor sanctioned a military intervention in Vietnam to restore Lê Chiêu Thống to the Vietnamese throne. Truong Buu Lam notes that Vietnamese kings "had to acknowledge China's suzerainty and become tributaries in order to avoid active intervention by China in their internal affairs" (1968, p. 179). The threat of China's intervention was peculiar not just to Vietnam but also to other tributary states that bordered China. For most of those tributary nations it was prudent for them to surrender part of their sovereignty to China in exchange for economic and trade benefits, military support in cases where their security was threatened by other nations and, more importantly, to avoid interference in their internal affairs by Chinese emperors (Lam 1968, p. 178; Cohen 1973, p. 476)—suggesting that the threat of China's intervention in their internal affairs was always imminent.

Notwithstanding, imperial China's foreign and domestic policies were entwined and driven by two fears: (a) barbarian attacks, and (b) internal revolts. The Chinese tended to think of "their foreign relations as giving expression externally to the same principles within the Chinese state and society.... [Hence] China's external order was so closely related to its internal order such that one could not survive without the other; when the barbarians were not submissive abroad, rebels might more easily arise within" (Fairbank 1968, p. 2, 3). It was therefore critical for Chinese emperors to maintain order and stability within the surrounding "barbarian" nations, as well as within China itself, and that entailed certain measures of intervention in the "barbarian" nations' internal affairs. However, with the rise of Confucius thinking, China's foreign and domestic politics was further inspired by the Confucian Code, which considered warfare to be a deplorable activity, and instead emphasised societal stability and order. Accordingly, "armed forces were made necessary only by the fear of barbarian attacks or internal revolts" (Kennedy 1988, p. 7).

More than being concerned with intrastate armed conflicts in foreign nations, as long as their interests were not at risk, Chinese emperors focused on containing internal revolts. As Liu writes, the revolts against emperors did not happen very often, but they did happen enough times to result in "cycles of order and disorder in the so-called twenty-four dynasties history" (1995, p. 205). The fear of internal revolts was further exacerbated by Confucians who according to Chan (1973, p. 62) sustained the doctrine of mass revolutions against inhumane leaders, an excuse that China also used to intervene in the internal affairs of its tributary states (Cohen 1973, p. 474). In concurrence, Yao wrote: "rulers could lose their throne if they lost people's hearts. In other words, if people are not happy with their emperors, they could overturn them" (Yao 2011, p. 220; see also Ivanhoe 2004, p. 272).

That fear of internal revolts is to a greater extent what led to the imperial code enacted during the middle Ming dynasty banning the construction and owning of seagoing ships and later any ships with more than two masts; all efforts were concentrated on containing any signs of internal revolt and to protecting the empire from outside aggressors rather than exploring unknown lands for profit, influence and gain. This was because for as long as there was a threat of internal revolt, barbaric attacks were considered imminent. It was not a misplaced concern of paranoid Chinese emperors because, as noted by John King Fairbank, "most dynasties collapsed under the twin blows of 'inside disorder and outside calamity' (*nei-luan wai-huan*), that is, domestic rebellion and foreign invasion" (Fairbank 1968, p. 3).

The banning of exploration ships and expeditions three years after the 1433 Zheng He expedition to Africa, possibly China's first engagement with the continent, which were financed and sanctioned by Emperor Cheng Zu of the Ming Dynasty (in which Zheng He stopped at the city states of Mogadishu and Brawa in Somalia and Malindi in Kenya), and the Middle East had long-term effects on China's relative economic and external intervention. Due to the ban "China did not seek information about the outside world. It neither fought external wars nor searched for external markets, and foreigners who came to China were welcome so long as they accepted the superiority of Chinese civilization" (Kornberg and Faust 2005, p. 8). Its decision to isolate itself from the outside world coincided with a decline in its economic growth and technological advancement. As put by Paul Kennedy, "the banning of overseas trade and fishing took away another potential stimulus to sustained economic expansion; such foreign trade as did occur with the Portuguese and Dutch in the following centuries was in luxury goods and (although there were doubtless many evasions) controlled by officials." Fast forwarding to the eighteenth century, Paul Kennedy continues: "In 1776—just as Abraham Darby's ironworks at Coalbrookdale were beginning to boom—the blast furnaces and coke ovens of Honan and Hopei were abandoned entirely. They had been great before the Conqueror had landed at Hastings. Now they would not resume production until the twentieth century" (1988, pp. 8–9). However, to imperial China that did not matter, because as far as the emperors were concerned, they were still the Middle Kingdom at the centre of their known global order, albeit lacking the wherewithal to intervene in other nations.

3.3 Incorporation of Imperial China into a Truly International System of States

Five centuries after the banning of exploration ships and two centuries since closure of the blast furnaces of Honan and Hopei, Deng Xiaoping reflected on the implications of China's self-isolation since imperial times in a speech at the Third Plenary Session of the Central Advisory Commission of the Communist Party of China in October 1984. He recounted:

> A closed-door policy prevents any country from developing. We suffered from isolation, and so did our forefathers. You might say it was an open policy of a sort when Zheng He was sent on voyages to the western oceans by Emperor Cheng Zu of the Ming Dynasty. But the Ming Dynasty began to decline with the death of Emperor Cheng Zu. In the Qing Dynasty, during the reigns of Kang Xi and Qian Long, there was no open policy to speak of. China remained isolated for more than 300 years from the middle of the Ming Dynasty to the Opium War, for nearly 200 years counting from the reign of Kang Xi. As a consequence, the country declined into poverty and ignorance … the lessons of the past tell us that if we don't open to the outside we can't make much headway.[5]

Indeed, the decision to isolate itself and discourage private enterprises at the end of the Ming Dynasty turned out to have far-reaching effects on China's position in a truly international system of states that emerged in the sixteenth century in Europe, and on its foreign policy regarding intervention in the internal affairs of other states. The decline in relative economic power caused by a lack of external trade, banning of explorations that could have opened new markets and sources of raw materials, and an isolationist foreign policy overly suspicious of foreigners and the foreign world made imperial China relatively weaker in terms of economic, military and technological advancement. As China looked inward, European powers such as Spain, Portugal, the Netherlands and Britain that were experiencing immense domestic economic growth were looking outward in search of markets, new sources of raw materials and labour—and, in the process, entangling themselves in other states' internal affairs.

As China's relative economic power declined, European powers such as Britain were becoming more dynamic and powerful, and aggressively expanding their interests and influence abroad, including into China. Using their preponderance of economic and military, especially naval, capabilities, they progressively but forcibly incorporated China into the global system of states that they dominated (Deng and Wang 1999, p. 11). Just as the African, Asian and Latin American polities were compulsorily assimilated into the international system of states in the eighteenth and nineteenth centuries, China found itself an engrafted weak member of that international system. It was no longer the powerful nation at the centre of its own global order, but one of the many relatively weak states under European domination. Furthermore, contrary to the *Sinocentric* approach of Chinese dynasties to a global order based on the Mandate of Heaven, the new international system of states based on the preponderance of material capabilities meant that China was no longer the centre of civilisation, and no longer were its emperors the "Sons of Heaven" ruling with a "Heavenly mandate." They also lost their latent right to intervene in the internal affairs of China's tributary states, and, even where it needed to intervene, China simply no longer had the means.

The culmination of China's incorporation into the modern international system of states happened in earnest in the years infamously referred to as the "century of humiliation" between 1839 and 1949. In that period, China came face-to-face with its two worst fears—fear of barbaric attacks, and fear of internal revolts that had influenced its domestic and foreign policy for centuries. Starting with the 1838 Yangtze River attack by Britain's gunboats, and subsequent attacks by the militarily and economically superior Japan, France and the Soviet Union, China was forced to make major concessions that opened its ports to foreign powers resulting in loss of tariff autonomy, territory and sovereignty. But more importantly, the "unequal concessions" exposed the decline in China's relative economic power. Besides foreign invasion, China also had to contend with internal revolts that resulted in the fall of its last emperor Henry Pu Yi, the twelfth and final ruler of the Qing dynasty. His fall led to the rise of Nationalists in 1911, and subsequently the Communists in 1949. It therefore goes without saying that from the beginning of the century of humiliation up to 1949 when the Communists took over, intervention in the internal affairs of states in the near and abroad was a luxury China could least afford—it was too busy fighting against foreign intervention in its own internal and foreign affairs to bother with other nations.

The century of humiliation had several other far-reaching effects on China's perception of the anarchic international system, and on its role in that global order. As observed by David Scott, "that period of humiliation and unfulfilled potential cast a long shadow that continues to affect Chinese foreign policy, strategic culture, and *weltanschauung* worldview" (2008, p. 3). The first implication is that "China was no longer in accord with the Mandate of

Heaven, nor was it a sovereign state in an international system dominated by Western powers" (Kornberg and Faust 2005, p. 8). It now constituted part of Third World countries under the overbearing influence, and, in worst cases, colonial dominance by European powers. The Mandate of Heaven that had previously legitimated China's hegemony over other nations and strengthened its claim as the centre of civilisation around which other nations orbited was no longer tenable. The tables had turned. A new global order where cultural superiority did not matter as much as economic, political and military superiority had emerged. So, as aptly put by Alison Adcock Kaufman, "where Chinese rulers and intellectuals had before had little concept of an 'international' arena, they now had to grapple with the notion that there existed a global system of power relationships whose dynamics—though almost entirely out of China's control—would determine its fate" (2010, p. 5).

Second, the transformation of China from being a prime civilisation at the centre of the tributary system in a global order whose parameters it largely defined to being one of the Third World countries in the lower tier of states in a Western-dominated anarchic international system also significantly impacted its foreign intervention policy. No longer did it have claim to possessing the latent right to intervene in the internal affairs of its bordering nations. Finding itself at the lower end of the international system of states, China had to adapt from being the ruler to being the ruled in a systemic order where, as put by Thucydides, "the standard of justice depends on the equality of power to compel and that in fact the strong do what they have the power to do and the weak accept what they have to accept."[6] China was therefore "not only forced into the international system dominated by European powers where it lost its tributary states, but also treated unequally and suffered in the hands of imperialist powers" (Zhao 2015, p. 976). Thus, the century of humiliation "replaced and overturned the country's previous preeminence and prestige as the 'Middle Kingdom'"[7] and the impact on its perception of intervention and state sovereignty was immeasurable.

3.4 Reimagining the International and Intervention: China Under Mao

In imperial times, states that formed part of China's tributary system were not considered sovereign and equal. They were regarded and treated as barbaric and inferior depending on how close they were to Chinese civilisation and culture. The concept of equality and state sovereignty was therefore unknown in *Pax Sinica* because in "the traditional Chinese world order … [they] did not use concepts corresponding to the Western ideas of nation, or sovereignty, or equality of states each having equal sovereignty" (Fairbank 1968, p. 5). But, as Mao declared the PRC in 1949, the *Pax Sinica* was long gone; in its stead was a Western-led global system of states premised, in principle, on both equal sovereignty and relative power distribution. Accordingly, the view of Mao and the Communist Party of China (CPC) regarding foreign, particularly Western, intervention was "one of national humiliation and international inequalities, as the imposition *on* one part of the international system (China) *by* another part of the international system (the West)" (Scott 2008, p. 8). The result was a replacement by the CPC of the suzerainty of China with a new emphasis on equality of states, respect of state sovereignty and non-intervention in the internal affairs of other states—reflecting its "inferior" position in the international system.

In a speech made at the First Plenary Session of the Chinese People's Political Consultative Conference on 21 September 1949, Mao Tse-tung delivered an opening address aptly titled *The Chinese people have stood up*, which reflected shifts in China's perception of state sovereignty and external intervention. He said:

> The Chinese have always been a great, courageous and industrious nation; it is only in modern times that they have fallen behind. And that was due entirely to oppression and exploitation by foreign imperialism and domestic reactionary governments… From now on our nation will belong to the community of the peace-loving and freedom-loving nations of the world and work courageously and industriously to foster its own civilization and well-being and at the same time to promote world peace and freedom. Ours will no longer be a nation subject to insult and humiliation. We have stood up.[8]

Less than a month later, on 1 October 1949, as he proclaimed the Central People's Government of the PRC, Mao announced that the newly established government was "willing to establish diplomatic relations with any foreign government willing to observe the principles of equality, mutual benefit, and mutual respect of territorial integrity and sovereignty."[9] The basis of China's relations and interaction with states in the international system was no longer premised on pre-eminence of its civilisation and "Mandate of Heaven" as in imperial times, but on the power dynamics of an anarchic international system in which China occupied the peripheries rather than the core.

Realising China's inferior position within the prevailing Western-led international order, Mao

> quickly embraced the concepts of territorial sovereignty and became a zealous defender of its sovereign rights in what the Chinese perceived to be a social Darwinian world, in which the status of a nation-state was determined by its economic and military strength … they sought to maximize China's security by expanding influence and control over its neighborhoods, and in some cases, far beyond … [Believing] that the world is unjust and unfair only in the sense that China was stagnant and weak. (Zhao 2015, p. 981; see also, Dreyer 2015, p. 1027)

In view of that, as China sought to increase its relative material power, it correspondingly sought to expand its influence beyond its borders—bringing in a new dynamic to its intervention behaviour in foreign states.

By arguing that "China had stood up," Mao and other CPC ruling elites kick-started a process of redefining China's role in a global system that it found itself thrust in. By all intents and purposes a weak and poor state, still fearful of imperialism and dominance by Western powers such as the United States, Britain, the then Soviet Union, and its long-time nemesis, Japan, China conceived of its role in international politics on the basis of the distribution of relative economic power in the international system. To the CPC, the dominant narrative was that for as long as China was weak relative to other states, as it was at that time, it remained susceptible to foreign domination, imperialism and what Deng Xiaoping referred to as "bullying" by developed countries.[10] Along the same lines as Deng Xiaoping, but decades later, President Xi "urged all Party members to firmly keep in mind that lagging behind leaves one vulnerable to attacks and only development makes a nation strong."[11] To escape the predicament that befalls weak "undeveloped" states, China, though relatively weak—economically and militarily—began spreading its revolutionary ideology into Africa and other Third World countries in order to counter US hegemonism in global affairs.[12] In that respect, it envisioned itself playing a significant role in international politics, carving a niche for itself in the Third World's struggle for political independence, and in its struggle against the Western hegemonism and power-ideological dominance.

In its formative years, the CPC ideologically aligned itself with the Soviet Union. So, when Mao was laying the foundation for the PRC, he pronounced in June 1949 that in terms of the guiding principles of China's foreign policy they belonged to "the anti-imperialist front, headed by the

Soviet Union." Having chosen the Soviet side, he then added that "the Chinese people must either incline towards the side of imperialism or that of socialism. There can be no exception to the rule. It is impossible to sit on the fence. There is no third road."[13] The implication of aligning itself with the Soviet Union was that in the early years of CPC rule, China was unable to articulate an independent foreign policy regarding its engagement with developing countries, especially in Africa. However, the Sino-Soviet cooperation on foreign policy principles did not last long. A combination of two international factors—the rise of the anti-colonial movement in Africa in the 1950s, and the Sino-Soviet fall-out in the 1960s[14]—gave China an opportunity to articulate the non-intervention principle abroad, as well as spread its own version of socialism in Africa. Prior to that, Africa was to China a region for which "a positive African policy was non-existent ... [because] apart from the question of distance, the new [Mao] regime was not yet strong enough to adopt any meaningful policy towards Africa, despite its ambition to universalize its revolutionary experience" (Ogunsanwo 1974, p. 4).

Nonetheless, apart from seeing the non-intervention principle as an instrument for protecting itself against Western and Soviet interference,[15] China also considered it to be an effective soft power strategy useful to securing a prominent place among Third World developing countries also struggling against United States and the Soviet Union's political and ideological dominance. The non-intervention principle therefore enabled China to be flexible and pragmatic in its foreign policy while gaining the admiration of states repulsed by the strict ideological demands of the United States and the USSR. It also helped China to carve a niche for its own politico-ideological influence in Africa through building bilateral relations with African states independent of the Soviet Union.

3.5 The Beginning of Intervention in African Conflicts by China

China's first momentous step towards engaging Africa was made at the Bandung Conference in 1955, where Premier Zhou Enlai pronounced the "Five Principles of Peaceful Co-existence,"[16] with emphasis on the principle of non-intervention in the internal affairs of other states. He explained: "as the Chinese proverb says: 'Do not onto others what you yourself do not desire.' We are against outside interference; how could we want to interfere in the internal affairs of others."[17] The principle resonated well with African countries that had either attained political independence or were still fighting against colonial rule. Three years after the Bandung Conference, the Bandung Principles as enunciated by Zhou Enlai were adopted by leaders of newly independent African countries at the Accra Meeting of Independent African States which was attended by Ghana, Liberia, Sudan, Ethiopia, the United Arab Republic (short-lived political union between Egypt and Syria), and Libya, Morocco and Tunisia and a delegation from Cameroon.[18] Among other factors, the emphasis on non-intervention guided China's efforts to gradually assume leadership of the Third World,[19] particularly of the subsequent Non-Aligned Movement, which comprised of developing countries that refused to ideologically side with either the United States or the Soviet Union. As a result, China attained greater support and diplomatic recognition from African countries, most of which had previously recognised Taiwan instead of the PRC.[20]

Having established itself as leader of the Third World,[21] China set to establish its own ideological and geopolitical dominance in Africa while professing that it did not interfere in African countries' internal affairs. However, as noted by Alaba Ogunsanwo, China's policy in Africa was interlocked to its international strategic interests, and "was a function of her triangular relationship with the United States and the Soviet Union" such that to a greater extent, African states were "used merely as pawns on the international chessboard" (1974, p. 3; see also Thrall 2015, p. 4, 6). To draw Africa into its sphere of influence, Mao elaborated the "Dual Intermediate Zones" theory in 1963 which posited that "a spacious intermediate zone existed between the United States and the USSR."[22] That intermediate zone consisted of African and Asian countries under colonial rule. Mao therefore argued to the satisfaction of several African leaders that "the most effective way to oppose the two superpowers was for all non-superpower countries in between the two political extremes they represented to unite in their struggle against imperialism,"[23] and "form a new international order" (Yu 1977, p. 1036). Satisfied with the reception of his Dual Intermediate Zones theory in Africa and the Global South, he then declared, "we must give active support to the national independence liberation movement in countries in Asia, Africa and Latin America as well as to the peace movement and to just struggles in all countries throughout the world."[24] In 1965, Defence Minister Lin Biao reiterated Mao's call to action, saying that China and other "socialist countries should regard it as their internationalist duty to support the people's revolutionary struggles in Asia, Africa and Latin America."[25] But then, China's support to "freedom movements" and "just struggles" included significant intervention in the other countries' internal affairs.

China's military support for African liberation war movements began in the late 1950s with assistance to Algeria's *Front de Libération Nationale* which fought for independence from France.[26] But, "with the worsening of Sino-Soviet relations in the early 1960s, China reversed its earlier policy of broad support for liberation organisations, and in general began to be more circumscribed in aiding movements that had links with Moscow. This led to a process of selecting suitable recipients for Chinese aid" (Taylor 2000, p. 93). The suitable ones were those that subscribed to Maoism and were not aligned with or receiving any support from the Soviet Union. As an illustration, in Angola, China supported the National Union for the Total Independence of Angola (UNITA) not only because its guerrilla strategies were similar to Mao's "revolution from the countryside," but also because UNITA's rival liberation movement, the Popular Movement for the Liberation of Angola (MPLA), had strong Soviet links.[27] China therefore supported UNITA and the *Frente Nacional de Libertação de Angola* (FNLA) even though the two groups were rivals of each other simply because they both fought against the Soviet-backed MPLA. In 1963, the leader of FNLA, Holden Roberto, was promised military support by the Chinese foreign minister, Chen Yi. Almost a decade later, in 1974 FNLA "received a 450-ton shipment of arms and benefitted from the assistance of 112 Chinese instructors based in former Zaire" (Campos and Vines 2008, p. 34). Meanwhile, in 1964, Jonas Savimbi, leader of UNITA, "met with Chairman Mao Zedong and Premier Zhou Enlai in China, where he received military training and became a disciple of Maoism" (Campos and Vines 2008, p. 34). Influenced by its anti-Soviet stance, China ended up joining the United States and apartheid South Africa in supporting UNITA, a decision that ended up tarnishing its image on the continent,[28] but, more importantly, exposed China as just like the United States and the Soviet Union in seeking to expand their influence over African countries.

As China's relative economic power increased by leaps and bounds in the 1960s, albeit not to levels comparable to the Soviet Union or United States, it became bolder in its geopolitical competition for influence in Africa. Its strategy of choice was to expand its support for liberation movements struggling for independence in Africa. In Zimbabwe, a country strategically located at the centre of Southern Africa, China supported the Zimbabwe

African National Liberation Army (ZANLA), the military wing of Zimbabwe African National Union (ZANU), because its rival, the Zimbabwe People's Revolutionary Army, military wing of the Zimbabwe African People's Union (ZAPU), followed Soviet Marxist-Leninist ideology. Initially, ZANU had sought military support from Moscow, but failing to get any, it turned to Beijing. The PRC took the opportunity to outdo the Soviets, seeing support for ZANU as a vehicle by which it could pursue its anti-Soviet objectives in Southern Africa.[29] It then started providing military training and strategic assistance to ZANLA. "It was [also] under Chinese tutorship that ZANLA's military strategy underwent a fundamental transformation from conventional military tactics to the Maoist model, which entailed the mass mobilisation of the population" (Zhang 2014, p. 6). The Maoist combination of guerrilla warfare and political education for the masses contributed to ZANU's triumph over ZAPU at independence in 1980.

To further strengthen its support for liberation movements in Africa, Chinese military instructors were sent from Beijing to several training camps in independent African countries such as Tanzania, Ghana and Congo-Brazzaville. Their instructions were to train liberation war fighters from other African countries still under colonial rule in Maoist ideology, guerrilla warfare and war strategies. In Tanzania, the Chinese military instructors set up training camps for the rest of Southern Africa and also did the same for West Africa in Ghana.[30] For example, a group of ZANU liberation war fighters were mainly trained in Tanzania. Besides providing training in African countries, some fighters were trained in China. Zimbabwe's president, Emmerson Mnangagwa, went to China in September 1963 for six months' training in military science. In 1966, another group of 11 fighters led by the ZANLA commander Josiah Magama Tongogara were trained in mass mobilisation, strategy and tactics at the Nanjing Academy in Beijing.[31] Similarly, as Mozambique's Frente *de Libertação de Moçambique* (FRELIMO) fought for independence from Portugal, its fighters received training from Chinese instructors in Tanzania, and they received weapons from China. "China also coordinated its military training for liberation groups with the Organisation of African Unity, providing the organisation's liberation committee with 75 percent of all the military aid that it received from countries outside of Africa during 1971 and 1972" (Shinn and Eisenman 2012, p. 165).

However, in its quest to outdo the Soviet Union and expand its influence across Africa, China ended up intervening in the internal politics of independent African states. Ian Taylor notes that "China adopted an anti-

Soviet policy towards the liberation organisations in reaction to Moscow and not to the local situation. Whenever a movement indicated a willingness to deal with Moscow, China encouraged a rival organisation by switching aid to them, thus aiming to thwart the Soviet Union. This became a competition for influence" (2000, p. 93). Because of its anti-Soviet fixation and desire to dominate the African continent, it supported anti-Soviet radical dissidents in Kenya, Uganda, Zanzibar, Senegal, Cameroon, Niger and the Congo,[32] much to the chagrin of newly independent African states. As a result, in 1966 Ghana expelled Chinese diplomats from Accra and suspended diplomatic ties with China on allegations that it was "interfering in its internal affairs by helping train Africans in secret military camps and supporting Nkrumah's effort to return to power" (Shinn and Eisenman 2012, p. 288). Other independent African countries that also suspended diplomatic ties with China in protest to its interference in their internal affairs include Benin (1966), Burundi (1963),[33] Democratic Republic of Congo (1961), Kenya (1967), Tunisia (1967) and the Central African Republic (1966).[34] In the end, African countries were "worried about trading one foreign master for another and regarded Beijing's radical fervour as potentially subversive" (Raine 2009, p. 19; see also Shinn and Eisenman 2012, p. 165).

Beijing justified the interventions as political support for movements fighting for self-determination. However, in international law, and to a sizeable number of African leaders, its support of liberation movements in their countries amounted to intervention. To settle the issue of whether support for rebels fighting for independence is intervention or not, the International Court of Justice ruled in a case involving US support for rebels in Nicaragua that "The United States of America, by training, arming, equipping, financing and supplying the *contra* forces or otherwise encouraging, supporting and aiding military and paramilitary activities in and against Nicaragua, has acted, against the Republic of Nicaragua, in breach of its obligation under customary international law not to intervene in the affairs of another State."[35] At international law, and in the view of several leaders of independent African states, China's support for some liberation movements and insurgents reflected its proactive interventionist policy.

Even by China's own interpretation of it non-intervention principle, "making direct contact with the opposition,"[36] in this case, liberation movements fighting against colonial governments, amounted to intervention. But, justifiable as it seemed, China's support for insurgent groups in countries such as Angola raised further suspicion and discontent against its involvement in ideological proxy wars alongside Moscow and Washington because it suggested that China's support for liberation movements was propelled by the primary motive to counter Soviet influence in the Third World,[37] and its desire to create a third ideological pole. The suspicion was confirmed when Deng Xiaoping said that China's support for liberation movements in the Third World was meant to rally "the world's people to oppose hegemonism, changing the world political balance, frustrating the Soviet hegemonists' arrogant plan to isolate China internationally, improving China's international environment, and heightening its international prestige"[38] (underlined for emphasis).

3.6 China First: Africa in Deng Xiaoping's China

Towards the beginning of the 1970s, a mélange of systemic and mostly domestic factors led to waning of China's support for liberation war movements in Africa. The most consequential domestic factor was definitely the Cultural Revolution which gained momentum from the late 1960s. Focusing on containing internal revolts and purging "anti-revolutionary" cadres within the CPC, support for African liberation movements drifted away from being a priority for Beijing. Under the overbearing effects of the Cultural Revolution, China's economy regressed; hence its ability to continue financing the "internationalisation" project in Africa was further constrained. As the Cultural Revolution drew to a close, and with the death of Mao on 9 September 1976—a man who had singly defined the issues and determined the course of Chinese foreign policy, especially its support to liberation war movements in Africa[39]—China's domestic and foreign policy took a shift. By 1975, Deng Xiaoping had already seized the opportunity and declared that it was "utterly wrong" for comrades in the Party to only make revolution without promoting production. He therefore declared that the overall national interest was to "turn China into a powerful socialist country with modern agriculture, industry, national defence, and science and technology by the end of this century."[40]

He also shifted China's foreign policy from being driven by political and ideological considerations to being influenced by economic interests, and from being geographically focused on the poor and developing Africa, to concentrating on engaging the developed and technologically advanced West. Part of his argument was:

> We have gone on opposing imperialism, hegemonism, colonialism and racism, working to safeguard world peace, and actively developing relations, including economic and cultural exchanges with other countries on the basis of the Five Principles of Peaceful Coexistence. After several years of effort, we have secured international conditions that are far better than before; they enable us to make use of capital from foreign countries and of their advanced technology and experience in business management.[41]

Following on from his argument that China should reengage the West, he toured Europe and, while addressing a press delegation in the Federal Republic of Germany on 10 October 1978, Deng Xiaoping urged China to open up to the outside world in order to advance itself.[42] From then on, China transfixed its efforts towards economic engagement with developed Western countries in order to achieve relative economic development instead of continuing with the isolationist and antagonistic policies of Mao.[43] With his focus on economically developing China, Deng Xiaoping also abandoned Mao's international revolution agenda which had focused on Third World countries in Africa and Asia.

China's shift from "internationalisation" of the revolution to domestic economic development was not just a response to domestic imperatives but also to systemic pressures. In relative terms, China was an economically and militarily poor country compared to the Soviet Union and the United States. It was therefore no longer able to measure up to the financial and military assistance given to most African countries by Moscow and Washington. In a talk with an economic and trade delegation of the government of Madagascar, Deng Xiaoping hinted on the withdrawal of Beijing from international engagements due to its weak relative economic status in the international system. He said, "at present, we are still a relatively poor nation. It is impossible for us to undertake many proletarian obligations, so our contributions remain small. However, once we have accomplished the four modernisations and the national economy has expanded, our contributions to mankind, and especially the Third World, will be greater."[44] This statement by Deng Xiaoping marked one of the first clearest admissions by a Chinese national leader that Beijing's level of engagement in international engagements was determined by its relative economic power, suggesting that for as long as China remained economically weaker than other global powers, its foreign policy remained limited until a time when its national economy has expanded.

Deng Xiaoping also reasoned that an economically poor China was vulnerable to bullying by other states at the international front. To avoid that situation, it needed to achieve comparable prosperity in order to restore "a position for China in international affairs."[45] Giving a speech at a meeting of the Central Committee of the CPC on 16 January 1980, Deng Xiaoping said, "the role we play in international affairs is determined by the extent of our economic growth. If our country becomes more developed and prosperous, we will be in a position to play a greater role in international affairs."[46] In 1984, he reiterated to the then President of Brazil, Joao Baptista de Oliveira, that when China achieves a gross national product, now known as the Gross National Income (GNI), of $1 trillion, it will be able to contribute more to mankind.[47] Furthermore, at the Third Plenary Session of the Central Advisory Commission of the CPC on 22 October 1984, Deng Xiaoping said, "what will the political situation be like once we have quadrupled the GNP? I am confident that there will be a genuine stability and unity. China will be truly powerful, exerting a much greater influence in the world. That's why we have to work hard. There are 16 more years until the year 2000."[48]

True to the objective, Deng Xiaoping's economic reforms and open-door policy enabled China to achieve an average annual GDP growth rate of 9.9% from 1978 to 2014, "one of the world's best" (Cheng 2014, p. vii). In 1984, when Deng Xiaoping told the President of Brazil that China will be truly powerful and ready to play a significant role in international affairs when it achieves a GNI of US$1 trillion, it still had a GNI of $257 billion. By 1998, two years before the targeted deadline, China quadrupled its GNI to slightly more than US$1 trillion. Table 3.1 illustrates the extraordinary growth of China's annual GNI from being a mere US$184.8 billion in 1975 when Deng Xiaoping urged his fellow CPC comrades to consider production more than revolution to becoming the world's second largest economy with an annual GNI of US$10,097 trillion in 2014.

In addition, China's percentage share of world trade grew from less than 1%[49] in 1978 to 12.1%, ahead of United States' 11.5% and Germany's 7.7% in 2013. In the same year, 2013, it became the world's biggest merchandise trader ahead of the United States, Germany and Japan.[50] In terms of trade with other regions, China-Africa trade surpassed the US$100 billion mark in 2008[51] and reached $210.2 billion in 2013, making China-Africa's foremost trading partner.[52] As predicted by Deng Xiaoping this increase in China's relative economic power resulted in extension of its interests and influence in Asia, Africa, Latin America and the Middle East,[53] thereby enabling it to exert a much greater influence in the world, and expand its contributions in the Third World.

Table 3.1 Comparative Gross National Income (Formerly Gross National Product) Atlas Method (current US$ in billions)

Country	*1975*	*1980*	*1985*	*1990*	*1995*	*2000*	*2005*	*2010*	*2014*
China	187.4	214.9	301.4	374.1	649.7	1181.5	2295.1	5811.0	10,265.0
France	363.6	723.7	556.5	1208.9	1542.6	1531.5	2273.8	2847.8	2849.0
Germany	529.8	1020.1	765.4	1694.8	2414.4	2154.7	2959.4	3662.4	3864.0
Russian Federation	–	–	–	–	392.1	250.3	638.5	1425.1	2142.0
United Kingdom	269.9	528.4	509.2	1044 7	1208.1	1701.0	2583.1	2597.5	2826.3
United States	1842.2	3048.1	4164.9	6029.5	7760.9	10,178.5	13,694	15,143.1	17,633.1
Japan	573.3	1261.1	1387.2	3440.8	5281.6	4595.2	5182.6	5562.9	5339.1

Source: World Bank. 2015, World Development Indicators. Available at: http://databank.worldbank.org/data/reports.aspx?source=2&country=&series=NY.GNP.ATLS.CD&period=#

3.7 Prosperous China and Re-emergence of Intervention in Africa

In terms of relative economic power and global status, the China of the twenty-first century is miles apart from the China of Mao and Deng Xiaoping in the twentieth century. Its economy has grown exponentially. In less than 60 years it has risen from being the "sick man of Asia" to becoming one of the world's major economies. In fact, according to the World Bank's 2014 development indicators, its GDP based on purchasing power parity stood at US$18 trillion ahead of United States' US$17 trillion[54]—eighteen times more than what Deng Xiaoping envisioned it to be by the turn of the century. That growth in economic power has expectedly resulted in expansion of its economic interests abroad as it searches for new markets and resources to keep the engine of its economy running. From being an isolationist underdeveloped country in 1949, it has also become the biggest trading partner of the United States, Asia and Africa, with extensive trade relations with European and Latin American countries.

By all standards, the China of today has far exceeded Deng Xiaoping's expectations, but what impact has it had on its role in global affairs? As discussed above, in 1978 and 1984 Deng Xiaoping respectively told a Madagascan delegation and the former president of Brazil, Joao Baptista de Oliveira, that when China quadruples its economy's size, it will be "truly powerful, exerting a much greater influence in the world," and playing a significant role in international affairs, particularly in the Third World. The questions that arise, and what this chapter has sought to do, are to explore from a historical perspective whether China's role in international affairs is determined by its relative economic power; and whether its understanding and practice of intervention in foreign intrastate armed conflicts particularly in Africa evolve with changes in its relative economic power. What is apparent is that China's role in international affairs, especially intervention in the internal affairs of other states, has historically been influenced by a combination of internal factors and its position in the international system, particularly its relative economic power.

The result of China's rapid economic growth since 1978 has been a subsequent expansion of its economic and political interests in Africa. Initially, the re-engagement with Africa was in response to the dilemma of its rising demand for primary commodities and insufficient domestic sources for those high-value commodities.[55] Second, it needed alternative import and export markets to sustain its growing economy.[56] In short China was in "pursuit of economic self-interest in the form of access to raw materials, markets and spheres of influence through investment, trade and military assistance" (Marks 2006). As a result, by the end of 2013, it had surpassed the United States as Africa's biggest trading partner, and its direct investment in Africa amounted to US$25 billion, with at least 2500 Chinese companies operating across the African continent in sectors that include finance and banking, telecommunications, infrastructure development, agriculture, manufacturing and commodity broking. In addition to economic interests, it also considered Africa to be "an important component in shaping its influence and prestige as a major power"[57] and in expanding its global influence.

The expansion into Africa was, however, not without significant geopolitical challenges. Despite most African countries having been independent for several decades, European "political influence, economic preponderance, and cultural conditioning remain[ed]. Britain and France, and with them the rest of the European Community, maintain[ed] a relatively high level of aid and investment, trade dominance, and a sizeable flow of teachers, businessmen, statesmen, tourists and technical assistants" on the continent.[58] In addition to the European powers, the United States, Russia, Japan and other rising powers such as India and Brazil also have significant stakes in the politics and economies of African countries. That means as a late-returnee to Africa, China lacked "the economic and political ties that Western Europe has with Africa as a legacy of colonialism, and the economic power that the United States wields because of its wealth and influence in international financial institutions" (French 2004). With options for economic and trading partners in Africa somewhat limited,[59] China was compelled to offer resource-rich African countries better terms than those offered by rival global powers.[60] For China, one of those better terms came in the form of promises not to interfere in the African countries' internal affairs, and, unlike the West, it did not attach political conditions (except the one-China policy) to its development assistance to African countries.[61] Just as in the 1950s, Beijing's emphasis on non-interference resonated well with African ruling elites,[62] some of whom were bogged down by Western demands for political and economic reforms in exchange for aid and development assistance.

Riding on its official foreign policy of non-intervention in other states' internal affairs, China first gained 'political, economic and military space' in countries described as "outposts of tyranny"[63] where Western presence and influence were weak.[64] These were countries ostracised either by the West for gross human rights violations, terrorism, bad governance and authoritarianism, or simply for being riddled with perennial political instability and intrastate armed conflicts.[65] Seeing countries such as the Democratic Republic of Congo, Sudan, Zimbabwe and Angola as opportunities, Beijing was quick to step into the vacuum left by Western powers.[66] Also taking advantage of the minimal competition from Western companies, whose activities in those countries were inhibited by their governments, multilateral sanctions or domestic pressure,[67] Chinese companies flourished as Beijing took "up political, economic and military space that was [once] occupied by Britain, France or the United States"[68] in resource-rich countries like Sudan.

Mutually invoking the historical Sino-Africa cooperation in their fight against colonialism, the CPC strengthened its economic and political ties with ruling political elites in Africa. As China gained access to strategic natural resources, political leaders in countries such as Zimbabwe, Libya, Sudan and Angola viewed China's enthusiasm to trade with them in spite of Western sanctions as a source of alternative development assistance, and legitimisation of their regimes.[69] By accentuating the principle of non-intervention in their internal affairs, "China offered [them] not just an alternative path to development, but also an alternative to the Western-authored, liberal international order—rejecting, for example, the concept of universal human rights."[70] As it gained in economic power and influence in global governance, China is expanding its tentacles beyond "pariah and authoritarian states" to include African countries such as Gabon, Equatorial Guinea, South Africa and Botswana that still are strongly aligned to the West.

As China expands its economic interests in Africa, more and more it is finding both its investments and nationals under threat from intrastate armed conflicts in some of its African trading partners. Examples of Chinese nationals being kidnapped for ransom and investments being caught in the crossfire of armed conflicts abound. For instance, when an intrastate armed conflict broke out in Libya in 2011, Zhong Manying, Director of the Department of West Asia and Africa under the Ministry of Commerce, reported that Chinese enterprises with businesses in property, railway, crude oil service and telecommunication valuing more than $20 billion were lost (MOFCOM, 2011). Among those Chinese enterprises were three state oil firms: China National Petroleum Company (CNPC), China Petrochemical Corporation (Sinopec Group) and China National

Offshore Oil Company (Martina and Buckley 2011). In Sudan, China invested US$20 billion mostly in the oil industry before a secessionist conflict resulted in split of the Sudan into two. Two-thirds of its investments ended up in the new state of South Sudan. A further intrastate armed conflict outbreak in South Sudan affected the operations of the state-owned CNPC, which is a major shareholder in two oil consortia—the Greater Nile Petroleum Operating Company and the Petrodar Operating Company.[71] Not only have the intrastate armed conflicts affected China's economic interests, its citizens working in Africa have also been targeted. For example, Chinese workers were kidnapped and others killed by rebels in Sudan.[72] In the Central African Republic, two Chinese workers were kidnapped in 2012[73] and, more recently, Chinese companies have had to evacuate their nationals and scale down operations due to the ensuing civil war in South Sudan.[74] More and more, as shall be discussed in the next three empirical chapters, China's adherence to its non-intervention principle is being put to the test, as it strives to protect its national interests in Africa.

3.8 The Cyclical Pattern in China's External Intervention Behaviour: A Recap

What is apparent, however, is that the general trajectory of China's actual intervention in the internal affairs of other states can be explained by its position in the international system and increases in its relative economic power. As promised by Deng Xiaoping in 1978 and reiterated by President Xi in 2015, as China's economic power increases, it is expanding its interests into Africa. In the process, its non-intervention policy is being put to the test, compelling it to intervene in some African conflicts, and forcing it to play a bigger role in international affairs. This means that the trend from imperial China is still relevant today. "When Chinese power prevailed, the empire was able to force its tribute system and its language of diplomatic discourse on surrounding peoples. When the empire was weak, the Chinese perception of the world had little effect on the course of events. The ultimate fact is the fact of power" (Schwartz 1968, p. 278). With "the continued growth of the Chinese economy and with China's deeper integration into the international system, the tendency to keep a low profile in various international situations changed … the old strategy of 'hiding one's brilliance and improving one's internal strength' (*tao guang yang hui*) is no longer viable" (Wang and Rosenau 2009, p. 23).

Already, "Chinese foreign policy under Xi Jinping appears to have moved beyond Deng's cautious and cautionary approach and is much in line with what one would expect from a reemerging power that accepts its status as a major global power on the rise" (Cook 2015, p. 113).

Writing in 2008, John G. Ikenberry noted that as China had quadrupled the size of its economy, with trillions of US dollars in reserve, its diplomacy was extending its reach to Asia, Africa, Latin America and the Middle East. The implication of that extraordinary economic growth is that China is now both a military and an economic rival to the United States, a factor that is heralding a shift in the distribution of global power and putting China on its way to becoming a formidable global power. President Xi noted that China was now supposed to protect its nationals and interests abroad, which in reality entails intervening in the internal affairs of other states. Correspondingly, it is taking a more liberal interpretation of the official non-intervention principle. In concurrence, Jian Yang notes that "China's foreign policy since the end of the Cold War has experienced major changes in a liberal direction" (2009, p. 31). Other authors also note that since the beginning of the 1990s, "Chinese foreign policy has become far nimbler and engaging than at any other time in the history of the People's Republic" (Medeiros and Fravel 2003). Structurally different levels of relative economic power point to divergent patterns in China's interpretation of its principle of non-intervention in the internal affairs of other states. With a rise in its relative economic power in the twenty-first century, there should be an increase in its intervention in foreign intrastate armed conflicts in Africa.

What is clear from this historical pattern is that in times of expansive rise in economic power, Chinese intervention in other states' affairs is more frequent, whereas in times of decline there is less significant intervention abroad. It can be argued that the periods of high economic growth in China are matched with higher activity abroad, making them extroversion times whereas the decline periods are matched with less or no activity abroad, making them introversion times. "The extroversion times are matched with greater activity, including interventions abroad" (Feste 2003, p. 188). Frank Klingberg (1996) describes this phenomenon as being foreign policy mood alternations from introversion to extroversion. From the analysis above, towards the end of the Ming dynasty, the century of humiliation and the period from Deng Xiaoping's leadership in 1978 to until the coming in of Hu Jintao can be described as withdrawn periods in China's foreign policy. These periods were "typified by the concern to prevent development or expansion of ... political and military concerns beyond its own borders,"[75] whereas the latter years of Hu Jintao and currently President Xi Jinping's reign constitute the extrovert periods of its foreign policy.

On the other hand, Mao Zedong's interventionist foreign policy in Africa suggests that even though the increase in relative economic power may be minute, a state can still intervene in the internal affairs of other states in order to expand and protect its interests abroad. This does not mean that political ideology and/or state interest may be autonomous push factors separate from relative economic growth and a state's position in the international system because unlike Xi Jinping who sees China as a global power able to compete with the United States in global governance, Mao narrowly defined China as the leader of the Third World with interests to protect there. In the Third World, China had a significantly superior "global" position, able to influence and intervene in their internal affairs on behalf of its geostrategic and ideological interests. As put by Gideon Rose, the increase in its relative economic power, however small, was the basis upon which it was able to expand its interests abroad. Mao's "withdrawal" from Africa during the Cultural Revolution and Great Leap Forward when China's economic power was significantly under strain suggests that economic power was the bedrock upon which China's interventionist foreign policy lay.

This cyclical pattern in China's foreign policy behaviour, in particular intervention in foreign conflicts, reflects the lateral pressure hypothesis and the neoclassical realist arguments that

> States expand when they think they can, when they perceive relative increases in national power, and when changes in the relative costs and benefits of expansion make it profitable for them to do so ... [because] as states grow wealthier and more powerful, they do not only seek greater worldwide political influence (control over territory, the behaviour of other states, and the world economy) commensurate with their new capabilities, but they will also be more capable of expanding their interests and, if necessary, of waging large-scale wars for this purpose. (Feste 2003, p. 189)

With its new economic power, China has international interests, and the capacity to project both military and non-military power to protect and advance those interests. Thus the "Chinese foreign policy establishment has come to see the country as an emerging global power with varied interest and responsibilities—and not as the victimised developing nation of the Mao Zedong and Deng Xiaoping era" (Medeiros and Fravel 2003). Hence, "as China's economy continues to grow and as its political ambition continues to develop, so will its influence around the world" (Wang and Rosenau 2009, p. 7). Thus, as put by Li Cheng, director of the John L. Thornton China Center of the Brookings Institute, "as a major power, China's voice should be heard, and views should be delivered ... [Since] along with its rising international status, China also shoulders more responsibilities and obligations in narrowing the rich-poor gap, promoting South-South cooperation and other global affairs."[76] This is because "the way Chinese policy changes and how it responds to the challenges of the twenty-first century will be critical not only to the future of conflict-affected and fragile states, but to global security and stability and, consequently, to China's own sustained economic growth and modernization" (Mariani 2015, p. 267).

Notes

1. Wing, SD 2016, 'French intervention in Mali: strategic alliances, long-term regional presence?' *Small Wars & Insurgencies*, vol. 27, no. 1, p. 72.
2. Yao, F 2011, 'War and Confucianism', *Asian Philosophy,* vol. 21, no. 2, p. 219.
3. Lam, TB 1968, 'Intervention versus tribute in Sino-Vietnamese relations, 1788–1790', in JK Fairbank (ed.), *The Chinese world order: Traditional China's foreign relations,* Harvard University Press, Cambridge, p. 165, 179.
4. Wang, YK 2011, *Harmony and war: Confucian culture and Chinese power politics*, Columbia University Press, New York, p. 70.
5. Deng, X 1984, 'Speech at the Third Plenary Session of the Central Advisory Commission of the Communist Party of China', 22 October 1984, in Deng, X 1994, *Selected Works of Deng Xiaoping: Volume III,* Beijing: Foreign Language Press, viewed 7 January 2016, https://archive.org/stream/SelectedWorksOfDengXiaopingVol.3/Deng03#page/n1/mode/2up
6. Thucydides 1985, *The Peloponnesian war*, Penguin, Basingstoke, p. 402.
7. Scott, D 2008, *China and the international system, 1840–1949: Power, presence, and perceptions in a century of humiliation,* State University of New York Press, New York, p. 2.
8. Mao, Z 1949, 'The Chinese people have stood up!', Opening address at the First Plenary Session of the Chinese People's Political Consultative Conference, 21 September, viewed 12 May 2014, https://www.marxists.org/reference/archive/mao/selected-works/volume-5/mswv5_01.htm

9. 'Proclamation of the Central People's Government of the PRC' 1949, *People's Daily*, 2 October, viewed 12 May 2014, https://www.marxists.org/reference/archive/mao/selected-works/volume-7/mswv7_003.htm
10. Deng, X 1979, 'China's goal is to achieve comparative prosperity by the end of the century', 6 December, in Deng, X 1983, *Deng Xiaoping wenxuan 1975–1982 (Selected Works of Deng Xiaoping 1975–1982)*, Beijing: Renminchubanshe, viewed 7 January 2016, https://archive.org/stream/SelectedWorksOfDengXiaopingVol.1/Deng02#page/n0/mode/2up
11. 'Xi pledges 'great renewal of Chinese nation' 2012, *Xinhua*, 29 November, viewed 13 May 2014, http://news.xinhuanet.com/english/china/2012-11/29/c_132008231.htm
12. Meredith, M 1984, *The first dance of freedom: Black Africa in the post war era*, Harper & Row, New York, p. 177.
13. Mao, Z 1949, 'On the people's democratic dictatorship', speech in commemoration of the twenty-eighth anniversary of the Communist Party of China, 30 June, viewed 12 May 2014, https://www.marxists.org/reference/archive/mao/selected-works/volume-4/mswv4_65.htm
14. Cohen, JA 1973, 'China and intervention: Theory and practice', *University of Pennsylvania Law Review*, vol. 121, no. 471, p. 492; Raine, S 2009, *China's African challenges,* Routledge, London, p. 16.
15. Yu, GT 1977, 'China and the third world', *Asian Survey,* vol. 17, no. 11, p. 1037; Pang, Z 2009, 'China's non-intervention question', *Global responsibility to protect,* vol. 1, no. 2, p. 245.
16. The Five Principles are: (1) mutual respect for territorial integrity and sovereignty, (2) non-aggression, (3) non-interference in internal affairs, (4) equality and mutual benefit, and (5) peaceful coexistence.
17. 'Supplementary speech of Premier Zhou Enlai at the Plenary Session of the Asian African-Conference', 1955, 19 April, History and Public Policy Program Digital Archive, PRC FMA 207-00006-02, pp. 1–13.
18. 'Resolutions of the Accra Meeting of independent African states' 1958, *New China News Agency*, 22 April, p. 27.
19. Hess, S, & Aidoo, R 2010, 'Beyond the rhetoric: Noninterference in China's African Policy', African *and Asian Studies*, vol. 9, no. 3, p. 361; Gill, B, Huang, C, & Morrison, JS 2007, 'Assessing China's Growing Influence in Africa', *China Security*, vol. 3, no. 3, p. 5; Raine, S 2009, *China's African challenges,* Routledge, London, p. 17.
20. Ogunsanwo, A 1974, *China's policy in Africa: 1958–71*, Cambridge University Press, Cambridge, p. 27; Raine, S 2009, *China's African challenges,* Routledge, London, p. 18.
21. Jakobson, L 2009, 'China's diplomacy toward Africa: Drivers and constraints', *International Relations of the Asia-Pacific*, vol. 9, no. 3, p. 407.
22. Mitchell, D & McGiffert, C 2007, 'Expanding the "strategic periphery": A history of China's interaction with the developing world', in Eisenman,

E Heginbotham, & D Mitchell (eds.), *China and the developing world: Beijing's strategy for the twenty-first century*, ME Sharpe, New York, p. 15.

23. Virrall, M 2012, 'Debunking the myth of China's soft power in China's use of foreign assistance from 1949 to the present', in H Lai & Y Lu (eds.), *China's soft power and international relations,* Routledge, London, p. 162.
24. Mao, Z 1956, 'Opening address at the Eighth National Congress of the Chinese Communist Party' 15 September, viewed 12 May 2014, https://www.marxists.org/subject/china/documents/cpc/8th_cong_opening.htm
25. Lin, B 1965, 'Long live the victory of people's war!', viewed 12 May 2014, http://www.marxists.org/reference/archive/lin-biao/1965/09/peoples_war/ch07.htm
26. Shinn, DH & Eisenman, J 2012, *China and Africa: A century of engagement,* University of Pennsylvania Press, Philadelphia, p. 164.
27. Legum, C 1976, 'The Soviet Union, China and the West in Southern Africa', *Foreign Affairs,* vol. 54, no. 4, pp. 745–762.
28. Raine, S 2009, *China's African challenges,* Routledge, London, p. 18.
29. Martin, D & Johnson, P 1981, *The struggle for Zimbabwe: the Chimurenga war,* Faber & Faber, London, p. 88.
30. Zacarias, A 1999, *Security and the state in Southern Africa,* Tauris Academic Studies, London, p. 76.
31. Johnson, P 2015, 'China in Zimbabwe, Africa: Past, present and future', The Herald, 24 November. Available at: http://www.herald.co.zw/china-in-zimbabwe-africa-past-present-and-future/
32. Shinn, DH & Eisenman, J 2012, *China and Africa: A century of engagement,* University of Pennsylvania Press, Philadelphia, p. 165.
33. 'Burundi draws Peking protest for cutting ties' 1965, *Chicago Tribune*, 1 February, viewed 15 May 2014, http://archives.chicagotribune.com/1965/02/01/page/3/article/burundi-draws-peking-protest-for-cutting-ties
34. Foreign Ministry of People's Republic of China 2004, 'Diplomatic ties between China and African countries', viewed 18 May 2014, http://www.fmprc.gov.cn/ce/ceza/eng/zghfz/zfgx/t165322.htm
35. Nicaragua *v.* United States of America (case concerning the military and paramilitary activities in and against Nicaragua), *International Court of Justice*, Judgment of 27 June 1986, viewed 18 May 2014, http://www.icj-cij.org/docket/?sum=367&p1=3&p2=3&case=70&p3=5
36. Fabricius, P 2014. 'Beijing's peacemaking efforts in South Sudan.' *Institute for Security Studies*, 6 November, viewed 21 December 2014, http://www.issafrica.org/iss-today/beijings-peacemaking-efforts-in-south-sudan
37. Corkin, L 2013, *Uncovering African agency: Angola's management of China's credit lines*, Ashgate, Surrey, p. 2.

38. Deng, X 1979, 'Uphold the Four Cardinal Principles', 30 March, in Deng, X 1983, *Deng Xiaoping wenxuan 1975–1982 (Selected Works of Deng Xiaoping 1975–1982)*, Renminchubanshe, Beijing.
39. Yu, GT 1977, "China and the third world", *Asian Survey,* vol. 17, no. 11, p. 1036.
40. Deng, X 1975, 'The whole Party should take the overall interests into account and push the economy forward', 5 March, in Deng, X 1983, *Deng Xiaoping wenxuan 1975–1982 (Selected Works of Deng Xiaoping 1975–1982)*, Renminchubanshe, Beijing.
41. Deng, X 1978, 'Hold high the banner of Mao Zedong Thought and adhere to the principle of seeking truth from facts', 16 September, in Deng, X 1983, *Deng Xiaoping wenxuan 1975–1982 (Selected Works of Deng Xiaoping 1975–1982)*, Renminchubanshe, Beijing.
42. Deng, X 1978, 'Carry out the policy of opening to the outside world and learn advanced science and technology from other countries', 10 October, in Deng, X 1983, *Deng Xiaoping wenxuan 1975–1982 (Selected Works of Deng Xiaoping 1975–1982)*, Renminchubanshe, Beijing.
43. Deng, X 1975, 'Strengthen Party leadership and rectify the Party's style of work', 4 July 1975, in Deng, X 1983, *Deng Xiaoping wenxuan 1975–1982 (Selected Works of Deng Xiaoping 1975–1982)*, Renminchubanshe, Beijing.
44. Deng, X 1978, 'Realize the four modernizations and never seek hegemony', 7 May, in Deng, X 1983, *Deng Xiaoping wenxuan 1975–1982 (Selected Works of Deng Xiaoping 1975–1982)*, Renminchubanshe, Beijing.
45. Deng, X 1979, 'China's goal is to achieve comparative prosperity by the end of the century', 6 December, in Deng, X 1983, *Deng Xiaoping wenxuan 1975–1982 (Selected Works of Deng Xiaoping 1975–1982)*, Renminchubanshe, Beijing.
46. Deng, X 1979, 'The present situation and the tasks before us', 16 January 1980, in Deng, X 1983, *Deng Xiaoping wenxuan 1975–1982 (Selected Works of Deng Xiaoping 1975–1982)*, Renminchubanshe, Beijing.
47. Deng, X 1984, 'We must safeguard world peace and ensure domestic development', 29 May 1984, in Deng, X 1994, *Selected Works of Deng Xiaoping: Volume III,* Beijing: Foreign Language Press.
48. Deng, X 1984, 'Speech at the Third Plenary Session of the Central Advisory Commission of the Communist Party of China', 22 October 1984, in Deng, X 1994, *Selected Works of Deng Xiaoping: Volume III,* Beijing: Foreign Language Press.
49. Zheng, B 2005, 'China's "peaceful rise" to great-power status', *Foreign Affairs,* vol. 84, no. 5, p. 18.
50. World Trade Organisation 2014, *World trade development, 2013*, World Trade Organisation, Geneva, page 15, viewed 7 April 2014, https://www.wto.org/english/res_e/statis_e/its2014_e/its14_highlights1_e.pdf;

Federal Ministry for Economic Affairs and Energy 2014, *Facts about Germany foreign trade in 2013*, viewed 7 April 2014, http://www.bmwi.de/English/Redaktion/Pdf/facts-about-german-foreign-trade-in-2013,property=pdf,bereich=bmwi2012,sprache=en,rwb=true.pdf; Wang, Y & Yao, Y 2003, 'Sources of China's economic growth 1952–1999: Incorporating human capital accumulation', *China Economic Review*, vol. 14, no. 1, pp. 32–52; Chow, GC & Li, K 2002, 'China's economic growth: 1952–2010', *Economic Development and Cultural Change*, vol. 51, no. 1, pp. 247–256.

51. Zhu, Z 2010, *China's New Diplomacy: Rationale Strategies and Significance*, Ashgate Publishing, Surrey, p. 22.
52. Ministry of Commerce People's Republic of China 2014, 'Chinese Premier Calls for Upgraded Version of China-Africa Cooperation', May 6, viewed 18 May 2014, http://english.mofcom.gov.cn/article/zt_africatour/news/201411/20141100802253.shtml
53. Ikenberry, GJ 2008, 'The rise of China and the future of the West: Can the liberal system survive?' *Foreign affairs*, vol. 87, no. 1, p. 26.
54. The World Bank 2014, *World Development Indicator – GDP ranking, PPP based*' viewed 7 April 2014, http://databank.worldbank.org/data/download/GDP_PPP.pdf
55. Choucri, N & North, RC 1975, *Nations in conflict: National growth and international violence*, WH Freeman: San Francisco, p. 15; Adem, S 2010, 'The Paradox of Chinas Policy in Africa', *African and Asian Studies*, vol. 9, no. 3, p. 336.
56. Gill, B, Huang, C, & Morrison, JS 2007, 'Assessing China's Growing Influence in Africa', *China Security*, vol. 3, no. 3, p. 9.
57. Jakobson, L 2009, 'China's diplomacy toward Africa: Drivers and constraints', *International Relations of the Asia-Pacific*, vol. 9, no. 3, p. 405.
58. Zartman, WI 1976, 'Europe and Africa: Decolonization or dependency?' *Foreign Affairs*, no. 54, no. 2, p. 325.
59. Zweig, D 2006, 'Resource diplomacy' under hegemony: The sources of Sino-American competition in the 21st century?' Working Paper, no. 18, Center on China's Transnational Relations, Hong Kong, p. 11.
60. Halper, S 2012, *The Beijing Consensus: Legitimizing authoritarianism in our time*, Basic Books, New York, p. xvi.
61. The 'no-condition' term has to be qualified. It does not mean that China's aid comes with no conditions attached. In most cases Chinese financial assistance comes with economic conditions such as the use of Chinese materials and contracting of Chinese companies. The no-condition refers to absence or lack of human rights, democracy and good governance conditions. For further discussion of the conditionality of Chinese financial assistance see: Hodzi, O, Hartwell, L, & De Jager, N 2012, '"Unconditional aid": Assessing the impact of China's development assistance to Zimbabwe', *South African Journal of International Affairs* 19, no. 1, pp. 79–103.

62. Taylor, I 2007b, 'Unpacking China's Resource Diplomacy in Africa', Working Paper, no. 18, Center on China's Transnational Relations, Hong Kong, p. 4.
63. 'Rice Names 'outposts of tyranny' 2005, *BBC News*, January 19, viewed 18 May 2014, http://news.bbc.co.uk/1/hi/world/americas/4186241.stm
64. Bayart, J 2000, 'Africa in the world: a history of extraversion', *African affairs*, vol. 99, no. 395, p. 265.
65. Givens, JW 2011, 'The Beijing Consensus is neither: China as a non-ideological challenge to international norms', *St Antony's International Review*, vol. 6, no. 2, p. 14.
66. Taylor, I 1998, 'China's foreign policy towards Africa in the 1990s', *The Journal of Modern African Studies*, vol. 36, no. 3, p. 453.
67. Kleine-Ahlbrandt, S & Small, A 2008, 'China's new dictatorship diplomacy: Is Beijing parting with pariahs?' *Foreign affairs*, vol. 87, no. 1, p. 41.
68. Zakaria, F 2008, *The Post-American World*, W.W. Norton, New York, p. 117. See also Jakobson, L 2009, 'China's diplomacy toward Africa: Drivers and constraints', *International Relations of the Asia-Pacific*, vol. 9, no. 3, p. 406.
69. Taylor, I 1998, 'China's foreign policy towards Africa in the 1990s', *The Journal of Modern African Studies*, vol. 36, no. 3, pp. 443–460.
70. Halper, S 2012, *The Beijing Consensus: Legitimizing authoritarianism in our time*, Basic Books, New York, p. xii; Foster, V, Butterfield, W, Chen, C, & Pushak, N 2009, *Building bridges: China's growing role as infrastructure financier for sub-Saharan Africa, Volume 5*, The World Bank, Washington D.C., p. viii.
71. Attree, L 2012, *China and conflict-affected states: Between principle and pragmatism*, Saferworld: London.
72. 'Sudan rebels kill 5 Chinese hostages' 2008, *The Telegraph*, 27 October, viewed 12 May 2014, http://www.telegraph.co.uk/news/worldnews/africaandindianocean/sudan/3270057/Sudan-rebels-kill-5-Chinese-hostages.html
73. Two Chinese kidnapped on Cameroon-C Africa border' 2012, *AsiaOne*, 15 October, viewed 22 March 2014, http://news.asiaone.com/print/News/AsiaOne%2BNews/Crime/Story/A1Story20121015-377828.html
74. '97 Chinese workers evacuated from South Sudan to Khartoum' 2013, *People Daily*, 25 December, viewed 22 March, http://english.peopledaily.com.cn/90883/8495532.html
75. Holmes, JE 1985, *The mood/interest theory of American foreign policy*, The University Press of Kentucky, Kentucky, p. 21.
76. Zhang, N 2016, 'China plays increasing role in global governance: US-based scholar', *People's Daily*, 1 April, 1 April 2016, http://en.people.cn/n3/2016/0401/c90883-9038862.html

Bibliography

Campos, I., & Vines, A. (2008). Angola and China: A pragmatic partnership. In J. Cooke (Ed.), *US and Chinese engagement in Africa: Prospects for improving US-China-Africa cooperation*. Washington, DC: Center for Strategic and International Studies (CSIS). Retrieved April 5, 2014, from http://csis.org/files/media/csis/pubs/080711_cooke_us_chineseengagement_web.pdf.

Chan, W. T. (1973). *A source book in Chinese philosophy*. Princeton: Princeton University Press.

Cheng, C. (2014). *China's economic development, 1950–2014: Fundamental changes and long-term prospects*. London: Lexington Books.

Ching, J. (2004). Confucianism and weapons of mass destruction. In S. H. Hashimi & S. P. Lee (Eds.), *Ethics and weapons of mass destruction: Religious and secular perspectives* (pp. 246–269). Cambridge: Cambridge University Press.

Cohen, J. A. (1973). China and intervention: Theory and practice. *University of Pennsylvania Law Review, 121*(471), 471–505.

Cook, M. (2015). China's power status change: East Asian challenges for Xi Jinping's foreign policy. *China Quarterly of International Strategic Studies, 1*(01), 105–131.

Deng, Y., & Wang, F. (1999). Introduction: Toward an understanding of China's world view. In Y. Deng & F. Wang (Eds.), *In the eyes of the Dragon. China views the world* (pp. 1–19). Lanham: Rowman & Littlefield.

Dreyer, J. T. (2015). The 'Tianxia Trope': Will China change the international system? *Journal of Contemporary China, 24*(96), 1015–1031.

Fairbank, J. K. (1968). A preliminary framework. In J. K. Fairbank (Ed.), *The Chinese world order: Traditional China's foreign relations* (pp. 1–10). Cambridge: Harvard University Press.

Feste, K. A. (2003). *Intervention: Shaping the global order*. Westport, CT: Praeger.

French, H. (2004). China in Africa: All trade, with no political baggage. *New York Times*, 8 August. Retrieved June 7, 2015, from http://www.nytimes.com/2004/08/08/international/asia/08china.html

Ikenberry, G. J. (2001). Review of saving strangers: Humanitarian intervention in international society, Wheeler, N.J. *Foreign Affairs*, Vol. 80, No. 6. Retrieved June 5, 2014, from http://www.foreignaffairs.com/articles/57287/g-john-ikenberry/saving-strangers-humanitarian-intervention-in-international-soci

Ivanhoe, P. (2004). "Heaven's mandate" and the concept of war in early Confucianism. In S. H. Hashimi & S. P. Lee (Eds.), *Ethics and weapons of mass destruction: Religious and secular perspectives* (pp. 270–276). Cambridge: Cambridge University Press.

Kaufman, A. A. (2010). The "century of humiliation," then and now: Chinese perceptions of the international order. *Pacific Focus, 25*(1), 1–33.

Kennedy, P. (1988). *The rise and fall of the great powers: Economic change and military power from 1500 to 2000*. London: Unwin Hyman.
Klingberg, F. L. (1996). *Positive expectations of America's world role: Historical cycles of realistic idealism*. Lanham: University Press of America.
Kornberg, J. F., & Faust, J. R. (2005). *China in world politics: Policies, processes, prospects*. Boulder: Lynne Rienner.
Lam, T. B. (1968). Intervention versus tribute in Sino-Vietnamese relations, 1788–1790. In J. K. Fairbank (Ed.), *The Chinese world order: Traditional China's foreign relations*. Cambridge: Harvard University Press.
Liu, S. (1995). Reflections on world peace through peace among religions—A Confucian perspective. *Journal of Chinese Philosophy, 22*, 193–213.
Mariani, B. (2015). China's role in UN peacekeeping operations. In C. P. Freeman (Ed.), *Handbook on China and developing countries* (pp. 252–271). Northampton: Elgar.
Marks, S. (2006). China in Africa-the new imperialism? *Pambazuka News*, March 2. Retrieved April 29, 2015, from http://www.pambazuka.net/en/category/features/32432
Medeiros, E. S., & Fravel, M. T. (2003). China's new diplomacy. *Foreign Affairs*, November/December Issue. Retrieved April 7, 2014, from https://www.foreignaffairs.com/articles/asia/2003-11-01/chinas-new-diplomacy
Ogunsanwo, A. (1974). *China's policy in Africa: 1958–71*. Cambridge: Cambridge University Press.
Perdue, P. C. (2015). The tenacious tributary system. *Journal of Contemporary China, 24*(96), 1002–1014.
Raine, S. (2009). *China's African challenges*. London: Routledge.
Schwartz, B. I. (1968). The Chinese perception of the world order, past and present. In J. K. Fairbank (Ed.), *The Chinese world order: Traditional China's foreign relations* (pp. 276–288). Cambridge: Harvard University Press.
Scott, D. (2008). *China and the international system, 1840–1949: Power, presence, and perceptions in a century of humiliation*. New York: State University of New York Press.
Shinn, D. H., & Eisenman, J. (2012). *China and Africa: A century of engagement*. Philadelphia: University of Pennsylvania Press.
Suzuki, C. (1968). China's relations with inner Asia: The Hsiung-nu, Tibet. In J. K. Fairbank (Ed.), *The Chinese world order: Traditional China's foreign relations* (pp. 180–197). Cambridge: Harvard University Press.
Taylor, I. (2000). The ambiguous commitment: The People's Republic of China and the anti-apartheid struggle in South Africa. *Journal of Contemporary African Studies, 18*(1), 91–106.
Thrall, L. (2015). *China's expanding African relations: Implications for US National Security*. RAND Corporation, California. Retrieved January 17, 2016, from http://www.rand.org/content/dam/rand/pubs/research_reports/RR900/RR905/RAND_RR905.pdf

Wang, H., & Rosenau, J. N. (2009). China and global governance. *Asian Perspective, 33*(3), 5–39.

Wang, Y. K. (2011). *Harmony and war: Confucian culture and Chinese power politics*. New York: Columbia University Press.

Womack, B. (2006). *China and Vietnam: The politics of asymmetry*. Cambridge: Cambridge University Press.

Yang, J. (2009). The rise of China: Chinese perspectives. In K. J. Cooney & Y. Sato (Eds.), *The rise of China and international security: America and Asia respond* (pp. 13–37). London: Routledge.

Yao, F. (2011). War and Confucianism. *Asian Philosophy, 21*(2), 213–226.

Yu, G. T. (1977). China and the third world. *Asian Survey, 17*(11), 1036–1048.

Zhang, C. (2014). China-Zimbabwe relations: A model of China-Africa relations? *South African Institute of International Affairs*, Occasional Paper 205. Retrieved December 7, 2014, from http://www.saiia.org.za/occasional-papers/643-china-zimbabwe-relations-a-model-of-china-africa-relations/file

Zhang, Y., & Buzan, B. (2012). The tributary system as international society in theory and practice. *The Chinese Journal of International Politics, 5*, 3–36.

Zhao, S. (2015). Rethinking the Chinese world order: The imperial cycle and the rise of China. *Journal of Contemporary China, 24*(96), 961–982.

CHAPTER 4

Libya

4.1 Introduction

The previous chapter traced the historical evolution of China's intervention behaviour vis-à-vis the trajectory of its transition from being the "Middle Kingdom" to a state within the modern international system. What became apparent is that as its relative economic power vacillated due to changes in its domestic economy, so did its intervention in African states' internal affairs. With Deng Xiaoping pursuing the "Socialist Modernisation" programme, Africa no longer fitted into the grand scheme of China's domestic and foreign policy. Simply put, what followed was a "decade of neglect by China"[1] because it "not only viewed Africa as largely immaterial in its quest for modernisation, but also saw that the rationale behind its support for anti-Soviet elements in the continent was no longer valid" (Taylor 1998, p. 444). It was only after the Tiananmen Square incident that China revived its political and diplomatic engagement with Africa, but still its role in the continent's internal affairs remained minimal. Its focus on Africa was, however, reinforced when, due to lateral pressure caused by high domestic economic growth, it aggressively sought new markets and sources of energy and other strategic primary commodities. Only then did it vigorously renew its re-engagement with resource-rich countries in Africa. With its gigantic oil and gas reserves and lucrative opportunities for Chinese multinational companies in the construction and telecommunications sector, Libya was a natural target for China's "going out" strategy.

O. Hodzi, *The End of China's Non-Intervention Policy in Africa*,
Critical Studies of the Asia-Pacific,
https://doi.org/10.1007/978-3-319-97349-4_4

Building on that broad history of Sino-Africa relations, and particularly on the thesis that China expands its interests abroad when its relative economic power increases, this chapter discusses China's intervention in Libya's 2011 intrastate armed conflict. It begins by exploring Sino-Libya diplomatic, political and economic relations from a historical perspective, and then focuses on China's economic interests in Libya and how the outbreak of the intrastate armed conflict in 2011 affected those interests in a manner and scale never before experienced by China in Africa. The latter part of the chapter examines China's unilateral, bilateral and multilateral intervention in the conflict. Overall, the main argument advanced in this chapter is that China's response to the Libyan intrastate armed conflict reflects an indecisive foreign policy on intervention in foreign conflicts that gravitated from non-interventionism to ambivalent interventionism.

4.2 Background of China-Libya Relations

Relations between China and Libya began in the 1950s through what began as indirect interactions at conferences such as the 1955 Bandung Conference[2] and the Afro-Asian People's Solidarity Conference held in late December 1957. China's drive to directly engage Libya, however, gained momentum as part of Beijing's wider "diplomatic offensive in North Africa … the region of Africa that had the largest number of independent states; Beijing believed it could persuade several to recognise the PRC" (Shinn and Eisenman 2012, p. 228). As a result of that concerted diplomatic offensive, China established its first African embassy in Cairo, Egypt, in 1956. A year later, a Commercial Officer at the Chinese embassy in Cairo, Chan Hiang-Kang, established China's first official trade relations with Libya, alongside other North African countries. The relations got a further boost when the International Liaison and Organisation Department of the Central Committee of the Communist Party of China and the State Council's Commission for Cultural Relations with foreign countries jointly organised visits to China for delegates from 27 African countries including Libya in 1958–1959. The visits by the African delegates "were naturally expected to support diplomatic recognition and the opening of trade relations after independence" (Ogunsanwo 1974, p. 35; see also Larkin 1973, p. 29). However, the outcome was not outright successful for China, because in 1959 the Kingdom of Libya under King Idris established and maintained full diplomatic relations with Taiwan.[3]

When Muammar Muhammad Abu Minyar al-Gaddafi (popularly known as Muammar Gaddafi) came into power after the 1969 coup d'état against King Idris, he was "a 27-year old signals officer driven by grand ambitions, fierce hatreds and a pathological penchant for meddling in the affairs of other countries, made possible by the huge flow of oil revenues at his disposal."[4] Partly because he was an anti-Communist and pro-Arab Unity nationalist—ideologies that were inimical to China, he was at first not keen on establishing diplomatic relations with China. He therefore maintained Libya's diplomatic ties with Taiwan until 1978. However, possibly due to a combination of acknowledgements by Zhou Enlai of Gaddafi's support for the anti-imperialist movement, and "China's support for the Arab states and the Palestinians against Israel,"[5] Muammar Gaddafi acquiesced to recognising the People's Republic of China in 1971. In fact, it was a unilateral decision that he made "while there was still an ambassador in Tripoli representing Taiwan."[6] Libya-Taiwan diplomatic relations still remained until August 1978 when the People's Republic of China and Libya officially established diplomatic ties.

On consummation of their diplomatic relations, China and Libya immediately entered into their first trade agreement, the agreement for cooperation on the economy, science and technology in August 1978, which came into force four years later.[7] In 1982, the countries signed the Agreement on Establishment of the Sino-Libyan Joint Committee on Economic, Trade, Scientific and Technological Cooperation, and the Sino-Libyan Mutual Cooperation Program. Further agreements were signed concerning the sending of Chinese medical teams to Libya between 1983 and 1994[8] and follow-on agreements on cultural cooperation (1985); scientific and technological cooperation (1990), and cultural and information cooperation (2001). In addition, although there were several exchange visits between the two countries in the course of Gaddafi's rule over Libya, official visits by heads of state of both Libya and China were rare. The only time Gaddafi made a state visit to China was in 1982, "during which the two countries signed an accord to set up a mixed committee for trade, economic, science and technological cooperation."[9] Two decades later, China's President Jiang Zemin and Vice-Premier Qian Qichen made a two-day state visit to Libya—the first visit by a Chinese President to the North African country.[10] In between, China's Vice-Premier Li Peng visited Libya in May 1984; in January 1996, Chinese Vice-Premier and Foreign Minister Qian Qichen visited Libya. In September of the same year, a delegation led by Zinati Mohammed Al

Zinati, Speaker of the General People's Congress of Libya, paid a goodwill visit to China. Libya's Secretary of Foreign Communication and International Cooperation, Abdul-Rahman Mohammad Shalgam, then visited China in May 2000; and the following year, in January 2001 China's foreign minister Tang Jiaxuan visited Libya.[11] The last visit by a high-ranking Chinese official before Gaddafi's fall in 2011 was by Foreign Minister Li Zhaoxing in January 2006. The fact that five years passed without high-level official visits between the two countries somewhat reflects the uneasy relations between China and Libya.

4.3 Troubled Diplomatic Relations

By the time a mass revolution against Muammar Gaddafi started in February 2011, China-Libya diplomatic relations had gone through turbulent times—causing China "occasional indignity."[12] For example, at the same time that Muammar Gaddafi was hosting China's foreign affairs minister Li Zhaoxing in Libya and confirming his country's commitment to the one-China policy, his son Sayf al-Islam Gaddafi, President of the Gaddafi International Foundation for Charity Associations and acting as his father's envoy, met President Chen Shui-bian in Taiwan. On behalf of his father, he went on to invite President Chen to visit Libya "in order to facilitate bilateral economic, science, technology, tourism, education and military exchanges, and exchange representative offices."[13] Much to the vexation of Beijing, President Chen made a transit stop in Tripoli four months later in May 2006.[14] Regarding that visit, Liu Jianchao, the PRC's Foreign Ministry spokesman, vented Beijing's anger in the following terms:

> Regardless of China's persuasion and strong opposition, Libya insisted on allowing Chen Shui-bian to stop over and discussed with him setting up representative offices on each other's territory… This is a serious violation of Libya's long-term commitment to the one-China policy and will exert a negative impact on China-Libya relations… We demand that Libya live up to its commitment and immediately cease all official exchanges with Taiwan in whatever form so as to maintain the overall China-Libya relations.[15]

Further infuriating China and causing it to lose face was that four months before President Chen's stopover in Libya, the spokesman of China's Foreign Ministry, Kong Quan, had confidently declared China's appreciation for the Libyan government's adherence to the one-China policy.[16] Nonetheless, despite China's stern rebuke over President Chen Shui-bian's visit to Tripoli, Libya did not cease relations with Taiwan. Instead, the Taiwan Commercial Office began operating in Libya just two years after President Chen's visit to Tripoli.[17]

Libya's foreign policy and relations with China, as they were with other countries, were generally unpredictable because of the prominent and direct role that Muammar Gaddafi played, which ensured that foreign relations were personality-driven and depended on his personal relations with leaders of the respective foreign countries.[18] For instance, when Gaddafi was incensed by China's lack of support for his "integrated Africa" initiative, under what he termed the United States of Africa, he publicly criticised China for attempting to "colonise" Africa for its own benefit and for its lack of support for integration and cooperation of African countries. Two years later, at the 2009 Fourth Ministerial Forum on China-Africa Cooperation (FOCAC), which was held in Sharm al-Shaykh, Egypt, Libya's foreign minister Moussa Koussa also complained about China's "divide and rule" of African countries. He remonstrated that Beijing does "not want the African Union, or African unity, but rather China wants to cooperate with Africa as separate nations, rather than as a union."[19]

Apart from accusing China of being divisive in its engagement with Africa, Gaddafi and his foreign minister continued to accuse China of colonising the continent. In an address to Oxford University students via satellite, Gaddafi contended that there was a geopolitical conflict between China and the United States over Africa and that the two countries were using different strategies and approaches to colonise the continent and benefit from its resources. He said:

> There is a colonialism that imposes itself by force [United States] and another that uses gentler methods [China]. There is a soft and a harsh colonialism. But in the final analysis, colonialism is one and the same. As I said, there are those who welcome China. We all seek a deterrent against the harsh approach of American penetration. This makes us take China's side. However, China must know that we are aware that it could turn into an imperialist power. If it wishes to settle in Africa or to plunder Africa's resources at a low price and sell its manufactured products at an exorbitant one, it will turn into a colonial power.[20]

His foreign minister, Moussa Koussa, put it in even more crude terms, arguing that reality on the ground suggested "something akin to a Chinese invasion of the African continent."[21] He then concluded his criticism by advising China not to resettle its citizens in Africa under the pretext of employment and investment.

Both accusations touched a nerve in China because it had carefully cultivated an image and identity as Africa's all-weather benevolent equal partner interested in mutually beneficial engagements unlike the "exploitative" West. Although there is no evidence of China's specific response to Gaddafi and Moussa Koussa's allegations that it was driving towards colonising Africa, China has consistently negated those accusations, arguing that it is Africa's development partner. Regardless, Libya's accusations against Beijing reflected the problematic nature of the two countries' relations. In fact, Maximilian Terhalle puts it that "Gaddafi's outspoken sympathies for and close ties with Taiwan and his well-known policy to raise resentments among African states against China's economic engagement on the continent made it somewhat easier for Beijing to vote in favour of the resolution [UNSC Resolution 1970]" (2015, p. 170). The UNSC Resolution 1970 (2011) imposed sanctions, asset freezes and an arms embargo on Libya, as well as on selected individuals that included Gaddafi, his sons, and close associates. However, as put by David H. Shinn and Joshua Eisenman in their book *China and Africa: A Century of Engagement*, despite their awkward relations, China was still "willing to suffer an occasional indignity because of Libya's significant oil resources in which China has shown increasing interest" (2012, p. 228). But exactly how much of those oil resources did China get from Libya?

4.4 China-Libya Economic and Trade Engagements

Libya's proven oil reserves are estimated at 43.7 billion barrels, the ninth largest reserves in the world.[22] According to the US Energy Information Administration, the country "holds the largest amount of proven crude oil reserves in Africa, the fifth-largest amount of proved natural gas reserves on the continent, and in the past years was an important contributor to the global supply of light, sweet (low sulfur) crude oil, which Libya mostly imports to European markets" (2015, p. 2). Before the intrastate armed conflict in 2011, Libya produced an estimated 1.65 million barrels per day of high-quality sweet crude oil, up from the 1.4 million barrels per day produced in 2000, and slightly lower than the 2008 average of 1.74 million barrels per day.[23] In mid-2011, oil production in Libya was reduced to its lowest level as mass demonstrations against the Gaddafi regime escalated to an intrastate armed conflict.

Before the intrastate armed conflict, approximately 85% of Libya's oil exports were destined for Europe, especially the West European countries of Italy, Germany, France and Spain.[24] Italy was the top destination. This dominance by West European countries of Libya's oil and gas exports was driven by two major factors: (1) Western Europe's need to diversify energy sources and reduce its dependence on expensive gas and oil from Norway and Russia; and (2) the opening up of the Libyan oil industry after lifting of international sanctions against the Gaddafi regime in 2003. Also, building on already existing economic relations between Libya and Europe, as well as a shift towards the West by the Gaddafi regime in the 2000s, European companies, especially Italian ENI, Spanish Repsol and Total from France, took the opportunity to dominate the Libyan energy sector. But in order to diversify its export oil market, the Libyan National Oil Corporation (NOC) maintained "a balance in its relationships between North American, European, Brazilian, Chinese, Russian, Turkish, Indian and other corporate entities that were investing in Libyan energy markets" (Campbell 2013, p. 6). This situation provided China with an opportunity to enter the Libyan oil industry, albeit on a smaller scale than the Europeans. Although it was a late entrant in Libya's energy sector, China still managed to increase its share of Libyan oil exports from 1.2% in 2008 to a peak of 13% in 2011. Western Europe, in particular Italy, however, remained the highest importers of Libyan oil. Figure 4.1 shows the major destinations of Libyan oil in percentage of its total oil exports from 2008 to 2013.

To Libya, China was one of its major oil buyers, but to China, Libyan oil constituted only a fraction of its total oil imports. As shown in Fig. 4.2, in 2010, Libyan oil represented only 3% of China's total crude oil imports. By the end of Libya's intrastate armed conflict in September 2011, Libyan oil exports to China had been drastically reduced to approximately 1% of China's imports. In 2013, it was further reduced to about 0.8% of total Chinese oil imports.[25]

Among China's African sources of oil, Libya fell far behind Angola, which has consistently remained the largest source of China's oil imports from Africa. At its peak, Angolan oil constituted 17% of China's total oil imports in 2010 and 14% in 2013. In contrast, to date Libya remains a small exporter of oil to China, and still is outside the league of China's largest African suppliers of oil—Angola, Equatorial Guinea, Nigeria, Democratic Republic of Congo and Sudan (Alessi and Xu 2015).

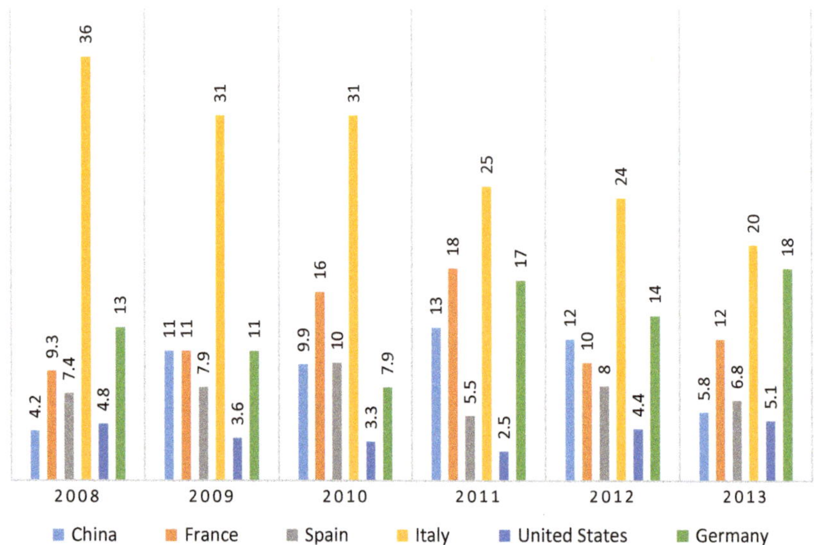

Fig. 4.1 Libya's petroleum crude exports by destination (%), 2008–2013

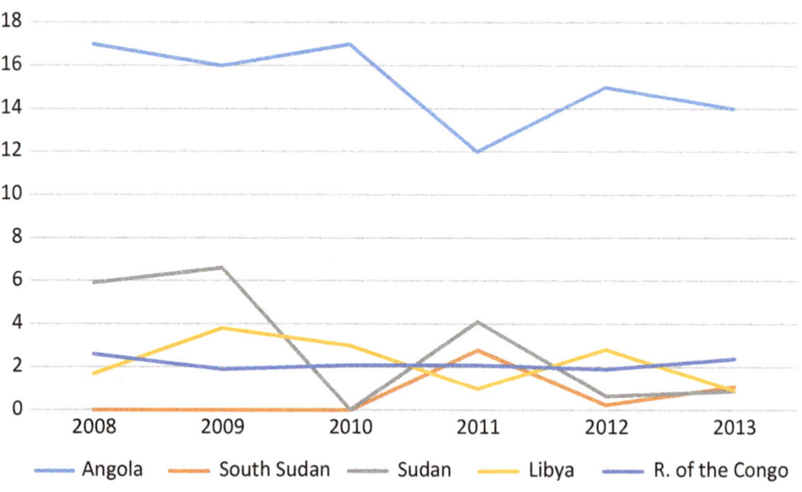

Fig. 4.2 China's petroleum crude imports from selected African countries (%), 2008–2013

Before the conflict in 2011, China made several unsuccessful attempts to increase its stake in the Libyan oil industry. For example, CNPC's "offered to assist Libyan counterparts in offshore exploration and the building of new pipeline system" (Engelbrekt and Wagnsson 2014, p. 3). It then "partnered with Libya's NOC to build pipelines and carry out exploration projects and was seen to have a strong relationship and business ties with the Gaddafi regime" (Jiang and Ding 2014, p. 28). Perhaps confident of its relations with the ruling elite in Libya, and seeking to further increase its stake, in 2008 CNPC attempted to acquire a controlling stake in the Verenex Energy Inc. of Canada, including its Libyan assets, but was blocked by Libya's NOC. Later into the deal, NOC chose to exercise its right of pre-emption, effectively blocking CNPC's bid to acquire Verenex Energy Inc.[26] "Verenex had been working on gas and oil exploration in the Ghadames Basin since 2006 and had reported several discoveries" (Taib 2010, p. 25.1). What bothered CNPC and the Chinese government is that Libya ended up paying far less than the $499 million that CNPC had offered, raising suspicion that the blockage was a political move by the Gaddafi regime to maintain ownership of oil reserves within the hands of the Libyan government as a matter of national interest. With attempts to increase its stake in the Libyan energy sector, China remained a comparatively small player, exploiting only a fraction of the Libyan oil exports.

4.5 China's Involvement in Libya's Industry

Beyond the oil industry, Chinese firms were major players in the construction and telecommunications sector of the Libyan economy. At the time of the conflict in February 2011 at least 75 Chinese private and state-owned firms were operating in Libya[27]—"mainly in the fields of telecommunications, irrigation and rail construction" (Engelbrekt and Wagnsson 2014, p. 3). Although Libya was not among the top 20 African destinations for China's Outward Foreign Investment,[28] it still provided a huge market for manufactured Chinese products and was a lucrative source of infrastructure development contracts for private and state-owned Chinese firms. This was "partly because the energy sector in Libya [had] already attracted scores of foreign companies, including giants such as BP, Shell, ExxonMobil, with the Chinese companies arriving too late to enter the market" (Zhang and Wei 2012, p. 44). Yin Gang, a senior researcher at the China Institute of Contemporary International Relations, concurred with Zhang and Wei's observation. He stated in an interview in 2011 that the most important relationship between Libya and China was not oil but the export of Chinese technology to Libya,[29] as well as infrastructural development—especially in the railway construction and telecommunications sector.

Unlike their Chinese counterparts in the energy sector, China's private and state-owned construction and telecommunication companies found Libya to be profitable. Contracted infrastructure development projects funded by the Libyan government attracted large Chinese private and state-owned enterprises, such as the Changshu Construction Group, a Jiangsu-based enterprise which was contracted to construct a university town in Libya. Other major Chinese state-owned enterprises with investments and construction projects in Libya included China Water Resources and Hydropower Construction Group, China Communications Construction Group, China Railway Construction Engineering Corporation, China State Construction Engineering Corporation, China Gezhouba Group Corporation, China Building Materials Group Import and Export Corporation, CNPC, China Metallurgical Group Corporation, the Workers International Engineering Co., Ltd., China Communications Construction Group, China Metallurgical Construction Co., China Civil Engineering Construction Corporation Limited; and two major private firms in the telecommunications sector—ZTE and Huawei. Of the major Chinese companies operating in Libya, 13, which included Metallurgical Corporation of China, China State Construction Engineering Corporation and China Railway Construction Corporation, are directly under the central government.[30] Table 4.1 gives a summary of the most significant projects and investments by Chinese firms in Libya.

The China-Africa Trade and Economic Relationship Annual Report of 2010 reported that China's imports from Libya increased by 22.6% to reach US$3.17 billion in 2009. It also reported that by 2009, Libya had the third largest project signed with a Chinese company in Africa—the Surt-Tripoli section, valued at US$24.2 billion; the other two major projects were the Central and western sections of the East-West expressway project in Algeria (US$62.5 billion) and the social housing project in Angola valued at US$35.4 billion.[31] By 2010, trade volumes between the two countries reached US$6.58 billion.[32] The boom in trade between Libya and China was such that the Afriqiyah Airline launched a twice-per-week direct flight from Tripoli to Beijing in order to cater to rising travel demands by Chinese business people and workers.[33] However, according to the Annual Report on the Development of Africa, jointly published by

Table 4.1 Investments by Chinese firms in Libya

Company name	*Ownership*	*Investment project*	*Investment amount*
China Railway Construction Corporation	State-owned	Railway construction and extension (352 km coastal railway from Khoms to Sirte; 172 km railway from Tripoli to Ras Ejder; 800 km railway between Misrata and Wadi Shatti)	US$4.237 billion
China State Construction Engineering Corporation	State-owned	Public housing construction (20 000 housing units in Benghazi)	¥17.6 billion (approx. US$2.67 billion)
China Gezhouba Group	State-owned	Public housing construction (7300 housing units in Eljebel Elgharbi and Nalut)	¥5.54 billion (approx. US$811 million)
China Metallurgical Group Corporation	State-owned	Public housing construction (5000 housing units in East Melita) and construction of cement factory in Misrata.	¥5.131 billion (approx. US$752 million)
China National Petroleum Corporation	State-owned	Entered Libya in 2002 and had five subsidiary companies operating before the civil war	Unknown
China Communications Construction Company	State-owned	Public housing project (5000 housing units in Misrata)	US$4.8 billion
Beijing Hongfu Group	Private Enterprise	Public housing project (5000 housing units)	¥3.4 billion (approx. US$498 million)
Ningbo Century Huafeng	Private Enterprise	Public housing project	¥3.354 billion (approx. US$491 million)
ZTE	Private Enterprise	Mobile communication network construction	US$92.7 million
Huawei	Private Enterprise	FTTH (fibre to the home) project	US$40 million

Source: Sohu, Inc. 2011, A List of Chinese Enterprises' Investments in Libya. Available at: http://business.sohu.com/20110823/n317112596.shtml

the Social Sciences Academic Press, the Institute of West Asian and African Studies of the Chinese Academy of Social Sciences, and the External Relations Bureau of the Ministry of Culture released in Beijing on 4 July 2012, "there was a sharp trade decline between China and Libya in 2011, a 58 percent year-on-year decrease."[34] Mei Xinyu, a researcher at the Ministry of Commerce affiliated Chinese Academy of International Trade and Economic Cooperation, confirmed that in the first eight months of 2011, trade between Libya and China fell by 51.4 percent year-on-year, amounting only to US$2.16 billion.[35]

4.6 Implications of the Libyan Armed Conflict on China's Economic and Trade Interests

Apart from drastic reductions in trade volumes between Libya and China there were several other direct and indirect implications of the Libyan armed conflict on China's economic interests there. Foremost, as the Libyan government struggled to contain the rebels, let alone maintain law and order, construction sites and commercial enterprises were indiscriminately looted and destroyed. In the first week of the conflict alone, a report in the *Global Times* suggested that 27 Chinese construction sites were pillaged and wrecked. The wanton destruction increased as the conflict intensified. A number of other Chinese companies started reporting not just destruction of their properties but also an increase in threat to their personnel—leading some to suspend or totally abandon project sites.

Some, especially the large Chinese firms, took several unorthodox measures, including hiring local militias as security details in a bid to protect their assets and at the very least mitigate losses. The China Communications Construction Company (CCCC), a state-owned enterprise that operated in Libya, recorded its on-site equipment, and signed material devolution agreements with local management commissions, the military and customers before evacuation. The China National Machinery Industry Corporation (SINOMACH) also made arrangements with local staff and residents to guard their assets as Chinese nationals were evacuated. But as the fighting intensified, those measures also proved to be ineffective. The situation was rather different for most small- and medium-sized enterprises that could neither afford private security nor had local political and military connections to have their assets protected in their absence.[36] For example, Century Huafeng, a medium-sized enterprise from the Zheijang province, reported extensive attacks, armed robbery and loss of all their documents to a fire. It ended up closing the site. This was the same with other small and medium enterprises that continued to suffer major losses due to lack of resources and inexperience in risk mitigation strategies in armed conflict situations such as was obtaining in Libya.

For some Chinese firms it was not destruction of property but just the threat of destruction that forced them to suspend operations. Large state-owned corporations such as the China State Construction Engineering Corporation announced suspension of operations because its 20,000 residential construction projects worth 17.6 billion yuan (US$2.68 billion) was under threat. The China Railway Construction Corporation left behind US$4.24 billion worth of unfinished projects in Libya. State-run Metallurgical Corporation of China suspended two projects worth 5.13 billion yuan,[37] while Sinohydro Corporation and the China Communications Construction Corporation also suspended their multibillion-dollar projects. Since most of these large firms worked on contracted projects financed by the Gaddafi government which also guaranteed their security, they found it fairly easy to suspend operations without fear of incurring as large losses as the small and medium enterprises.

In addition, UN sanctions against Libya's NOC, and other Libyan oil companies decreased income from oil and gas upon which the Libyan economy was overly dependent. Further sanctions and asset freezes against major Libyan financial investment vehicles controlled by the Gaddafi regime as well as the Central Bank of Libya translated the intrastate armed conflict into an economic crisis. As a result, Libya's real GDP shrunk by 27.8% in 2011, and oil production plummeted to almost zero. The consequential reduction of the Libyan government's revenue was particularly detrimental to Chinese firms because most of their Libyan projects were contracted projects commissioned and financed by the Libyan government. With sources of revenue drastically reduced and fiscal focus flatly placed on containing the rebellion, the Libyan government's capacity to meet its financial and contractual obligations to Chinese firms was further reduced. Because "overseas contracted projects are characterised as long-lasting and requiring input in the prophase"[38] Chinese companies had already expended large amounts of their money ahead of time setting up fixed assets such as offices and purchasing equipment and materials such as construction equipment and raw materials. Most Chinese companies ended up losing those initial investments, and, despite assistance from the Chinese government, they are still struggling to get compensation for their losses from the Libyan government.

Loss of revenue due to UN sanctions and the combined effect of suspension and abandonment of projects due to intensified fighting between rebels and Gaddafi's forces meant further losses of revenue by Chinese firms. In particular, revenue in the form of "performance bonds, advance payment bonds, to maintain the normal operation of projects"[39] was lost due to *force majeure*, a common clause in business contracts that relieves both parties of their contractual obligations when events such as war that are beyond the control of both parties prevent them from fulfilling their contractual obligations. The loss of revenue meant that Chinese firms could not pay their suppliers and other contractors, giving the Chinese firms poor global credit ratings.

To pacify reports that Chinese investments in Libya had gone to waste, Zhu Weidong, deputy-director of the African Law and Society Research Centre at the Xiangtan University in Hunan Province, wrote in *Global Times* that the losses were not as severe because most Chinese companies had received 15% of their payments in advance from Libyan outsourcers in order to purchase necessary materials and equipment before construction projects began. He explained that apart from three companies that had completed over 30% of their projects, such as Beijing Hongfu Group, Beijing Construction Engineering Group and China State Construction Engineering Group, which had completed 50% of its contracted project, the rest of the enterprises did not incur major loses. However, data published by the Ministry of Commerce showed that 50 projects undertaken by 75 Chinese companies worth approximately US$18.8 billion had been severely affected by the Libyan conflict.[40]

Further exacerbating the loss for Chinese companies operating in Libya is that domestic banks made compensation claims against some Chinese companies. Media in China reported that Sahara Bank, which is part of the French bank BNP Paribas, had already made compensation claims for advance payment guaranteed by the bank against several Chinese companies. Affected companies included the state-owned engineering and construction company China Gezhouba Group Corporation, as well as Sinohydro Corporation, and the Beijing Hongfu Construction and Engineering Group. Hu Jiangu, director of the Chinese Academy of International Trade and Economic Cooperation under the Ministry of Commerce, explained that it was improper for Sahara Bank to make such claims because there still was half a year before the guarantee expired. He also argued that advance payment guarantees are for use by local Libyan developers who would have made advance payments to Chinese enterprises engaged in construction projects, and get bank guarantees to hedge risks against that payment. Nonetheless, Sahara Bank made a claim of about 400 million yuan (US$61 million) against Beijing Hongfu Construction and Engineering Group. Other sources suggested that the biggest claim of an undisclosed amount was against China Gezhouba Group. Overall, the net effect of such claims is that credit ratings of Chinese companies were negatively affected.[41]

In addition to losses of revenue, assets and equipment, Chinese companies also incurred evacuation and resettlement expenses for their Chinese workers in Libya. Although Chinese nationals were not specifically targeted, the intensity of the fighting and destruction of some Chinese projects made it impossible for their safety and security to be guaranteed. Also, there was a growing anti-foreigner sentiment across Libya, particularly against nationals of countries that were perceived as supporting the Gaddafi regime. As highlighted above, major Chinese firms were somewhat aligned to the Gaddafi regime because they were contracted and paid by his government. All these factors increased threats against Chinese nationals. Chinese firms were therefore compelled to arrange for the evacuation and resettlement of their workers to secure areas within Libya, and, if they had the means, back to China. Although the Chinese government ended up assisting with the evacuation of Chinese nationals from Libya, most companies had already started the evacuation process before. In the end, approximately 36,000 Chinese nationals who had been working on various projects in both private and state-owned companies were evacuated.

4.7 China's Intervention in Libyan Armed Conflict

The monumental impact of the Libyan intrastate armed conflict on Chinese businesses and economic interests was largely undisputed; but in a bid to avoid public discontent, China's Ministry of Commerce attempted to play down the nature of companies affected and the extent of their losses. Zhong Manying, Director of the Department of West Asia and Africa under the Ministry of Commerce, put the figure of affected Chinese firms at a modest 26, and disputed that China had direct investments in Libya or that state-owned companies had been affected. However, reports soon emerged suggesting that as many as 75 Chinese firms, including at least 13 state-owned enterprises, had approximately US$18–20 billion worth of investments at the time of the conflict in Libya. Those media reports, as well as the fact that about 36,000 Chinese nationals were marooned in Libya, increased pressure on Beijing to show effort towards protecting and guaranteeing the security of Chinese nationals and interests abroad—putting to test its non-intervention principle.

That it was the first time China had been confronted by an intrastate armed conflict in Africa which had such a direct, visible and grand scale effect on its interests and nationals abroad became obvious as the conflict intensified. Besides exposing China's unpreparedness, lack of contingency planning and inability to take concrete and decisive action regarding foreign intrastate armed conflicts, the Libyan conflict put China in an embarrassing Catch-22 situation. On the one hand, its foreign policy principle of non-intervention in the internal affairs of other states proscribed it from taking any direct action in Libya, but on the other hand, there was increasing domestic pressure for the PRC to protect Chinese nationals and interests abroad, and also incessant calls internationally for Beijing to act like a responsible global power able to actively participate in global efforts towards resolving conflicts. Both the international and domestic demands for China to take action entailed some level of intervention in the internal affairs of Libya, putting Beijing in a quandary—whether to take action and risk flouting its own foreign policy principle of non-intervention, or not take any action to protect its nationals and interests abroad and risk losing credibility among the Chinese. Balancing the different interests proved to be tricky for Beijing and, as discussed below, it reflected itself in its ambivalent interventionist strategies as it got to grips with a changing perception of foreign intrastate armed conflicts as threatening to its interests abroad.

4.7.1 Non-intervention

China's first response to the Libyan conflict was non-action, and non-interventionist because China's relations with African countries are predicated on the principle of non-intervention in their internal affairs, and that includes intrastate armed conflicts. There were some exceptions though, as discussed in Chap. 4 during Africa's struggle for independence, and, when China was engaged in competition against the Soviet Union over geopolitical influence in Africa, it supported anti-Soviet liberation war groups and rebels across the continent. That was in the 1950s, 1960s and 1970s; since then, there have been rare cases of significant Chinese intervention in Africa's intrastate armed conflicts. Part of the reason is that unlike armed conflicts in its immediate Asian region, intrastate armed conflicts in Africa posed no particular direct threats to China's sovereignty, territorial integrity, economic and political interests, or even to its nationals working there. Before the outbreak of Libya's intrastate armed conflict, threats to China's national interests and nationals working and living in African countries were minor and limited to isolated cases of kidnappings, robberies and, in rare cases, murder, which normally was of a civilian nature. In such cases, the responsibility to protect Chinese nationals and its overseas investments fell on the Chinese firms operating abroad and mostly on the hosting African state. So, since there had never been an intrastate armed conflict that threatened its interests and nationals at a scale as that of Libya, Beijing generally viewed intrastate armed conflicts in Africa as non-threatening to its nationals and national interests there. Thus, Beijing and most Chinese firms in Africa emphasised commercial risk management rather than political and security risk management.

The focus on commercial risk rather than political and security risk made sense because in most cases major Chinese investments were a result of bilateral consultations between the Chinese government and the respective African government in which the investments would be based. Libya was not an exception. Huge energy and infrastructure development projects, especially by Chinese state-owned enterprises, were often a result of state-to-state consultations between Beijing and Tripoli. In addition, because it was the Libyan government that contracted Chinese firms to undertake infrastructure development projects, such as building of university towns and rail construction, it guaranteed their security. It was therefore a foregone conclusion that the security of the Chinese firms and nationals working on those projects was the responsibility of the Libyan government. So, when the Libyan intrastate armed conflict began, the Chinese government made frantic demands on Gaddafi's regime to guarantee the security of Chinese investments in that country as well as to ensure the safety of Chinese nationals working there.

In cases where intrastate armed conflicts and political instability threatened Chinese investments and nationals in countries such as the Democratic Republic of Congo, Sudan or Nigeria, Beijing's strategy was to prop up regimes in those countries through financial, diplomatic and, sometimes, military assistance, as well as through formal and informal networks with ruling elites in those countries. For as long as those ruling elites remained in power, Chinese interests, nationals and investments in those countries were secure. The existence of such an interreliant relationship between the security of China's foreign investments and the security of regimes in some African countries was, however, problematic. A major challenge for China is still that if the regime that guaranteed security of its interests, firms and nationals is overthrown, then its interests, investments and nationals operating in that country would be exposed, or in some cases targeted by the new regime for their (perceived) support of the fallen regime. It is therefore not surprising that at the beginning of Libya's intrastate armed conflict, Chinese foreign policymakers perceived it to be another internal conflict that the Gaddafi regime was able to quash without much ado; hence they were convinced that for as long as the Gaddafi regime remained in power, its nationals and investments were secure, meaning there was no need for Beijing to take any intervention action until it was clear that the Gaddafi regime was losing power.

As in all cases where China evoked non-interventionism, it was notably silent regarding the Libyan conflict, something that reflected its initial confidence in the ability of the Gaddafi regime to restore order. The media in China also largely ignored the conflict until foreigners working in Libya were targeted in xenophobic attacks. With about 36,000 Chinese nationals who were working on various projects worth approximately US$20 billion under threat, it seemed only natural that the media turned its attention to their plight. In addition to heightened media attention to threats of losing major investments and Chinese nationals, domestic public opinion[42] and growing popularity of the issue on Weibo forced the Chinese government to at least acknowledge the Libyan conflict and consider taking some level of action to avoid domestic public discontent. Being careful to avoid picking any sides in the conflict or issuing statements perceivable as interference in the Libyan intrastate armed conflict, Beijing issued several statements urging parties in the conflict to resolve their differences amicably and guarantee the security of civilians, particularly Chinese nationals. However, with intensification of the conflict, Beijing's calls for dialogue and protection of foreigners rang hollow because they were devoid of action.

Three other reasons explain China's silence at the beginning of the conflict and then the tepid statements urging parties in the Libyan conflict to resolve their differences peacefully that followed. First, it considered the Libyan state to be more centralised, and capable of reining in the protestors than had been the case for the Zine El Abidine Ben Ali and Hosni Mubarak regimes in Tunisia and Egypt respectively. Indeed, in the initial stages of the protests, the Gaddafi regime appeared in control and able to restrict the protests within particular areas such as Benghazi. Also, Gaddafi's defiance and violent crackdown on protestors gave an impression that he was determined to quash the demonstrations before they spread across Libya. Focusing on Gaddafi's ruthlessness and determination, Chinese foreign policy makers saw no need to intervene or take a decisive position regarding the conflict. They reasoned that the protests and demonstrations against the Gaddafi regime were a passing phase, and, based on previous effects of other Arab Spring protests in countries neighbouring Libya, it was Beijing's view that the Libyan conflict was not worthy meddling into the murky waters of Arab conflicts; hence it adopted political passivity and avoided taking any concrete position or action regarding the protests as it had done in the case of Tunisia and Egypt. Also, China regarded the Gaddafi regime to be more powerful and stable and incapable of being overthrown by a group of protestors.

The second reason is that China separated business from politics. Its deputy foreign minister, Zhou Wenzhong, had said, "business is business. We try to separate politics from business" (Whalley 2011, p. 235). The underlying philosophy of that principle was that for as long as internal conflicts did not affect its business interests there was no need to intervene. Since previous conflicts of a similar nature in Tunisia and Egypt had not significantly affected Chinese investments or threatened Chinese nationals living in those countries, there was no need for Beijing to take action. Not taking action meant that China would let the Gaddafi regime deal with the conflict on its own. Moussa Koussa, the former Libyan foreign affairs minister, criticised China for taking that position in African matters. He argued that "genuine cooperation must include politics … and should not be limited to building roads and schools. It is true that this is required, but international cooperation is not based on constructing buildings and giving aid, but rather through political positions" (Shichor 2014, p. 128).

The third reason is that "there was no love lost between Beijing and the Gaddafi regime" (Calabrese 2013, p. 10). As discussed above, Gaddafi had visited Beijing only once in 1982, and the last high-ranking officials from Beijing had last visited Libya in 2006. Besides, diplomatic relations were tense due to continued semi-official relations between Libya and Taiwan. To China, Muammar Gaddafi was nothing to get concerned about except when he (Gaddafi) justified his government's crackdown on protestors by saying "the unity of China was more important than those people on Tiananmen Square." To that, Beijing responded by censoring all media reference to the crackdown on protestors in Libya, and, in particular, Gaddafi's reference to Tiananmen Square. Apart from that censorship, China did not make any significant changes to its stance of non-intervention in the initial phases of the Libyan conflict until the conflict escalated and Chinese businesses were at threat.

4.7.2 Transition from Non-intervention to Pragmatic Intervention

Mass revolutions in Tunisia and Egypt left Beijing's foreign policy of non-intervention in the internal affairs of other states unscathed—the majority of protests in the Arab world had not turned into full-scale intrastate armed conflicts. But Libya turned out to be different. As the Gaddafi regime began using heavy military equipment and live ammunition to disperse protestors[43] in order to re-assert its authority, the mass protests escalated into an armed conflict that attracted global attention. Also, in protest against Gaddafi's harsh military tactics, professional army personnel defected with their weapons and joined civilian protestors, adding a new military dynamic to the mass protests. To replace the defectors and strengthen his forces, Gaddafi used the country's oil wealth to recruit a private army of mercenaries from sub-Saharan African countries such as Niger, Chad and Mali. In retaliation, protestors organised themselves into armed rebel armies, which in turn escalated the protests into a full-fledged armed conflict. This had not been the case in Morocco, Tunisia, Egypt or Algeria, but, as put by Jack A. Goldstone, when protestors started using violent action, the Gaddafi regime was emboldened in its use of more violent force even against unarmed civilians, as it depicted them "as a threat to social order and justified using repressive tactics against them" (Goldstone 2012, p. 115). Using mercenaries[44] and special guard units loyal to him, Gaddafi vowed to track down and kill the protestors "house by house" like rats,[45] which resulted in indiscriminate violence against civilians perceived to be anti-Gaddafi. Faced with such a formidable and determined Gaddafi force, the armed protestors then sought international support to militarily fight against the Gaddafi regime, leading to internationalisation of the conflict.

A combination of internationalisation of the Libyan conflict and increasing inability of the Gaddafi regime to guarantee security of foreign investments and foreign nationals all drew Beijing's attention. In addition, the threat to Chinese nationals raised domestic demands for Beijing to protect its nationals abroad, effectively bringing to question China's perception of, and response to, threats emanating from African intrastate armed conflicts. What also drew the ire of Chinese officials is that as soon as rebels organised themselves into the NTC, they issued veiled warnings to China because of its passiveness to their struggle against the Gaddafi regime. Because some of Chinese investments and projects in Libya were a result of its bilateral arrangements with the Gaddafi regime rather than being pure business contracts, they were vulnerable to changes of government.[46] With several of its state-owned enterprises such as CNPC and the China Railway Construction Company having won large contracts, and over 75 other Chinese companies operating in the country, in addition to over 35,000 Chinese nationals in Libya, China's strict adherence to its foreign policy principle of non-intervention in Libya's armed conflict was put to the test. Also put to the test was its long-held perception that foreign intrastate armed conflicts, or more generally political issues in African countries, were non-threatening to its interests in those countries.

The above factors combined to put pressure on Beijing to take action in order to protect both its foreign investments and nationals in Libya.[47] The factors also compelled China to consider political instability in Africa to be threatening to its interests there, thus its perception of the intrastate armed conflicts in Libya metamorphosed from being regarded as a non-threatening internal issue to being regarded as threatening. The effect was a reconsideration of its absolute non-intervention approach to the Libyan conflict. But what proved to be a challenge for Beijing, and what influenced the rest of its responsive action to the Libyan conflict, was the need to strike a balance between protecting its interests in Libya and maintaining its foreign policy of non-intervention in the internal affairs of other states. It is here that pragmatism proved to be an asset for China. From passive and tepid statements urging parties to the Libyan conflict to resolve their disputes through dialogue, Beijing experimented with both multilateral and bilateral actions aimed at protecting its interests in Libya. In particular, it found multilateral interventions to be a discreet intervention option which struck a delicate balance between its identity as a non-interventionist power and intervening to protect its nationals and investments under threat in Libya.

4.7.3 China's Complicity in Multilateral Intervention in the Libyan Intrastate Armed Conflict

To strike a balance between non-intervention and protecting its interests and nationals in Libya, Beijing chose United Nations-led multilateral intervention. The first UN multilateral action that China supported was imposition of sanctions against members of Gaddafi's family and inner circle. On 26 February 2011, a few weeks after the Libyan mass demonstrations escalated, China opted not to veto UN Security Council Resolution 1970 (2011) when it was tabled for adoption at the 6491st meeting of the Security Council. Among other things, the resolution condemned "the gross and systematic violation of human rights, including the repression of peaceful demonstrators, expressing deep concern at the deaths of civilians, and rejecting unequivocally the incitement to hostility and violence against the civilian population made from the highest level of the Libyan government." Having placed responsibility for the "hostility and violence" against the civilian population on political leaders in Gaddafi's government, the Security Council referred the situation to the International Criminal Court (ICC) for investigation and imposed an arms embargo, asset freeze and travel ban on Gaddafi, his family and close officials.

Beijing's support for imposition of sanctions and referral of the Libyan situation to the ICC was in stark contrast to its principle of non-intervention in Libya's internal conflict, since, as previously put by its Deputy Foreign Minister, Zhou Wenzhong, China is "against embargoes" (Whalley 2011, p. 253). This is because previously China had vetoed UNSC resolutions that sought to impose sanctions on countries such as Zimbabwe, Burma, North Korea and Sri Lanka for gross human rights violations and violence against civilians. Its argument in those several cases was that imposition of sanctions against a sitting head of state amounted to interference in his/her country's internal affairs. It further reasoned that such resolutions did not assist in resolving conflicts, but instead tended to escalate the situation. Speaking after vetoing a resolution that sought to impose sanctions against Mugabe and his government in Zimbabwe, China's Foreign Ministry spokesman Liu Jianchao argued that "passing a sanctions resolution against Zimbabwe would not help to encourage the various factions there to engage in political dialogue and negotiations and achieve results."[48] Considering that initially China advocated political dialogue amongst warring parties in Libya, and that the Libyan government was not agreeable to sanctions being imposed against its leaders or that the situation be referred to the ICC, "it was impossible for China to support UN intervention" (Shih and Huang 2014, p. 147). Except that it did.

Against its tradition of non-intervention and opposition to sanctions, China still voted in favour of sanctions against Gaddafi's regime.[49] Its ambassador to the United Nations justified his country's deviance by arguing that regional organisations such as the Arab League, the AU and the Secretary General of the Organisation of the Islamic Conference were in favour of the resolution as a way of compelling Gaddafi to come to the negotiating table. In proffering that argument China sought to absolve itself of the responsibility to explain why it had deviated from its non-intervention principle. Furthermore, based on its UNSC voting history, China is not known to be influenced by pressure from regional or non-international organisations, but by its own interests. So even though it explained its support of the resolution on the basis that it was in the interest of cooperation with the international community, and stability of Libya, the overarching reason is that the resolution enabled protection of its investments and nationals in Libya. It also allayed concerns from the international community that it was passively condoning the massacre of civilians by the Gaddafi regime.

With domestic pressure increasing over China's seeming inability to protect its nationals and interests abroad, Resolution 1970 was also critical to disproving its critics. The resolution "expressed concern for the safety of foreign nationals and their rights in the Libyan Arab Jamahiriya.... [Urging] the Libyan authorities to ensure the safety of all foreign nationals and their assets and facilitate the departure of those wishing to leave the country."[50] In fact Ambassador Li Baodong's statement after voting for Resolution 1970 confirmed that the immediate cessation of violence through peaceful means such as dialogue was important insofar as they guaranteed that the safety and interests of foreign nationals in Libya were assured throughout the process.[51] Thus, China's voting in favour of the resolution was also meant to prove to its citizens concerned about the welfare of their compatriots in Libya that it was taking serious efforts to protect them and secure national interests abroad.

Despite Beijing's justification, Resolution 1970 was a collective intervention into the internal affairs of Libya, to which Beijing took part by voting in favour of the resolution. From a functional perspective, the UNSC resolution tilted the balance of power in the Libyan conflict in favour of the rebels rather that the Gaddafi regime because the arms embargo, asset freeze and travel ban were imposed only on officials in Gaddafi's regime. By cutting off the supply of weapons, and financial resources, the UNSC resolution set up Gaddafi to fail in the ensuing intrastate armed conflict. China's complicity in the collective intervention in Libya's intrastate armed conflict is confirmed by attempts by Beijing to exonerate itself from the subsequent military intervention by NATO. Ambassador Li Baodong justified China's support of the UNSC intervention in Libya by saying that China had voted in favour of the resolution after taking into account the special situation in Libya, and regard for concerns and views of Arab and African countries. Still that did not change the fact that according to China, imposition of sanctions on the government of another state is interference in that country's domestic affairs. In fact, that was the basis China had vetoed other UN resolutions that sought to impose sanctions on President Mugabe of Zimbabwe, the military junta in Burma and the leaders of North Korea. According to Joel Wuthnow, China acted to protect its investments and nationals because "on Libya, China observed a leader acting erratically and endangering not only oil producing facilities in rebel-held eastern part of the country, but also the lives of some 40,000 of Chinese citizens, who would later have to be evacuated" (2013, p. 131).

The second UN-mandated multilateral intervention was declaration of a no-fly zone in Libya. Instead of voting in favour, this time China abstained, resulting in adoption of UNSC Resolution 1973 (2011) on 17 March 2011. The resolution was compelled by failure of the Gaddafi regime to comply with Resolution 1970 (2011) as well as continued escalation of state-sponsored violence against civilians, and systematic human rights violations such as arbitrary detentions, enforced disappearances, torture and summary executions. Circumstances leading to adoption of the resolution are important to understanding why China's abstention signified its intent to use multilateral institutions to resolve the Libyan conflict. First, building on its argument that on Libya it was guided by wishes of regional organisations, China claimed to have abstained because the Council of the League of Arab States had resolved at an extraordinary session held in Cairo, Egypt, on 12 March 2011 to "call on the Security Council to bear its responsibility towards the deteriorating situation in Libya, and to take the necessary measures to impose immediately a no-fly zone on Libyan military aviation, and to establish safe areas in places exposed to shelling as a precautionary measure that allows the protection of the Libyan people and foreign nationals residing in Libya."[52]

However more importantly, China and the rest of UNSC members were aware that Mustafa Abdel-Jalil, leader of the NTC, had lobbied regional organisations, the European Union and the United States to impose a no-fly zone on Libya. For example, on March 10, Mustafa Abdel-Jalil met Nicholas Sarkozy, the then president of France; subsequent to their meeting, Sarkozy announced France's recognition of NTC as the legitimate government of Libya. Nicholas Sarkozy then lobbied other EU members at the EU summit in Brussels on 11 March 2011 to support the no-fly zone proposal, arguing that "the strikes would be solely of a defensive nature if Mr. Gaddafi makes use of chemical weapons or air strikes against non-violent protesters."[53] True to NTC's wishes, Resolution 1973 (2011) authorised member states "acting nationally or through regional organisations or arrangements, and acting in cooperation with the Secretary-General, to take all necessary measures ... to protect civilians and civilian populated areas under attack in the Libyan Arab Jamahiriya, including Benghazi, while excluding a foreign occupation force of any form on any part of Libyan territory."[54] It then imposed a no-fly zone in the airspace of Libya in order to help protect civilians and authorised Member States to strictly enforce the arms embargo and an asset freeze on Libyan government institutions such as the Libyan Investment Authority, the Libyan Foreign Bank, the Libyan NOC and Libyan Africa Investment Portfolio, as well as the assets of officials within the Gaddafi inner circle. Of the fifteen countries in the UN Security Council, ten voted in favour of the Resolution with five (China, Brazil, Germany, India and Russia) abstaining. With knowledge of NTC's lobbying of regional organisations as well as European powers and the United States, it was insincere for China to argue that in abstaining it was merely following the wishes of regional organisations, when it was clear that the no-fly zone was intended to incapacitate the Gaddafi regime for the benefit of the NTC.

By decapitating Gaddafi's air force, Resolution 1973 skewed the armed conflict in favour of the NTC, which by that time was already engaged in a full armed combat against the Gaddafi regime. China's withholding of its veto on Resolution 1973 was in more ways than one a passive consent to a multilateral military intervention in the Libyan conflict. As put by US Defence Secretary Robert Gates, "a no-fly zone begins with an attack on Libya to destroy the air defenses. That's the way you do a no-fly zone. And then you can fly planes around the country and not worry about our guys being shot down. But that's the way it starts."[55] Chinese diplomats at the United Nations and foreign policy makers in Beijing were aware of these dynamics, and its abstention was calculated to give the impression that it was opposed to the intervention but only gave in in order not to spoil international efforts towards resolving the conflict. This was a convenient excuse for China because it helped it maintain the façade and re-assure African countries opposed to the resolution that it still adhered to principles of non-intervention.

China's insincerity soon emerged when NATO began bombing Gaddafi's air force installations just as Robert Gates had warned. As soon as African countries started complaining against what they termed Western military intervention in Libya, China quickly joined them, arguing that it had supported the resolution out of the impression that it was meant to protect civilians rather than institute regime change. If indeed China believed that, which is highly unlikely, it was naive of its foreign policy makers to think that by abstaining it was not participating in military intervention in the Libyan intrastate armed conflict because China's abstention from UNSC Resolution 1973 paved way for NATO's military intervention in Libya. China's "abstention over Resolution 1973 allowed it to walk a tight rope between supporting intervention and adhering to its non-interference principle" (Kassim 2014, p. 35). As a result of that abstention, Yun Sun argues, that "China sees its acquiescence as directly contributing to the fall of Muammar Qaddafi" (2012, p. 1). For that is what China had done: it had together with other Western powers militarily intervened in the Libyan intrastate armed conflict and effectively assisted the NTC to topple the Gaddafi regime.

4.7.4 Engagement with the NTC and Mediation Attempts

At the height of the Libyan intrastate armed conflict, China made unprecedented steps towards reaching out to both parties in the conflict. *Xinhua* described the reaching out to warring parties in Libya as "taking a practical and constructive approach to the Libya issue by mediating between the two conflicting sides."[56] By any stretch of the practice of mediation, China's reaching out to both the Gaddafi regime and the NTC was in no way a mediation effort. In many respects it turned out to be more of a public relations exercise meant to curry favour with the NTC which Beijing had snubbed since its formation. Part of the reason for its action is that as the conflict intensified, it became clear that the NTC was gaining international recognition as the legitimate representative of Libya from countries such as France, Britain, the United States and some Arab countries. Beijing therefore reasoned that continued snubbing of the NTC was not going to be in its best interest, especially after the NTC announced that in the reconstruction phase it was going to give preference to businesses from countries that had supported its struggle against the Gaddafi regime. Up to that point China had not made any direct contact with the NTC or openly supported its struggle against Gaddafi; it therefore made the unprecedented step to make contact with them even though Gaddafi's regime was still in power. This was contrary to Beijing's own non-intervention principle which inhibits contact with opposition groups in another country because it constitutes intervention in that country's internal affairs.

The first confirmed contact between China and the NTC happened on 2 June 2011 when China's Ambassador to Qatar, Zhang Zhiliang, met NTC Chairman Mustafa Abdel-Jalil in Doha, Qatar.[57] A statement by China's Foreign Ministry spokesperson Hong Lei confirmed the meeting but did not provide intricate details except that "the two sides exchanged views on the Libyan situation" and that "the Libyan crisis can be resolved through political means and that the future of Libya is decided by the Libyan people."[58] Following the first meeting in Doha, Li Lianhe, a Chinese diplomat in Egypt, met with Mustafa Abdel-Jalil when he visited the headquarters of NTC in Benghazi on 6 June 2011. As part of his visit he inspected the humanitarian situation and property of Chinese businesses in Benghazi.[59] Subsequently, on 22 June 2011, Mustafa Abdel-Jalil visited Beijing on a two-day visit, during which he met Yang Jiechi, China's foreign minister. In the meeting, Foreign Minister Yang said, "since its creation, the NTC has increased its representativeness and gradually become a major political force. China sees it as an important dialogue partner."[60] In addition, a statement by China's Foreign Ministry spokesman, Hong Lei, confirmed that to China, the NTC was indispensable to resolving the conflict in Libya for the benefit of its businesses, hence its readiness "to stay in contact with all parties including the Libyan National Transitional Council to push for an early political settlement of the Libyan crisis."[61]

In honour of its pledge to stay in contact with the NTC, on 6 July 2011 Chen Xuedong, Director-General of the Department of West Asian and North African Affairs in China's Ministry of Foreign Affairs, met members of the NTC including deputy head of the NTC Executive Office, Ali al-Isawi, and head of the Executive Board's foreign affairs office. The meeting had two main objectives: the first was to implore the NTC to support the AU's mediation efforts. To that effect, Chen reiterated China's recognition of the NTC as an "important dialogue partner" critical to resolving the conflict in Libya through political dialogue and settlement. The second and more important reason for the meeting came to light when Chen sought assurances from the NTC that it would guarantee the safety of Chinese nationals and assets in areas that it controlled.[62] The NTC officials undertook to protect Chinese nationals working in Libya and their property and expressed appreciation for China's efforts to strengthen relations and promote a peaceful settlement of the Libyan crisis.[63]

Although the Chinese foreign minister had met with Libya's foreign minister (General People's Committee for Foreign Liaison and International Cooperation of Libya) Abdul Ati Al-Obeidi, a special envoy of the Gaddafi regime, in Beijing on 8 June 2011,[64] it is Beijing's contact with the NTC that is an exception to its non-intervention policy. By China's own definition of interference in the internal affairs of another state, establishing ties and maintaining relations with the NTC while the Gaddafi regime was still in power was a direct intervention in the Libyan intrastate armed conflict. *Global Times*, a media outlet that "often reflects conservative, and even nationalistic, opinions that do not represent the official line,"[65] justified China's engagement with both the NTC and the Libyan regime in the following terms: "closer contact with Libya's two camps shows China is dedicated to helping seek peaceful and quicker solution to the protracted civil strife in the North African country." Nonetheless, the most significant motivating factor in meeting both sides was revealed in China's official media, which suggested that maintaining close contact with both sides to the Libyan conflict enabled China to comprehensively keep abreast with the current condition of its investments and assets.

The coinciding of China's "mediation" efforts with international recognition of the NTC at the expense of the Gaddafi regime implied a pragmatic intervention by China meant to mend fences with the NTC before it assumed total control of Libya. That way, whichever side won, Chinese investments would have been secured. Articles jointly published in *Global Times* and *Xinhua* concurred: "It is only natural that China is keeping a close eye on its investments there"[66] by keeping "closer contact with both sides… China assess the latest development in Libya more comprehensively, know the current condition of its investments and assets there more clearly, including uncompleted infrastructure projects and equipment, and better protects its lawful and justifiable investment interests there."[67] Another article published in *Xinhua* also argued that the "mediation" was pragmatic because "Libya's prolonged civil war … posed serious threats to foreign investments, including those of China, in the country."[68] The "mediation" was therefore meant to protect Chinese interests and nationals in Libya rather than seriously mediate between the warring parties. The main motivation was to gather information on the state of its investments as well as to ensure their security.

Furthermore, three years later, Zhong Jianhua, China's Special Envoy for African Affairs, confirmed that China had indeed violated its own non-intervention principle when he said: "I think for the last two or three decades we were quite rigid about non-interference in the internal affairs of other countries ... we try to avoid making direct contact with the opposition ... when you talk to a rebel force that means stepping into internal affairs."[69] Yin Gang, an African affairs expert at the Chinese Academy of Social Sciences' Institute of West Asian and African Studies, interpreted Beijing's meeting with opposition leaders in foreign countries which have intrastate armed conflicts as part of its mediation efforts.[70] But, as put by Zhong Jianhua, meeting rebels or opposition forces amounts to intervention in another country's internal affairs. However, He Wenping, Director of African Studies at the Chinese Academy of Social Sciences, in justification of the PRC's reaching out to the NTC while Gaddafi was still in power, said: "once things became clear, and we knew that even the people in Tripoli supported the NTC (National Transitional Council), there was no reason for China not to support the NTC, and then we recognised the NTC and give them support."[71] He Wenping "often reflects China's position on African issues" (Shinn 2013), thus her statement confirms arguments that China recognised the NTC only in order to protect its investments and guarantee its businesses' return to Libya.

Also suggesting China's mediation efforts were insincere are allegations published in a Final Report of the Panel of Experts established pursuant to Security Council Resolution 1973 (2011) concerning Libya. Media reports suggested that the Gaddafi regime had tried to secure arms from China in violation of the arms embargo. Although *The Guardian* newspaper noted that further research was required to determine whether or not the violation occurred, other media reports insisted that the state-owned China North Industries Corporation, China Precision Machinery Import-Export Company and China Xinxing Import and Export Company negotiated with Libyan officials in Beijing to buy arms worth approximately US$200 million in July 2011 in breach of the UNSC arms embargo.[72] According to Denny Roy, documents implicating the state-owned Chinese companies were discovered by anti-Gaddafi forces in Tripoli. He argues that "the Chinese companies proposed delivering the weapons through intermediary countries such as South Africa or Algeria to shield China from criticism" (Roy 2013, p. 244). Jiang Yu, spokeswoman of the Chinese Foreign Ministry, admitted that "the Gaddafi regime sent representatives to China in July to meet individuals from relevant Chinese companies without the knowledge of Chinese government departments."[73] She, however, refuted claims by Omar Hariri, head of the transitional government's military council, and the Libyan military spokesman, Abdulrahman Busin, that the guns had been delivered to Libya and that they had "hard evidence of deals going on between China and Qaddafi,"[74] arguing that no contracts were signed and no weapons were delivered.[75] She maintained that "China exercises strict management over all military exports."[76] It is, however, questionable whether Libyan officials would visit Beijing and have meetings with state-owned arms companies without the knowledge of the Chinese government.

4.7.5 *Evacuation and Protection of Chinese Nationals*

The magnitude of threat to Chinese nationals in Libya was greater than at any point in the history of China-Africa engagement. As it became clear that the intrastate armed conflict in Libya was intensifying and that foreigners were in danger, domestic pressure on the Chinese government to secure the lives of Chinese nationals increased. In fact, one of the major reasons China had supported UN intervention in Libya and engaged in low-key mediation efforts was to secure its nationals in Libya. As put by Maximilian Terhalle, "another key driver behind's China's support of UN intervention in Libya was to protect its citizens" (2015, p. 170). In February 2011 China chartered planes from Air China and buses and ocean liners from Greece and Malta in order to evacuate Chinese citizens in Libya. Most of the Chinese nationals stranded in Libya were employees of Chinese companies operating there.[77] In total China evacuated 35,860 nationals from Libya with assistance from countries such as Greece, Malta, Egypt, Tunisia, Turkey and Jordan that provided transportation and temporary shelter to the evacuated Chinese nationals. The PLA as well as Chinese companies operating in Libya such as China Communications Construction Group and the China Railway Construction Corporation contributed to the evacuation of the Chinese nationals.[78]

Some media reports suggested that the Chinese Defence Ministry had authorised the Chinese Navy to conduct escort missions in the Aden Gulf in order to provide support and protection to ships evacuating Chinese nationals in waters surrounding Libya.[79] The 4000-ton missile frigate *Xuzhou* was diverted from the coast of Somalia on 24 February 2011 "in the Asian power's first naval operation in the Mediterranean Sea and its first deployment of military hardware in a civilian evacuation mission."[80]

The *Xuzhou* is armed with weapons that include HHQ-16 surface-to-air missiles and carries a Z-9 helicopter. According to Jeremy Page the evacuation reflected the mounting domestic pressure on Beijing to protect its growing foreign interests and increasing numbers of Chinese citizens working abroad. More importantly, it illustrated the Chinese Navy's ability to operate far beyond China in order to protect the country's perceived foreign interests.[81] President Hu Jintao was quoted as saying: "spare no efforts to ensure the safety of life and properties of Chinese citizens in Libya."[82] In order to coordinate evacuation efforts, "the State Council of China set up the emergency command headquarters to the Libyan crisis to lead all relevant organisations to create solutions and negotiate with the Libyan government to protect Chinese expatriates and overseas assets" (Zhang and Wei 2012, p. 48). The implication is that while evacuation might not be considered as intervention in the strict sense of armed interventions such as the NATO-led military intervention, it involved a violation of Libyan sovereignty, and was done without the consent of the Libyan government. But the most significant implication is that it transformed China's perception of threats emanating from African intrastate armed conflicts from considering them as inconsequential to its interests in Africa, to regarding them as detrimental to both its economic interests and citizens there, thus compelling it to modify its non-intervention policy.

4.8 The Ambivalence of China's Intervention in Libya

China's ambivalent multilateral and unilateral intervention in the Libyan intrastate armed conflict reflected a state struggling to reconcile "the nexus of intervention, state sovereignty and the use of force" (Richardson 2012, p. 45). In effect, the Libyan conflict

> Set its own precedent for international dilemmas in implementing UN Security Council resolutions in support of the doctrine of the "Responsibility to Protect," on the one hand, and the involvement of Western military intervention to implement it, on the other. The former present[ed] moral pressure, and the latter creat[ed] discomfort. It is almost as if the solution is more problematic than the problem. (Aybet 2011)

China was largely unprepared, and to a greater extent was inexperienced to deal with that paradox, because before the Libyan conflict, concerning Africa China had successfully portrayed an imagery of being able to strike a balance between safeguarding its expanding economic interests in Africa, and respecting the host African countries' sovereignty through non-intervention in their internal affairs. But as highlighted above, the intrastate armed conflict in Libya and its accompanying threats to China's economic interests scuttled that delicate balance, exposing Beijing's unpreparedness, lack of concrete foreign policy strategy and inability to decisively deal with threats emanating from foreign intrastate armed conflicts.

As discussed above, the Libyan conflict also tested China's overriding perception that intrastate armed conflicts in Africa were not a threat to its economic interests or nationals there. The shock of realising that they actually were a threat to its interests seems to have had a transformational effect on how Beijing considered and responded to the threat, and on how it reacted to subsequent intrastate armed conflicts in Mali and South Sudan. Part of the transformational effect was an incipient change to its overall perception of foreign intrastate armed conflicts in Africa as threats to its national interests. Because in most cases the change in threat perception is not usually distinct but gradual, in the case of China, the process of that threat perception transformation was characterised by a distinct sense of lack of clarity and consistency between rhetoric and action on how to intervene and safeguard its interests in a way that balances "its traditional commitment to 'non-interference' with its responsibilities as a great power" with interests abroad (Pang 2009, p. 237).

The effect of the re-calibration and re-thinking process is usually characterised by lack of clarity on foreign policy. Thus, as China was compelled to respond spontaneously to the threatening effect of the Libyan intrastate armed conflict, it did not "know when, where and how to use its power" (Wang 2013). The result was ambivalence in its intervention behaviour, which reflected itself in the difference between China's rhetoric and actions in Libya. On the one hand it condemned intervention in Libya's domestic affairs, but on the other, it supported multilateral intervention that affected the direction, duration and outcome of the intrastate armed conflict in a direct way. On the one hand it condemned Western manoeuvres towards ousting the Gaddafi regime, but on the other, it engaged and recognised the Libyan opposition when Gaddafi was still the leader of Libya in blatant violation of its own non-intervention principle. It can therefore be argued that based on how it responded to the Libyan conflict, China's foreign policy was ambivalent, "did not reflect a clear and well-developed policy ... [and] strong rhetoric [was] often used to compensate for weak or incoherent policies."[83] Thus, "China should be counted in the group of ambivalent interventionists" (Engelbrekt 2014, p. 51).

NOTES

1. Taylor, I 2007b, 'Unpacking China's Resource Diplomacy in Africa', Working Paper, no. 18, Center on China's Transnational Relations, Hong Kong, p. 1.
2. Ogunsanwo, A 1974, *China's policy in Africa: 1958–71*, Cambridge University Press, Cambridge, p. 8.
3. Shichor, Y 2014, 'Respected and suspected: Middle Eastern perceptions of China's rise' in N Horesh & E Kavalski (eds.), *Asian Thought on China's Changing International Relations*, Palgrave Macmillan, London, p. 128.
4. Meredith, M 2011, *The state of Africa: A history of the continent since independence,* Simon and Schuster, London, p. 350.
5. Ogunsanwo, A 1974, *China's policy in Africa: 1958–71*, Cambridge University Press, Cambridge, p. 244.
6. Shinn, DH & Eisenman, J 2012, *China and Africa: A century of engagement,* University of Pennsylvania Press, Philadelphia, p. 238.
7. 'Brief introduction to relations between China and Libya' 2002, *Xinhua*, 5 April, viewed 16 May 2014, http://news.xinhuanet.com/english/2002-04/05/content_346047.htm
8. Ibid.
9. 'Backgrounder: Major events in Sino-Libyan relations' 2002, *Xinhua*, 13 April, viewed 16 May 2014, http://news.xinhuanet.com/english/2002-04/13/content_358002.htm
10. 'Chinese president starts state visit to Libya' 2002, *Xinhua*, 13 April, viewed 16 May 2014, http://news.xinhuanet.com/english/2002-04/13/content_357037.htm
11. 'Backgrounder: Major events in Sino-Libyan relations' 2002, *Xinhua*, 13 April, viewed 16 May 2014, http://news.xinhuanet.com/english/2002-04/13/content_358002.htm
12. Shinn, DH & Eisenman, J 2012, *China and Africa: A century of engagement,* University of Pennsylvania Press, Philadelphia, p. 228.
13. 'Taiwan president accepts Gaddafi's invitation to visit Libya' 2006, *Kuwait News Agency*, 18 January, viewed 16 May 2014, http://www.kuna.net.kw/ArticlePrintPage.aspx?id=1630090&language=en
14. 'Taiwan's Chen stops over in Libya' 2006, *BBC News*, 11 May, viewed 16 May 2014, http://news.bbc.co.uk/2/hi/asia-pacific/4760471.stm
15. 'China demands Libya cease official ties with Taiwan' 2006, *Xinhua*, 11 May, viewed 16 May 2014, http://news.xinhuanet.com/english/2006-05/11/content_4534843.htm
16. People's Republic of China 2006, *China appreciates Libya's adherence to one-China policy*, 19 January, viewed 18 May 2014, http://www.gov.cn/misc/2006-01/19/content_164701.htm
17. Ministry of Foreign Affairs Republic of China (Taiwan) 2008, *Taiwan Commercial Office in Tripoli began functioning in Libya on February 13,*

viewed 18 May 2014, http://www.mofa.gov.tw/en/News_Content.aspx?n=1EADDCFD4C6EC567&sms=5B9044CF1188EE23&s=F6E2F3C7AD839690

18. Blanchard, CM 2010, *Libya: Background and US relations,* DIANE Publishing, p. 21.
19. Al-Awsat, A 2009, 'Q & A with Libyan Foreign Minister Musa Kusa', *Asharq al-Awsat,* 10 November, viewed 18 May 2014, http://english.aawsat.com/2009/11/article55252921; Hook, L & Dyer, G 2011, 'Chinese oil interests attacked in Libya', *Financial Times,* 24 February, viewed 18 May 2014, http://www.ft.com/intl/cms/s/0/eef58d52-3fe2-11e0-811f-00144feabdc0.html
20. Gaddafi, M 2007, 'The brother leader addresses the students of Oxford University discussing the issues facing Africa in the twenty-first century', *AlGaddafi.org,* viewed 18 May 2014, http://english.algaddafi.org/the-brother-leader-addresses-the-students-of-oxford-university-discussing-the-issues-facing-africa-in-the-twenty-first-century.html
21. Al-Awsat, A 2009, 'Q & A with Libyan Foreign Minister Musa Kusa', *Asharq al-Awsat,* 10 November, viewed 18 May 2014, http://english.aawsat.com/2009/11/article55252921; Hook, L & Dyer, G 2011, 'Chinese oil interests attacked in Libya', *Financial Times,* 24 February, viewed 18 May 2014, http://www.ft.com/intl/cms/s/0/eef58d52-3fe2-11e0-811f-00144feabdc0.html
22. Blanchard, CM 2010, *Libya: Background and US relations,* DIANE Publishing, p. 21.
23. U.S. Energy Information Administration 2015, *Country analysis brief: Libya,* U.S. Energy Information Administration, 19 November, viewed 10 January 2016, https://www.eia.gov/beta/international/analysis_includes/countries_long/Libya/libya.pdf
24. U.S. Energy Information Administration 2011, *Libya is a major energy exporter, especially to Europe,* U.S. Energy Information Administration, 21 March, viewed 10 January 2016, https://www.eia.gov/todayinenergy/detail.cfm?id=590
25. Jiang, J & Sinton, J 2011, 'Overseas investments by Chinese national oil companies', *IEA Energy Papers,* no. 2011/03, OECD Publishing, Paris, viewed on 10 June 2015, p. 27, http://www.oecd-ilibrary.org/docserver/download/5kgglrwdrvvd.pdf?expires=1456063139&id=id&accname=guest&checksum=EA84CD4E1E7E7AD5D92BCC1CF35BC439
26. Ibid.
27. Pierson, D 2011, 'Libyan strife exposes China's risks in global quest for oil', *Los Angeles Times,* 9 March, viewed 10 June 2015, http://articles.latimes.com/2011/mar/09/business/la-fi-china-oil-20110310
28. Zhang, J & Wei, WX 2012, 'Managing political risks of Chinese contracted projects in Libya', *Project Management Journal,* vol. 43, no. 4, p. 43.

29. Branigan, T 2011, 'China looks to protect its assets in a post-Gaddafi Libya', *The Guardian*, 23 August, viewed 10 June 2015, http://www.theguardian.com/world/2011/aug/23/china-assets-post-gaddafi-libya
30. Song S 2012, 'China seeks compensation in Libya', *Global Times*, 7 March, viewed 10 June 2015, http://www.globaltimes.cn/content/699098.shtml
31. FOCAC 2011, 'China-Africa Trade and Economic Relationship Annual Report 2010', *FOCAC*, 22 June, viewed 10 June 2015, http://www.focac.org/eng/zxxx/t832788.htm
32. Mei, X 2011, 'China-Libya ties still vital', *China Daily*, 2 November, viewed 10 June 2015, http://www.chinadaily.com.cn/opinion/2011-11/02/content_14020093.htm
33. FOCAC 2010, 'Direct flight route between China and Libya launched', *FOCAC*, viewed 10 June 2015, http://www.focac.org/eng/zxxx/t766530.htm
34. FOCAC 2012, 'China-Africa trade hits historic high', *FOCAC*, 6 July, viewed 10 June 2015, http://www.focac.org/eng/zxxx/t948493.htm
35. Mei, X 2011, 'China-Libya ties still vital', *China Daily*, 2 November, viewed 10 June 2015, http://www.chinadaily.com.cn/opinion/2011-11/02/content_14020093.htm
36. Zhang, J & Wei, WX 2012, 'Managing political risks of Chinese contracted projects in Libya', *Project Management Journal*, vol. 43, no. 4, p. 49.
37. 'China counting financial losses in Libya' 2011, *Global Times*, 4 March, viewed 10 June 2015, http://www.globaltimes.cn/content/629817.shtml
38. Zhang, J & Wei, WX 2012, 'Managing political risks of Chinese contracted projects in Libya', *Project Management Journal*, vol. 43, no. 4, p. 46.
39. 'Chinese enterprises in Libya investment list' [中国企业在利比亚投资情况一览] 2011, *SOHU Finance*, 23 August, viewed 10 June 2015, http://business.sohu.com/20110823/n317112596.shtml
40. Zhu W 2011, 'Business losses in Libya bloated by careless media', *Global Times*, 21 April, viewed 10 June 2015, http://www.globaltimes.cn/content/647393.shtml
41. Li, Q 2011, 'Compensation claims may weigh on business losses in Libya: report', *Global Times*, 28 March, viewed 12 June 2015, http://www.globaltimes.cn/content/638773.shtml
42. Sun, Y 2014, *Africa in China's foreign policy*, Brookings Institute, Washington D.C., p. 10.
43. Mekay, E 2011, 'Gaddafi hits with deadly force', *Al Jazeera*, 21 February, viewed 12 June 2015, http://www.aljazeera.com/indepth/features/2011/02/2011221133437954477.html
44. UN Security Council 2011, *Security Council resolution 1973 (2011) [on the situation in the Libyan Arab Jamahiriya]*, 17 March, S/RES/1973(2011), viewed 12 June 2015, http://www.refworld.org/docid/4d885fc42.html
45. Fahim, K & Kirkpatrick DD 2011, 'Gaddafi's grip on the capital tightens as revolt grows', *New York Times*, 22 February, viewed 12 June 2015,

http://www.nytimes.com/2011/02/23/world/africa/23libya.html?pagewanted=all

46. 'China counting financial losses in Libya' 2011, *Global Times*, 4 March, viewed 12 June 2015, http://www.globaltimes.cn/content/629817.shtml
47. Sun, Y 2014, *Africa in China's foreign policy*, Brookings Institute, Washington D.C. p. 10.
48. Buckley, C 2008, 'China defends veto of Zimbabwe resolution', *Reuters*, 12 June, viewed 13 June 2015, http://www.reuters.com/article/us-china-zimbabwe-idUSPEK14214420080712; see also, United Nations 2008, *Security Council fails to adopt sanctions against Zimbabwe leadership as two permanent members cast negative votes*, United Nations Security Council, 11 July, viewed 13 June 2015, http://www.un.org/press/en/2008/sc9396.doc.htm
49. Wuthnow, J 2013, *Chinese diplomacy and the UN Security Council: Beyond the veto*, Routledge, London, p. 2; Morris, H, Blitz, J, Dombey, D, Saleh, H & Peel, M 2011, 'UN unanimously backs Gaddafi sanctions', *Financial Times*, 26 February, viewed 23 May 2016, http://www.ft.com/intl/cms/s/0/cf73de4e-40c2-11e0-9a37-00144feabdc0.html#axzz49RyXsZMD
50. United Nations Security Council Resolution 1970 (2011), viewed 13 June 2015, http://www.un.org/en/ga/search/view_doc.asp?symbol=S/RES/1970(2011)
51. United Nations 2011, 'In swift, decisive action, Security Council imposes tough measures on Libyan regime, adopting Resolution 1970 in wake of crackdown on protesters', *United Nations*, 26 February, viewed 13 June 2015, http://www.un.org/press/en/2011/sc10187.doc.htm
52. Council of League of Arab States, 2011, *The outcome of the Council of the League of Arab States meeting at the Ministerial level in its extraordinary session on the implications of the current events in Libya and the Arab position*, Council of League of Arab States, 12 March, viewed 12 June 2015, http://responsibilitytoprotect.org/Arab%20League%20Ministerial%20level%20statement%2012%20march%202011%20-%20english(1).pdf
53. Watt, N 2011, 'Nicolas Sarkozy calls for air strikes on Libya if Gaddafi attacks civilians' *The Guardian*, 11 March, viewed 13 June 2015, http://www.theguardian.com/world/2011/mar/11/nicolas-sarkozy-libya-air-strikes
54. UN Security Council 2011, *Security Council resolution 1973 (2011) [on the situation in the Libyan Arab Jamahiriya]*, 17 March, S/RES/1973(2011), viewed 12 June 2015, http://www.refworld.org/docid/4d885fc42.html
55. Sanger, DE & Shanker, T 2011, 'Gates warns of risks of a no-fly zone', *New York Times*, 2 March, viewed 12 June 2015, http://www.nytimes.com/2011/03/03/world/africa/03military.html?pagewanted=all
56. Wu, X & Yu, Z 2011, 'China adopts pragmatic, constructive approach on Libya', *Xinhua*, 24 June, viewed 12 June 2015, http://news.xinhuanet.com/english2010/china/2011-06/24/c_13948400.htm

57. 'China receives Libyan opposition leader, recognizes NTC as "important dialogue partner"' 2011, *Xinhua*, 22 June, viewed 12 June 2015, http://lr.china-embassy.org/eng/majorevents/t832931.htm
58. 'Obama chided on Libya, China meets rebels' 2011, *UNHCR Refugees Daily*, 5 June, viewed 22 June, http://www.unhcr.org/cgi-bin/texis/vtx/refdaily?pass=52fc6fbd5&id=4dec6a3d5; Lowe, C, Harvey, J, & Maclean, W 2011, 'China meets Libya rebels in latest blow to Gaddafi', *Reuters*, 3 June, viewed 22 June 2015, http://www.reuters.com/article/us-libya-idUSTRE7270JP20110603
59. 'China ready to receive Libya opposition envoys' 2011, *China Daily*, 9 June, viewed 22 June 2015, http://europe.chinadaily.com.cn/china/2011-06/09/content_12670100.htm; 'China adopts pragmatic, constructive approach on Libya' 2011, *Global Times*, 24 June, viewed 22 June 2015, http://www.globaltimes.cn/content/663177.shtml
60. 'China recognizes Libya's NTC "important dialogue partner" as it receives opposition leader' 2011, *Xinhua*, 22 June, viewed 22 June 2015, http://en.people.cn/90001/90776/90883/7417683.html
61. People's Republic of China Ministry of Foreign Affairs 2011, *Foreign Ministry Spokesperson Hong Lei's Regular Press Conference on June 21, 2011*, viewed 22 June 2015, http://www.fmcoprc.gov.hk/eng/xwdt/wjbt/t833157.htm
62. Huang, J 2011, 'Senior envoy visits Benghazi', *Global Times*, 8 July viewed 22 June 2015, http://www.globaltimes.cn/content/665213.shtml
63. FOCAC 2011, 'Director-General of the Department of West Asian and North African Affairs of Chinese Foreign Ministry Chen Xiaodong visits Benghazi', *FOCAC*, 12 July, viewed 24 June 2015, http://www.focac.org/eng/zxxx/t838566.htm
64. FOCAC 2011, 'Special Envoy of the Libyan government, Secretary of the General People's Committee for Foreign Liaison and International Cooperation to visit China", *FOCAC*, 8 June, viewed 24 June 2015, http://www.focac.org/eng/zfgx/t828702.htm
65. Evron, Y 2014, 'Sino-Israeli defense relations: In search of common strategic ground', in DC Chau & TM Kane (eds.), *China and international security: history, strategy, and 21st-century policy*, Praeger, Santa Barbara, p. 251.
66. 'China adopts pragmatic, constructive approach on Libya' 2011, *Global Times*, 24 June, viewed 24 June 2015, http://www.globaltimes.cn/content/663177.shtml
67. Wu, X & Yu, Z 2011, 'China adopts pragmatic, constructive approach on Libya', *Xinhua*, 24 June, viewed 12 June 2015, http://news.xinhuanet.com/english2010/china/2011-06/24/c_13948400.htm
68. Ibid.
69. Fabricius, P 2014. 'Beijing's peacemaking efforts in South Sudan.' *Institute for Security Studies*, 6 November, viewed 21 December 2014, http://www.issafrica.org/iss-today/beijings-peacemaking-efforts-in-south-sudan

70. Zhou, L 2014, 'Chinese diplomats make exception to non-interference rule by meeting South Sudan opposition', *South China Morning Post*, 5 November, viewed 5 November 2014, http://www.scmp.com/news/china/article/1632138/chinese-diplomats-make-exception-non-interference-rule-meeting-south
71. Martin, P & Cohen, D 2011, 'Through Chinese eyes: He Wenping (part 3)', *The Interpreter*, 2 December, viewed 12 June 2015, http://www.lowyinterpreter.org/post/2011/12/02/Through-Chinese-eyes-He-Wenping-%28Part-3%29.aspx
72. 'China confirms weapons firms met Gaddafi envoys in July' 2011, *BBC News*, 5 September, viewed 12 June 2015, http://www.bbc.com/news/world-asia-pacific-14785688; Branigan, T 2011, 'Chinese arms companies 'offered to sell arms to Gaddafi regime', *The Guardian*, 5 September, viewed 12 June 2015, http://www.theguardian.com/world/2011/sep/05/chinese-arms-companies-weapons-gaddafi-regime
73. Anderlini, J 2011, 'China confirms Libya arms sale talks', *Financial Times*, 5 September, viewed 12 June 2015, http://www.ft.com/intl/cms/s/0/77a3e566-d7bb-11e0-a06b-00144feabdc0.html#axzz40VnGnbau
74. Wines, M 2011, 'China says state-run arms makers talked to Libyans', *New York Times*, 6 September, viewed 12 June 2015, http://query.nytimes.com/gst/fullpage.html?res=9E0CEEDF1F3AF935A3575AC0A9679D8B63
75. Branigan, T 2011, 'Chinese arms companies 'offered to sell arms to Gaddafi regime', *The Guardian*, 5 September, viewed 12 June 2015, http://www.theguardian.com/world/2011/sep/05/chinese-arms-companies-weapons-gaddafi-regime
76. Wines, M 2011, 'China says state-run arms makers talked to Libyans', *New York Times*, 6 September, viewed 12 June 2015, http://query.nytimes.com/gst/fullpage.html?res=9E0CEEDF1F3AF935A3575AC0A9679D8B63
77. 'China sends plane to bring back Chinese citizens in Libya' 2011, *Global Times*, 23 February, viewed 13 June 2015, http://www.globaltimes.cn/content/626214.shtml; 'China arranges logistics backup for evacuation of citizens in Libya' 2011, *Global Times*, 24 February, viewed 13 June 2015, http://www.globaltimes.cn/content/626637.shtml
78. 'China strives to evacuate nationals from Libya, gets aid from foreign governments' 2011, *Global Times*, 26 February, viewed 13 June 2015, http://www.globaltimes.cn/content/627666.shtml; 'Chinese army likely to join more overseas evacuations after Libya mission: PLA generals' 2011, *Global Times*, 5 March, viewed 13 June 2015, http://www.globaltimes.cn/content/630167.shtml; '35,860 Chinese nationals in Libya evacuated: FM' 2011, *Global Times*, 3 March, viewed 13 June 2015, http://www.globaltimes.cn/content/629380.shtml
79. 'China strives to evacuate nationals from Libya' 2011, *Global Times*, 25 February, viewed 13 June 2015, http://www.globaltimes.cn/content/627198.shtml

80. Page, J 2011, 'Libyan turmoil prompts Chinese naval first', *The Wall Street Journal*, 25 February, viewed 13 June 2015, http://blogs.wsj.com/china-realtime/2011/02/25/libyan-turmoil-prompts-chinese-naval-firsts/
81. Ibid.
82. Hook, L & Dyer, G 2011, 'Chinese oil interests attacked in Libya', *Financial Times*, 24 February, viewed 13 June 2015, http://www.ft.com/intl/cms/s/0/eef58d52-3fe2-11e0-811f-00144feabdc0.html
83. Wang, Z 2013, 'Does China have a foreign policy?' *New York Times*, 18 March, viewed 13 June 2015, http://www.nytimes.com/2013/03/19/opinion/does-china-have-a-foreign-policy.html

Bibliography

Alessi, C., & Xu, B. (2015). *China in Africa*. Council on Foreign Relations, Washington, DC. Retrieved March 14, 2016, from http://www.cfr.org/china/china-africa/p9557

Aybet, G. (2011). Turkey and the ambivalent, reluctant military intervention over Libya. *Today's Zaman*, 24 March. Retrieved March 14, 2014, from http://www.todayszaman.com/op-ed_turkey-and-the-ambivalent-reluctant-military-intervention-over-libya-by-gulnur-aybet_239022.html

Calabrese, J. (2013). China and the Arab awakening: The cost of doing business. *China Report, 49*(1), 5–23.

Campbell, H. (2013). *NATO's failure in Libya: Lessons for Africa*. Pretoria: Africa Institute of South Africa.

Engelbrekt, K. (2014). Why Libya? Security Council Resolution 1973 and the politics of justification. In K. Engelbrekt, M. Mohlin, & C. Wagnsson (Eds.), *The NATO intervention in Libya: Lessons learned from the campaign* (pp. 41–62). London: Routledge.

Engelbrekt, K., & Wagnsson, C. (2014). Introduction. In K. Engelbrekt, M. Mohlin, & C. Wagnsson (Eds.), *The NATO intervention in Libya: Lessons learned from the campaign* (pp. 1–14). New York: Routledge.

Goldstone, J. A. (2012). Protest and repression in democracies and autocracies: Europe, Iran, Thailand and the Middle East 2010–11. In S. Seferiades & H. Johnston (Eds.), *Violent protest, contentious politics, and the neoliberal state* (pp. 103–118). Surrey: Ashgate.

Jiang, J., & Ding, C. (2014). *Update on overseas investments by China's national oil companies. Achievements and challenges since 2011*. IEA Partner Country Series, OECD Publishing, Paris. Retrieved June 10, 2015, from http://www.iea.org/publications/freepublications/publication/PartnerCountrySeriesUpdateonOverseasInvestmentsby ChinasNationalOilCompanies.pdf

Kassim, Y. R. (2014). *The geopolitics of intervention: Asia and the responsibility to protect*. Singapore: Springer.

Larkin, B. D. (1973). *China and Africa, 1949–1970: The foreign policy of the People's Republic of China*. California: University of California Press.

Ogunsanwo, A. (1974). *China's policy in Africa: 1958–71*. Cambridge: Cambridge University Press.

Pang, Z. (2009). China's non-intervention question. *Global Responsibility to Protect, 1*, 237–252.

Richardson, C. J. (2012). A responsible power? China and the UN peacekeeping regime. In M. Lanteigne & M. Hirono (Eds.), *China's evolving approach to peacekeeping* (pp. 44–56). London: Routledge.

Roy, D. (2013). *Return of the dragon: Rising China and regional security*. New York: Columbia University Press.

Shichor, Y. (2014). Respected and suspected: Middle Eastern perceptions of China's rise. In N. Horesh & E. Kavalski (Eds.), *Asian thought on China's changing international relations* (pp. 123–140). London: Palgrave Macmillan.

Shih, C., & Huang, C. (2014). *Harmonious intervention: China's quest for relational security*. Surrey: Ashgate Publishing, Ltd.

Shinn, D. (2013). China confronts terrorism in Africa. *China-US Focus*, 18 November. Retrieved September 3, 2018, from https://www.chinausfocus.com/peace-security/china-confronts-terrorism-in-africa

Shinn, D. H., & Eisenman, J. (2012). *China and Africa: A century of engagement*. Philadelphia: University of Pennsylvania Press.

Sun, Y. (2012). Syria: What China has learned from its Libya experience. *Asia Pacific Bulletin*, No. 12. Retrieved September 3, from https://www.eastwestcenter.org/system/tdf/private/apb152_1.pdf?file=1&type=node&id=33315

Taib, M. (2010). The mineral and oil industry of Libya. In *U.S geological survey, area reports – International – Africa and the Middle East: U.S geological survey minerals yearbook 2008* (Vol. III, pp. 25.1–25.6). U.S Government.

Taylor, I. (1998). China's foreign policy towards Africa in the 1990s. *The Journal of Modern African Studies, 36*(3), 443–460.

Terhalle, M. (2015). *The transition of global order: Legitimacy and contestation*. London: Palgrave Macmillan.

U.S. Energy Information Administration. (2015). *Country analysis brief: Libya*. U.S. Energy Information Administration, 19 November. Retrieved January 10, 2016, from https://www.eia.gov/beta/international/analysis_includes/countries_long/Libya/libya.pdf

Wang, B. W. (2013). The Dragon brings peace? Why China became a major contributor to United Nations peacekeeping. *Stimson Center Spotlight*, 12 July. Retrieved July 24, 2015, from http://www.stimson.org/spotlight/the-dragon-bringspeace-why-china-became-a-major-contributor-to-united-nationspeacekeeping-/

Whalley, J. (2011). *China's integration into the world economy*. New Jersey: World Scientific.

Wuthnow, J. (2013). *Chinese diplomacy and the UN security council: Beyond the veto*. London: Routledge.

Zhang, J., & Wei, W. X. (2012). Managing political risks of Chinese contracted projects in Libya. *Project Management Journal, 43*(4), 42–51.

CHAPTER 5

Mali

5.1 Introduction

As the intrastate armed conflict in Libya ended with the death of Muammar Gaddafi, another armed conflict emerged in Mali. Although different in nature, the Malian and Libyan conflicts were interlinked in that weapons and Tuaregs who had fought as mercenaries for the Gaddafi regime returned to aid the struggle for independence of Northern Mali. While the government of Mali struggled to contain the Tuareg rebellion, a group of disgruntled Malian soldiers mutinied and overthrew the government in Bamako. The internationalisation of the conflict, and the fact that it had emerged hardly six months after the Libyan intrastate armed conflict, made it impossible for China to ignore it as it had done with previous Tuareg rebellions and coup d'états in Mali. Besides, China had had unbroken diplomatic relations with Mali since 1960. Furthermore, there were Chinese nationals and investments in Mali, with the possibility of the conflict spiralling into neighbouring countries such as Niger, where China has uranium mining concessions (Shaw 2013). Again, the question of how China responds to threats posed by intrastate armed conflicts on its interests, both direct and indirect, emerged.

This chapter examines China's intervention in the Malian intrastate armed conflict. Like the previous chapter, it begins by giving a historical analysis of Sino-Mali diplomatic, political and economic relations since diplomatic relations were established in 1960. In giving the historical

O. Hodzi, *The End of China's Non-Intervention Policy in Africa*,
Critical Studies of the Asia-Pacific,
https://doi.org/10.1007/978-3-319-97349-4_5

analysis of Sino-Mali relations, the focus is on China's response to previous Tuareg rebellions and coup d'états in Mali. The aim is to draw comparisons with its intervention in the 2012 coup d'état and the Tuareg rebellion. The argument pursued in this chapter is that with hindsight concerning the effect of the Libyan crisis on its interest there, China was more alert to the threats the Malian armed conflict potentially had to its interests in Mali and the Sahel region.

5.2 China-Mali Political and Diplomatic Relations

Since establishing diplomatic relations on 27 October 1960, China and Mali maintained uninterrupted ties despite adverse internal and external political dynamics in Mali. To start with, in its external relations, even at the peak of Sino-Soviet wrangling in the 1960s, Mali maintained ties with both China and the Soviet Union. It was, however, not just Mali that played both sides; other independent African states did the same—maintaining political, economic and military relations with both China and the Soviet Union, and at times playing the two against each other. During the Cold War era, African leaders, according to Lucy Corkin, were "experts in appearing to emulate the ideologies of their patrons in order to coax out further material support,"[1] and Mali's first president, Modibo Keita, played that game well. He received extensive aid, political support[2] and military equipment from the Soviets as well as China despite warnings of the Soviet Union's imperialist tendencies from Beijing. But unlike other independent African countries, and to its advantage, Mali pragmatically and consistently avoided taking sides in the 1960s Sino-Soviet squabbling—something that Alaba Ogunsanwo refers to as "a practical application of the non-alignment principle developed in the period of the cold war" (1974, p. 217). Nonetheless, a common anti-imperialist ideology[3] in the formative years of Malian independence and President Modibo Keita's "socialist ideology and mode of production, with heavy emphasis on the role of the public sector in the economy"[4] inclined Mali towards Mao's China rather than towards the Soviet Union or France, its former colonial power.

To show the depth of their political and diplomatic relations, Sino-Mali high-level official visits were common. Official visits between the two countries started off with Premier Zhou En-lai's official tour of ten African countries (Egypt, Algeria, Morocco, Tunisia, Ghana, Mali, Guinea, Sudan,

Ethiopia and Somalia) between 14 December 1963 and 4 February 1964. As part of the maiden official trip by a Chinese national leader to Africa, Premier Zhou visited Mali from 16 to 21 January 1964. At the time of his visit, several agricultural projects such as rice and sugarcane growing, as well as infrastructure development projects, were already underway, all funded by Chinese money and overseen by Chinese technicians. To show its appreciation for the assistance rendered by China, the Malian government went all out to show its indebtedness to Premier Zhou, Vice-Premier Chen Yi and their entourage. Mali declared "a holiday for all government offices and public and private enterprises in Bamako and its outskirts..., [in order] to accord a welcome deserving the great Chinese-Malian friendship."[5] In the Malian town of Koulikoro, the Mayor, Mamadou Diarrah, made Premier Zhou an honorary citizen of Koulikoro. But amidst that pomp and fanfare, in his meetings with President Keita, Premier Zhou "enunciated the eight principles observed by the Chinese Government in providing economic and technical assistance to other countries."[6] He also "shared with Keita China's experiences on governance and economic development, which covered the capacity building of the governing party, the elimination of the residues of colonialism and the importance of safeguarding economic independence" (Zeng 2014). The thoughts were then encapsulated in a joint communique that the two parties published on 21 January 1964.

Impressed by President Keita's anti-imperialist and anti-colonial rhetoric and appreciation for China's assistance by Malians, Premier Zhou and Chairman Liu Shao-chi invited President Keita to visit China. Within months of Premier Zhou's departure from Bamako, President Modibo Keita led a delegation of 51 on a tour of Asia, with Beijing being the main destination. It was during his visit in Beijing that the Sino-Mali Treaty of Friendship was signed in November 1964. With this agreement, several trade and economic agreements were reached. In the same mould as the TAZARA railway, China agreed to fund construction of the Guinea-Mali railway. The agreement for its financing and construction was signed in May 1968 by China's finance minister Li Hsien-nien and by the Guinean and Malian foreign ministers in the presence of Premier Zhou Enlai. Three months after the signing ceremony, Chinese technicians conducted the preliminary surveys of the rail project in Mali and Guinea. But four days after they left Bamako, President Modibo Keita was overthrown on 19 November 1968 in a coup d'état led by Captain Yoro Diakité.[7] All in all, from 1960 until 1968, when President Keita's rule was ended, 55 Chinese delegates had visited Mali; excluding the 51 delegates that visited China with President Keita in September 1964, 56 Malian delegates visited China (Ogunsanwo 1974, p. 269, 270).

On taking over power from President Modibo Keita on 19 November 1968, Captain Yoro Diakité suspended the constitution and handed over power to a 14-member *Comité Militaire de Libération Nationale* (CMLN—Military Committee of National Liberation). Under the leadership of Lieutenant Moussa Traoré, the CMLN governed Mali from 1969 to 1979. In June 1974, Malians approved a new constitution that paved the way for a transition to a civilian government. However, in a bid to maintain political power, Traoré's government sponsored the *Union Démocratique du Peuple Malien* (UDPM—Malian People's Democratic Union) which Moussa Traoré led. Unsurprisingly he won the 1979 elections, as well as the successive elections until he was deposed in 1992. In all this turmoil, China maintained relations with the ruling regime of the day, without any sense of obligation to the deposed governments.

Unlike his predecessor, Modibo Keita, Moussa Traoré had a pragmatic foreign policy approach. He rejuvenated relations with France and opened ties with the United States and other Western powers while maintaining close connections with both the Soviet Union and China. In comparison, Sino-Mali relations measured by official visits between the two countries increased more during Moussa Traoré's leadership than in Modibo Keita's. For example, in June 1973, Moussa Traoré visited China and met with Chairman Mao; he also visited China in August 1981, June 1986 and January 1989. China seemed to positively reciprocate Traoré's visits because Chinese government, military and CCP officials, including "Zhang Dazhi, commander of the Chinese artillery (May 1971), Geng Biao, Vice-premier (October 1978), Huang Hua, Vice-premier and concurrently minister of foreign affairs (November 1981), Liu Kai, assistant to minister of national defence (March 1982), Tian Jiyun, Vice-premier (December 1984), Wang Hanbin, Vice-chairman of the National People's Congress (September 1989, Qian Qichen, Member of the State Council and concurrently minister of foreign affairs (January 1992),"[8] visited Mali on official state and party business.

Despite the seemingly cordial relations between Moussa Traoré's regime and Beijing, there was silence from Beijing when he was deposed by junior officers led by Amadou Touré in 1992. Having overseen reform of the constitution and a democratic election, Amadou Touré handed over power to the democratically elected government of Alpha Oumar Konaré.

President Konaré made two state visits to China, in December 1992 and September 1996. Other Malian high-level officials that visited China during the Konaré regime include Prime Minister Ibrahim Boubacar Keita (August 1994 and October 1999), Ali Nouhoum Diallo, Speaker of the National Assembly (July 1995), Moussa Balla Coulibaly, Chairman of Economic, Social and Cultural Council (March 2000),[9] and Moctar Ouane, Minister of Foreign Affairs and International Cooperation (August 2009). Also, "in 2009, Minister of Territorial Administration and Local Communities General Kafougouna Kone, Minister of Communications and New Technologies Diarra Mariam Flantié Diallo and Minister of Health Oumar Ibrahima Toure visited China."[10] From China, "General Liu Jingson, commander of Lanzhou Military Zone (July 1995), Major General Chen Youqing, Political Commissar of Communications Department of the Headquarters of the General Staff (December 1995), General Zhou Kunren, Political Commissar of the General Logistics Department (July 2000) and General Chen Bingde, Commander of Jinan Military Zone (June 2002) paid visits to the Republic of Mali one after the other."[11] The highlight of Sino-Mali political relations during President Amadou Toumani Touré's time in power occurred in February 2009 when President Hu Jintao arrived in Bamako for a one-day state visit.[12]

5.3 Sino-Mali Economic and Trade Relations

Beyond politics, Sino-Mali relations came to be more economically defined soon after Mali's independence. In February 1961, just a year after Mali's independence, the two countries signed a goods and exchange payment agreement, which "called for the export to Mali of machinery, farm machines and tools, scientific instruments and electrical appliances, chemicals, drugs and medical apparatus, metalware, and steel products, etc., but this could better be described as aid, as Mali had at that time relatively little to export to China in return" (Ogunsanwo 1974, p. 86). The 1961 agreement was consummated in November 1964 when the two countries signed a treaty of friendship during President Keita's visit to China at the invitation of Premier Zhou Enlai. Following the treaty of friendship, a host of other economic and trade agreements, including Chinese technical and financial assistance for construction of a radio transmitter, a cinema, and a hotel in Mali, were agreed upon. The Chinese government bore three-quarters of the projects' costs, and it also agreed to send technicians to work on the projects. The rest of subsequent projects were funded partly through a US$3 million credit facility requested by President Keita's government, and was advanced to the Central Bank of Mali. The credit facility was one of the first cases of an African country requesting loans and development assistance from China, and it set the tone for subsequent Sino-Mali engagements.

China was also quick to bring to fruition the economic and trade undertakings it made to Mali soon after establishing diplomatic relations. By January 1962, three months after signing the Sino-Mali economic and technical cooperation agreement in September 1961, Chinese agricultural experts arrived in Bamako to start working on irrigation projects that included rice and sugar plantations. Following a resounding success of the sugar plantation project, China provided further economic and technical assistance for the building of Mali's first sugar refinery in the Segou region. At its completion in 1964, Mali was able to process 400 tonnes of sugarcane daily, enabling it to export sugar in the region and beyond. Other notable Chinese-supported projects included a match factory completed in Bamako in 1967, a textile mill built in Segou in 1968, a tea plantation and cement works. But since Mali lacked strategic mineral resources, China concentrated on infrastructure development and agricultural projects such that "the presence of Chinese agricultural and technical personnel remained the symbol of Chinese commitment" to its relationship with Mali (Ogunsanwo 1974, p. 216).

As Mali is landlocked, semi-desert and a poor country lacking in both financing and skilled personnel, President Modibo Keita was impressed by the Chinese development assistance model. Instead of merely providing funds and expecting Mali to complete the projects on its own, as Western governments did, China provided both financing and personnel to implement their aid and infrastructure projects. Chinese aid and technical assistance in the agricultural, infrastructure and rail construction sectors thrived. And from its early days of independence "when most external actors limited their activity to supplying the equipment with which Mali was supposed to embark on economic development, China went further to build factories which they only handed over after completion" (Anda 2000, p. 218). These actions endeared China to both civilian and military leaders in Mali. In fact, President Modibo Keita was highly appreciative of the Chinese model of development assistance, and he made it known to Premier Zhou Enlai when he visited Mali in January 1964. At a function held in Premier Zhou's honour, President Keita paid "warm homage to the P.R.C. for the low cost of its technical assistance, for the readiness of its technicians to adapt themselves to the life of our people, for the speed and competence with which the projects undertaken by the People's China are carried out one by one, and all these things are done without the slightest intention of interfering in our internal affairs" (Ogunsanwo 1974, pp. 159–160).

To Mali, then and to date, China epitomised a benevolent development partner, uninterested in seeking hegemony or intervention in its internal affairs, unlike France and other Western countries. Unlike its neighbour Niger which has rich uranium reserves, Mali had "relatively little to export to China,"[13] because its "mineral sector [was] dominated by the production of gold. No other mineral commodities [were] produced in significant quantities in the country" (Soto-Viruet 2012, p. 28.1). Accordingly, China's economic and trade relations with Mali were better described as aid and assistance. By the time the crises of 2012 began, China and Mali had had 50 years of unbroken diplomatic and economic relations—making China one of Mali's four biggest trading partners. In the course of those five decades, Mali benefitted from three debt reliefs provided by China in 2001, 2006 and 2008. The indebtedness of Mali and debt reliefs given by China does not mean China suffered losses; it still derived benefits from the bilateral relationship. According to Beijing's Eight Principles of China's Assistance to African Countries espoused by Premier Zhou Enlai during his visit to Africa in 1964, China did not consider "its financial aid as a unilateral grant, but rather a mutual and reciprocal process from which China also benefits" (Zeng 2014).

By the turn of the twenty-first century, trade and economic relations between the two countries had significantly developed from just being aid and assistance to joint ventures in Mali's agricultural sector and the construction industry created huge opportunities for Chinese state- and private-owned enterprises. The sector that recorded the largest boom in Sino-Mali relations is the construction industry. In 2002, Mali was advanced a loan by the Chinese government to construct five football stadiums that were used when Mali hosted the 2002 Africa Cup of Nations, Africa's biggest football tournament. Major Chinese investments were also in rail construction. Interestingly, major construction deals were reached even after the 2012 intrastate armed conflicts in Mali, suggesting that China's intervention in Africa is not just driven by perception of threat to current economic interests but also to anticipated interests. In December 2015, the state-owned China Railway Construction Limited (CRC) announced that Mali and Senegal had signed a US$2.7 billion contract for CRC to rehabilitate the Bamako-Dakar railway line.[14] Also, Chinese investments in Malian agricultural sector flourished, making cotton China's biggest import from Mali. From a trade value of US$23.35 million in 2002, Sino-Mali trade grew to approximately US$130 million in 2010.

5.4 Insurrections and Coup d'États: A Test to China's Non-intervention Principle

Since 1960, Mali has had persistent internal insurrections[15] including three successful coup d'états, and multiple Tuareg rebellions in Northern Mali. Throughout all these events, China maintained its non-intervention posture, continuing diplomatic and political relations with each successive government. However, it was not long before attempts were made by ruling elites in Mali to drag a reluctant China into their internal politics. The first case happened when President Keita, who was facing popular dissent due to his government's widespread corruption, declining economy, and his own version of a "cultural revolution," persuaded China to support his people's militia project, as he feared a looming popular uprising. Military overthrow of governments in the West African region, particularly the coup d'état against President Kwame Nkrumah of Ghana, had made a military rebellion in Mali imminent. To counter that possibility, President Keita established a "people's militia" twice the size of the country's army. Turning to China for support of the "people's militia," three military delegations from Mali visited Beijing between October 1966 and July 1968. By the third visit in 1968, China agreed to provide Mali with uniforms and weapons, but before the militia was consolidated, President Keita was overthrown in a military coup by junior army officers led by Lieutenant Moussa Traoré in November 1968. Considering that Modibo Keita's socialist policies were rhetorically moulded along Chairman Mao's economic and political ideology, one would have expected China to come to his rescue; instead China issued no public statement and maintained diplomatic ties with the new Traoré regime as if power had been transferred to Lieutenant Moussa Traoré procedurally.

When he announced his takeover of power from President Modibo Keita to cheering Malians, Moussa Traoré promised rapid development, revival of the economy and an end to corruption. However, ten years into his rule, a failing economy, stagnant development, widespread corruption and abuse of power resulted in internal resistance and an attempted coup against his own government. When the 1978 attempt by the military to overthrow him failed, Moussa Traoré became even more heavy-handed, ruthlessly purging political and military opponents and banning opposition political parties. In the process of wanting to maintain political power, he triggered a string of protests and widespread riots between 1991 and 1992 that eventually resulted in his ouster by the military in 1992. Again, China, which had maintained good diplomatic ties with Moussa Traoré as discussed above, simply moved on with the new regime without even a public statement being issued concerning the coup d'état.

On taking over power from Moussa Traoré, Colonel Amadou Toumani Touré, the coup leader, immediately instituted a transitional committee that oversaw adoption of a new constitution, facilitated the holding of democratic elections and then oversaw transition of power to a civilian government in that same year.[16] Alpha Omar Konaré won those elections and established Mali's first democratically elected government since independence. His election ushered in a period of political stability, and successive democratic transitions of power from one civilian government to the other until 2012.[17]

In 2002, Amadou Toumani Touré returned to power after winning a landslide in an election marred by political fraud and irregularities. But his government's failure to contain the Tuareg rebellion in northern Mali, "as well as the lack of resources at the disposal of the army to deal with the brewing insurgence,"[18] led to his ouster in 2012. He was toppled in a military rebellion led by Captain Amadou Haya Sanogo, who declared himself leader of a transitional authority called the *Comité national pour le redressement de la démocratie et la restauration de l'État* (CNRDR—National Committee for the Return of Democracy and the Restoration of the State).[19] However, due to regional and international pressure, the CNRDR agreed to hand power over to a civilian transitional government led by President Dioncounda Traoré, the country's former Speaker of parliament, following an agreement brokered by the Economic Community of West African States (ECOWAS) between Sanogo and Touré, in which they both agreed to resign. Nonetheless, soldiers loyal to Amadou Toumani Traoré attempted to wrestle back political power, leading to a violent backlash from the military junta that had installed President Dioncounda Traoré. International and regional pressure again resulted in presidential elections that Ibrahim Boubacar Keita won in August 2013.[20]

Amidst the above seriate of coup d'états and insurrections, the Tuareg in northern Mali were engaged in a persistent and prolonged armed struggle for self-determination against the successive Malian governments since Modibo Keita's reign. Between 1962 and 1964, the first Tuareg rebellion started but was ruthlessly crushed by the better equipped Malian military. Since then, there were intermittent but largely unsuccessful Tuareg insurrections until 2013 when they briefly declared unilateral independence. The Tuareg, a nomadic people inhabiting northern Mali and adjacent parts of the Sahara Desert in Niger, Burkina Faso and Algeria, were politically and culturally excluded by Malian governments. Also, being "nomads of the white race, [they could] neither conceive nor accept to be commanded by blacks whom [they] always had as servants and slaves" (Lecocq 2005, p. 54). Determined to achieve independence from southern Mali, their struggle for self-determination was led by the following major groups: *Mouvement Populaire de l'Azaouad*—Popular Movement of Azawad—(MPA); *Tuareg Front Populaire pour la Libération de l'Azaoud*—Tuareg Front for the Liberation of Azawad (FPLA); *Alliance Touareg Niger-Mali*—the Niger-Mali Tuareg Alliance (ATNM); and the National Movement for the Liberation of Azawad (MNLA).

A combination of regional and domestic factors produced a favourable environment for a major Tuareg offensive against Bamako. Domestically, they took "advantage of the power vacuum caused by the coup and the incertitude surrounding Bamako … [to carry] forward their task for an independent State" (Roberto et al. 2013, p. 76). Regionally, the fall of the Gaddafi regime propelled the Tuareg rebellion in two ways. First, there was an overflow of small arms and heavy weaponry such as NR-160 rockets, BM-21 multiple-launch rocket systems, 9M22M rockets and UB-32 rocket launchers from Libya.[21] Militants who raided Libyan government's armouries sold the weapons to Islamic groups and the Tuareg. Second, the Tuareg who had been working in Libya's oil and construction industry returned to Mali due to increased xenophobic attacks as the Gaddafi regime crumbled. Returning to Mali also were Tuareg mercenaries who had fought in the Libyan war on behalf of the Gaddafi regime.[22] These diverse Tuareg groups returned with military weapons, and equipped with modern fighting and insurgent experiences.[23] Joining forces with the MNLA, which was formed in 2010, along with Islamic armed groups including Ansar Dine (formed in 2012), Al-Qaida in the Islamic Maghreb (AQIM) and the *Mouvement pour l'unicité et le jihad en Afrique de l'Ouest* (MUJAO) they seized control of northern regional capitals of Kidal, Gao and Timbuktu before taking total control of the rest of northern Mali. By 6 April 2013, they had declared independence of northern Mali, renaming it Azawad with Gao as its capital. It was only through the military intervention of France that Malian government's authority was re-established in northern Mali (Francis 2013, p. 3).

5.5 From Indifference to "Concern"

From the military overthrows of Modibo Keita to the present government of President Ibrahim Boubacar Keita, and from the first Tuareg rebellion in independent Mali in 1962 to the Tuareg declaration of independence in April 2013, China was careful not to entangle itself in the murky terrain of Malian politics. Professing strict adherence to its foreign policy principle of non-intervention in the internal affairs of other states, it avoided siding with any regimes in Mali. In fact, in the first two coup d'états China did not issue any public response, either in favour of or condemning the military takeovers of governments in Mali. Diplomatic relations remained, and so did its development projects. Only in one incident did the overthrow of a president result in disruptions of Chinese projects in Mali. When President Keita was overthrown in November 1968 the joint Guinea-Mali rail project funded and constructed by the Chinese was suspended. The suspension was, however, not a Chinese initiative but a result of Guinea's unwillingness to work with the new military government of Moussa Traoré. As a result of the rail project's suspension, a few Chinese technicians working on the project left Bamako—but the majority of their Chinese colleagues working on other projects remained.

China approached the Tuareg rebellion in northern Mali with the same attitude as it did the SPLM's struggle for independence of South Sudan—it regarded Tuareg's struggle for independence as Mali's internal affair. Because of its friendly relations with successive Malian governments—military and civilian—it simply ignored, or at best was indifferent to, the Tuareg struggle for greater autonomy and self-determination. As in the case of its reaction to southern Sudan's own struggle for independence from the Sudan, China maintained its rhetoric on respect for national and territorial integrity of its partners, as well as its non-intervention principle in the internal affairs of other states. On that basis, China contended that it could not support secessionist groups. But as will be argued in the next chapter on South Sudan, Beijing's policy regarding support to opposition groups in Africa was not consistently implemented. Nonetheless, in Mali,

Beijing was consistent in its indifference to the Tuareg rebellion, concentrating instead on managing its relations with successive Malian regimes to which it generally "developed vested interests in the stability of a friendly African state … [Such that] for the African state concerned, friendship with China removed a potentially dangerous and powerful external source of inspiration for rebellious and discontented elements" (Ogunsanwo 1974, p. 174).

Overall, Beijing's indifference to military overthrows of governments and the Tuareg rebellion in Mali was strategic and pragmatic, leading to unintended benefits. For example, at the time Modibo Keita was overthrown, his government had approved the Soviet Union's 1968 invasion of Czechoslovakia despite China's advice not to. The new regime of Moussa Traoré immediately reversed the approval and castigated the Soviet Union for being imperialist, much to the glee of Beijing. Similarly, by ignoring the Tuareg rebellion, China continued to foster and maintain cordial relations with successive Malian governments—shrewdly preventing the Tuareg rebellion from tainting its relations with Bamako. By and large, the volatility and instability of the Malian political landscape caused China to be careful of its engagement with the different regimes, choosing not to take any sides for as long as they took no action to strain relations with Beijing.[24]

The biggest test of China's indifferent approach to the Malian coup d'états and Tuareg insurrections came in 2012 when Mali plunged into chaos under the pressure of "three distinct but interrelated types of conflicts that coalesced to produce the 2012–3 crises" (Francis 2013, p. 2). The three crises included: (1) the Tuareg takeover of northern Mali, (2) a coup d'état that overthrew President Amadou Toumani Touré's government and (3) an attempt by Islamist jihadists to establish an Islamic, Sharia law–based state. Occurring just a few months after the Libyan intrastate armed conflict, there was overwhelming evidence that the Tuareg had advanced more aggressively than before due to the fall of Gaddafi. Accordingly, there was significant international focus on Mali as well as fears that the conflict could engulf the whole Sahel region (Shaw 2013). In addition, fears that Mali could become an Islamic terrorist hub were amplified when it emerged that al-Qaeda-linked Islamist groups captured Northern Mali and were advancing towards Bamako.

Initially China was indifferent to the triple crises in Mali, but when it became apparent that the Tuareg rebellion had been successful as it declared the independent state of Azawad, at the backdrop of the military overthrow of Amadou Toumani Touré's government, China's position changed to what can be described as a tepid expression of concern. What proved the tepidness of its concern is that unlike France, Britain and the United States that issued statements condemning the coup d'état in Mali, China's reaction was solicited by a journalist in the regular Ministry of Foreign Affairs press conference on 22 March 2012. In a brief statement, Hong Lei, China's Foreign Ministry spokesperson, said: "China is concerned about the soldier's riot in Mali and hopes the situation will subside and return to normal as soon as possible. We maintain that relevant issues should be resolved through dialogue and consultation."[25] China's statement, although it was in response to a journalist's question, marked a departure from its practice in the previous two coup d'états and multiple Tuareg rebellions. Hitherto, it had avoided issuing public statements against Tuareg rebellions or coup d'états in Mali.

A day after China expressed its concern about the army riots in Bamako, General Amadou Sanogo announced on Malian state television and radio that the CNRDR had taken over control of the government from Amadou Toumani Touré. The third successful coup d'état in Malian history had been completed. General Amadou Sanogo's takeover of government was met with widespread condemnation from several African countries, the AU, ECOWAS, the United Nations, France and the United States. The US Department of State straightaway issued a statement announcing that it stood "with the legitimately elected government of President Amadou Toumani Touré."[26] An immediate suspension of financial aid to Bamako, and suspension of the military assistance programme which provided the Malian army with counter-terrorism training and intelligence operations in the Sahel, followed the Department of State's statement.[27] France, the most influential power in Mali, mobilised the European Union and together they imposed strict restrictions on the military junta and cut off all non-essential aid. In Africa, the response was even swifter. ECOWAS representatives from Cote d'Ivoire, Burkina Faso, Benin and Niger convened an emergency meeting in Abidjan, Cote d'Ivoire, on 29 March 2012; on the following day they "threatened to close Mali's borders and cut off its access to the regional central bank, on which Mali relied for currency" (Chivvis 2016, p. 69). The threat of sanctions was acted upon on 3 April 2012, which effectively cut Mali's fuel supply, and access to cash from the regional central bank. In protest, South Africa closed its Bamako embassy on 22 March 2012.[28] In addition, two of the most important organisations to Mali—ECOWAS and the AU—suspended Mali's membership and began making plans for military intervention to restore democracy.

Compared to other states' responses and action against the military junta in Mali, China's own response was a far cry away. Noting the difference between its response and other major powers', Beijing departed from its "tepid concern" and issued its strongest statement against the military junta in Mali: "We are opposed to the unconstitutional takeover of power,"[29] the Foreign Ministry spokesperson said. But instead of being backed by punitive action against the military government of General Sanogo, China added the traditional and official plea in such events[30]; it called upon "relevant parties in Mali to restore normal order as soon as possible and safeguard national unity and stability for the sake of the fundamental interests of the country and the people."[31] Compared with responses from other international capitals such as Washington, London and Paris, Beijing's response exuded apparent indifference to the implications of its rhetorical opposition to the military takeover of the Malian government.

In addition, despite major powers and the UNSC imposing measures against the military junta, China remained unperturbed. In fact, when a counter-coup was attempted by military guards loyal to the deposed Amadou Touré, the PRC Foreign Ministry through its spokesperson Liu Weimin again called on parties in the Malian conflict to "exercise restraint, properly handle their disputes by peaceful means including dialogue and consultation, and jointly safeguard constitutional order, so as to ensure a smooth political transition."[32] The continued failure by China to take concrete measures against the military government in Mali raised concerns that it was a free-rider,[33] trying to "maximize its interests through minimal involvement … while staking a claim to the moral high ground"[34] by "making hollow calls for a political resolution,"[35] but not acting as a responsible global power, and being "highly reluctant to take on more burdens—whether economic, political, or military—preferring to free-ride" (Kleine-Ahlbrandt 2009).

Beijing's position regarding the intrastate armed conflict in Mali shifted only when its nationals and interests in Mali appeared to be under threat—suggesting that China's response was primarily motivated by concerns over protection of its own interests. To address those threats and mitigate losses, possibly to avoid the Libyan debacle, the Foreign Ministry of the People's Republic of China issued a security alert on its website. It urged "Mali to take effective measures to ensure the safety and lawful rights and interests of Chinese institutions and nationals there"[36] Beyond issuing a security alert, the Foreign Ministry's spokesperson Hong Lei announced several steps taken by the Chinese government in Beijing, the embassy of China in Bamako and Chinese enterprises operating in Mali. The Chinese embassy in Bamako proactively engaged Chinese firms and nationals in Mali to assess their needs and security status. But as the security situation deteriorated in weeks that followed, the Ministry of Commerce warned Chinese firms of the escalating security risks in Mali and urged them to exercise vigilance. It also cautioned against non-essential travel to Mali, advising Chinese nationals to temporarily leave the country and consider returning when the security situation improves. The proactivity in taking measures to protect Chinese nationals and interests in Mali before extensive losses had occurred suggests the change in China's perception of threats posed by intrastate armed conflicts in Africa to its nationals and interests there. On the other hand, it also reflected that China was largely self-focused in its response to international security issues.

5.6 From Concern to Rhetorical Support for Mediation

The onward advance towards Bamako by the MNLA and its Islamist allies after they captured strategic towns in Northern Mali compelled China to urge ECOWAS to lead mediation efforts. To that effect it issued a statement through its Foreign Ministry spokesperson expressing appreciation and support for "efforts made by the African Union, ECOWAS and regional countries to mediate the Mali issue."[37] What China did not publicly acknowledge was that the mediation efforts by ECOWAS combined dialogue with the threat of political, diplomatic and economic sanctions as well as military intervention. One could argue that this was deliberate because China considers both the imposition of sanctions and military action as intervention in the internal affairs of another state. When the Chinese Foreign Ministry's spokesperson was asked to comment on ECOWAS's demand that the military hand over power or else face sanctions such as closure of borders and freeze on central bank accounts and military action, Hong Lei avoided commenting on the sanctions and military action; instead he said: "China supports the ECOWAS-led peaceful mediation for the Malian crisis. We hope parties concerned in Mali will establish a dialogue channel with the ECOWAS as soon as possible to seek an end to the crisis through negotiation, and avoid confrontation as well as serious impact on people's life."[38] Reading between the lines, the ECOWAS sanctions were in every respect "confrontational," with potential to cause "serious impact on people's lives." Yet it was only through imposition of sanctions that Captain Sanogo was willing to negotiate reinstatement of the constitution and hand over power to a transitional government.[39]

The rationale behind China's support for ECOWAS mediation, while deliberately avoiding express support for imposition of sanctions or taking any punitive action against the military regime as other states had done, was to preserve its bilateral relations with Mali and avoid breaching its non-intervention principle. The basis for exercising caution against giving full and express consent or even implied consent as it had done in the case of the NATO-led intervention in Libya is that it wanted to avoid sharing the blame in case Mali descended into chaos; at the same time it also wanted to be in support of regional and international initiatives towards restoring democracy in Mali. It also wanted to portray and maintain its image as a neutral power that does not interfere in the internal affairs of other states. But as put by Paul Haenle, director of Carnegie-Tsinghua Center for Global Policy, rhetorical support for mediation efforts being taken by others was not commensurate with China's global status.

Indeed, China's support for ECOWAS mediation efforts turned out to be mostly rhetorical. The European Union, France and the United States provided financial, diplomatic or logistical support to ECOWAS, but the Chinese government offered nothing. It simply played no significant role in facilitating mediation efforts by ECOWAS. David Shinn maintains that China's support of mediation efforts rather than punitive measures against the military regime was in accordance with its non-interference policy. Understandably, China was concerned that sanctions or military intervention would escalate the conflict, effectively destabilising the region, as had been the case in Libya. The interconnectedness of the Malian conflict with the downfall of Gaddafi as a result of sanctions and military intervention by NATO and other Western powers also seemed to cement China's concerns against confrontational measures against Captain Sanogo. So, as noted by a senior researcher at the Institute for Peace and Security Studies in Addis Ababa, to avoid the controversy of a failed military intervention, Beijing simply settled on giving rhetorical support to ECOWAS, while hoping that the situation did not escalate in a manner that would cause extreme damage to its interests in Mali and the Sahel region.

Nonetheless, ECOWAS countries had a strong preference for military intervention. As Captain Sanogo announced plans to hold a national meeting to decide the country's democratic transition schedule, ECOWAS began plans for a military intervention of Mali. However, within the ruling and political elites in Mali, there was no consensus on the proposed ECOWAS-led military intervention. In particular, Captain Sanogo and other military leaders controlling key ministerial portfolios, including Defence, Home Security and Territorial Administration,[40] opposed ECOWAS intervention, arguing that it was an affront to Mali's state sovereignty. At best Captain Sanogo wanted ECOWAS' role in Mali to be limited to training and logistical support for Malian troops. The transitional government also opposed the ECOWAS-led military intervention in Mali because even though power had been handed over to them as demanded by the AU and ECOWAS, Captain Sanogo and his military junta had remained influential in the background. In protest against pressure from Captain Sanogo and the military junta to oppose military intervention by ECOWAS, the transitional government's prime minister resigned in November 2012, and a new one, Django Sissoko, was immediately appointed in his stead (Francis 2013, p. 3).

5.7 Multilateral Action

In spite of pressure from the military junta, the leader of the transitional government, President Dioncounda Traoré, defiantly supported military intervention by ECOWAS. On 1 September 2012, he sent an official invitation to ECOWAS and France to militarily intervene in Mali in order to quell the Tuareg rebellion.[41] In what turned out to be a replay of the Libyan case, the UNSC unanimously adopted Resolution 2071 on 12 October 2012. It authorised ECOWAS and the AU to make an actionable plan for military intervention in Mali. China voted in favour of that Resolution. But before the AU and the ECOWAS African-led International Support Mission to Mali (AFISMA) became operational, Tuareg separatists and their Islamic allies advanced towards Bamako, capturing strategic towns of Konna and Diabaly on the way. They took advantage of divisions and political bickering among political and military leaders in Mali over military intervention by ECOWAS.[42] In response, the UNSC issued a press statement expressing the determination of members of the Security Council "to pursue the full implementation of its resolutions on Mali, in particular resolution 2085 (2012) in all its dimensions." Resolution 2085 (2012) authorised the AFISMA to assist the armed forces of Mali in regaining of control over its northern territory.[43] Taking note of the changed context, they then called "for a rapid deployment of the African-led International Support Mission in Mali (AFISMA)."[44] However, the continued inability of the Malian military to stop the Tuareg and their Islamist allies from advancing towards Bamako, "coupled with failure of the deployment of troops from African countries ... forced France to act unilaterally, but with the approval of the international community, including Russia, China and African regional actors" (Francis 2013, p. 5; see also, Okemuo 2013, p. 219). China had also voted in favour of both Resolution 2071 (2012) and Resolution 2085 (2012), all of which authorised military intervention in Mali.

Regarding France's military intervention in Mali there appeared to be confusion in Beijing. Although Beijing supported it at the UN Security Council, it remained adamant that military intervention without consent of the target state is illegitimate. "You cannot imagine China would support any bombing. It's against our principles,"[45] is how He Wenping, Director of African Studies at Chinese Academy of Social Sciences, had put it in a discussion on China's role in international peace and security. She then warned that unless opposed, "French forces' involvement in Mali will provide the case for legalization of a new interventionism in Africa."[46] Along similar lines, researchers at China's Naval Military Research Institute, Li Jian and Jin Jing, retorted that France was behaving like the African gendarmerie, and that its military intervention in Mali was a ploy to consolidate its control over Malian gold mines and oil reserves. Further drawing comparisons with the military intervention in Libya, they made an argument that France's eagerness to militarily intervene in African countries constituted an attempt to re-colonise and secure its strategic interests in Africa. What also exacerbated these concerns is that "France did not give any explanation why it was going it *cavalier seul* rather than within the EU framework" (Okemuo 2013, p. 219).

In its defence, France argued that its military intervention in Mali was at the invitation of Mali's interim government led by President Dioncounda Traoré,[47] thus it was not a violation of Mali's sovereignty. "France had answered to the request for military assistance issued by the Malian authorities by providing, within the bounds of international law, the support of its armed forces to the Malian units engaged in the fight against terrorist groups" (Okemuo 2013, p. 236). The intervention met the traditional requirement of consent of the country concerned. Furthermore, there was near-consensus in ECOWAS and the AU that French forces intervene alongside troops from Mali, Niger, Chad and other predominantly West African countries. In fact, ECOWAS adopted Resolution A/Res. Msc.1/01/13 that expressed gratitude to France for militarily intervening in Mali.[48] In further defence, the Permanent Representative of France at the UN, Gérard Araud, argued that his country's intervention in Mali was a bridging operation required in Mali before deployment of AFISMA. Thus, France's "Serval operation mark[ed] a clear contrast with the nation's modus operandi in the Libyan conflict" (Ping 2014).

The incongruence between China's rhetoric of anti-military intervention in Mali and its actual behaviour, such as voting in favour of a post *facto* authorisation of the intervention,[49] exposed the lack of an elaborate foreign policy position on intervention in foreign conflicts in Beijing. Realising that an outright support of France's intervention in Mali was detrimental to its image in Africa, Beijing continued to emphasise concerns of "a potential abuse of the UN mandate, like what happened in Libya."[50] He Wenping said, "we have some concerns about the intervention… These concerns are based on problems that have arisen as a result of foreign intervention in other countries such as Libya and Côte d'Ivoire. The whole African continent now has a heavy foreign military presence, with increasing numbers of military bases and drones."[51] Arguably, considering what had happened in Libya, if China was serious about raising these concerns it would have vetoed the French military intervention in Mali. However, as it became clear that the French were effective in pushing MNLA and the Islamists back into the Northern Mali hinterland, thus restoring peace and order which was necessary to safeguard the security of Chinese nationals, institutions and investments there, there was an about-turn in China's position. He Wenping retorted that none of Chinese officials had opposed France's intervention in Mali because "the French military intervention was necessary … [since] the situation was urgent."[52] This sudden change in opinion implied that China had improvised or tailored the non-intervention principle in African intrastate armed conflicts in order to protect its immediate interests there.

5.8 Conclusion: Striking a Balance Between Intervention and Non-intervention

Struggling to articulate its role in the Malian intrastate armed conflict in order to secure its interests there vis-à-vis its non-intervention principle, Guo Xueli, charge d'affaires at the Chinese embassy in Bamako, announced that China was considering providing military support to the Malian army. In an interview broadcast on television in Bamako, Guo Xueli said: "we are going to bring our assistance to the extent possible, specifically in the military, where we already have a very old cooperation."[53] Researchers at China's Naval Military Research Institute disagreed—causing another embarrassing discord among foreign policy elites in China. In a commentary published in the *Global Times* soon after, Li Jian and Jin Jing retorted that appeals for China to contribute troops were Western ploys to manipulate China and were against China's principle of non-intervention in the internal affairs of other states. In summation they wrote, "the West will not allow us to get involved in its traditional spheres of influence and deploying troops would also conflict with the guiding principle of our foreign affairs."

Conceding that safeguarding Chinese interests in Mali and the Sahel region could not be entrusted to France and the West, Li Jian and Jin Jing urged Beijing to "look at the situation from a broad, global perspective, and carefully consider how we can safeguard the national interests that China has developed in this complex and disorderly region."[54] China's interests in Mali included investments in agriculture and in the construction industry. Prospecting of oil in Northern Mali, and threats that the Tuareg rebellion could spread to Niger where China has uranium and oil interests, added to Chinese anxiety over the Malian conflict. So, in order to safeguard those broad interests, Li Jian and Jin Jing proposed that China focus on economic construction, livelihood issues and infrastructure development in order to present itself as a "constructive, cooperative and responsible major power."

The discord among Chinese foreign policy makers and academics reflected the underlying conflict between protection of its interests abroad and maintaining the non-intervention principle. In order to balance those two conflicting imperatives, instead of supporting the military in Mali, which would have been interpreted as unilateral military intervention, Beijing opted to actively participate in UN-authorised peacekeeping and peace enforcement operations.[55] When the UN Security Council extended United Nations Multidimensional Integrated Stabilization Mission in Mali's (MINUSMA) mandate "to protect the United Nations personnel, notably uniformed personnel, installations and equipment and ensure the safety, security and freedom of movement of United Nations and associated personnel,"[56] China grabbed the opportunity.

For the second time in its UN peacekeeping history since 1990, China sent a separate protection unit to the UN peacekeeping mission in Mali to protect both Chinese and other international UN personnel. Official Chinese statements referred to them as "security forces" from the PLA, but in actuality they were a combat troop authorised "to take all necessary means to carry out its mandate, within its capabilities and its areas of deployment."[57] Previously, China had "sent a peacekeeping force consisting of 395 personnel to the Mission, of which there is a 170-person police unit, a 155-person engineering unit and a 70-person medical unit"[58] to MINUSMA. However, as put by Earl Conteh-Morgan (2001), the sending of the combat troops by China under the UN peacekeeping and enforcement operation reflected "a shift from a strict adherence to the doctrine of state sovereignty and the principle of non-intervention." In an editorial published in the *South China Morning Post*, Minnie Chan also concurred that "sending troops to Mali, in West Africa, indicated a major shift in China's peacekeeping approach,"[59] which according to Niall Duggan suggested that "China's new intervention policy is bound by the principle of sovereignty and territorial integrity" (Duggan 2018, p. 222).

Seen from the historical trajectory of the 1970s total rejection of international peacekeeping, hesitant participation in the 1980s and then sustained involvement since the 1990s,[60] China's deployment of combat troops in Mali reveals a major shift from the doctors, military observers and engineers it deployed before. That it happened a few months after a similar deployment in South Sudan implies a changing perception in Beijing concerning intervention in foreign intrastate armed conflicts. Previously, China had a policy that the PLA does not operate in foreign territory, as doing so would amount to intervention in those foreign countries. But, as put by Hanauer and Morris (2014, p. 44), there is a growing realisation in Beijing that peacekeeping provides its security and military personnel the opportunity to gain combat experience in volatile countries. Chris Alden and Yixiao Zheng concur. They note that "Chinese participation in UN peacekeeping operations serves a variety of institutional purposes… Given the lack of actual combat experience for the PLA … there is a genuine need for Chinese troops to gain real-life combat experience. In fact, China's White Paper on Defence takes up this concern directly, noting that these missions would contribute to efforts build up the PLA's combat capabilities, since they would allow the PLA troops to gain more real-work combat experience" (Alden and Zheng 2018, p. 53). In addition, UN Peacekeeping operations create avenues for China to subtly protect its nationals and interests abroad in a non-threatening, "non-interventionary" legitimate manner.

Accordingly, China's involvement in the multilateral intervention in Mali has been explained by several authors as being motivated by four factors: (1) securing natural resources; (2) maintaining trade and economic benefits or interests; (3) exposing its troops to international operations and (4) projecting itself as a responsible global power. Empirical evidence suggests the first two points played a major role in China's intervention in Mali, even though it had no significant direct economic interests in Mali to the magnitude comparable to South Sudan and Libya. It has regional economic interests, and strong interests in the Uranium deposits in Northern Mali and parts of Niger adjacent to the parts controlled by the Tuareg in Northern Mali. In Mali, unlike South Sudan and Libya, China's economic and strategic interests were regional such that the risk of transnational spread of the Malian intrastate armed conflict into neighbouring countries where it controlled large stakes in Uranium and other strategic commodities compelled China to intervene and support interventions by other powers in order to control the conflict. "In Mali and the broader Western African region, China is especially interested in protecting Chinese civilians, their economic interests, and to contribute to regional stability as the best condition to protect their economic interests."[61] Thus, as put by Vincenzo Bove et al., "the risk of transnational spread of a civil war can make states with strong interests in a region intervene to contain the conflict" (2015, p. 2). Also, the renewal of oil explorations in Mali gives it an interesting dynamic that has attracted intervention not just from China but also France which previously ignored past Tuareg rebellions that occurred before oil exploration began in the mid-2000s (Bove et al. 2015, p. 3).

As put by Ted Galen Carpenter, the vice-president for Defence and Foreign Policy Studies at Cato Institute, China's intervention in Mali, as is the case in other African countries, is driven by its growing economic stake and increased presence of Chinese nationals, thus "Beijing wants to promote greater stability in countries where businesses and people may be at risk."[62] While this is an immediate motivation, the underlying cause is the gradual change in China's perception of intrastate armed conflict in Mali as being a threat to its interests there. This explains why in just over a year, Chinese engagement in the Malian intrastate armed conflict went from an indifferent and passive response to rebellion and coup d'états in Mali since 1960, to expressions of concern over military takeover of the government by Captain Sanogo; then from support for French military intervention to sending 500 combat troops under the multidimensional and integratedUN peacekeeping operation MUNISMA, which is authorised to take all necessary "steps to prevent the return of armed elements" to northern Mali (Shinn 2013). It appears that as the intrastate armed conflict intensified, the conflict's threat to Chinese interests in Mali and the region increased, compelling Beijing to improvise its intervention accordingly.

Notes

1. Corkin, L 2013, *Uncovering the African agency: Angola's management of China's credit lines*, Routledge, London, p. 2.
2. Roberto, WM, Closs, MB & Ronconi, GBA 2013, 'The situation in Mali', *UFRGS Model United Nations Journal*, vol. 1, p. 73.
3. Ogunsanwo, A 1974, *China's policy in Africa: 1958–71*, Cambridge University Press, Cambridge, p. 216.
4. Boko, SH 2002, *Decentralization and reform in Africa*, Springer, New York, p. 12.
5. 'Premier Chou En-lai in West Africa' 1964, *Peking Review*, no. 5, p. 6, viewed on 5 August 2015, https://www.marxists.org/subject/china/peking-review/1964/PR1964-05.pdf
6. Ibid., p. 7.
7. Azam, J, Morrisson, C, Chauvin, S, & Rospabé, S 1999, *Conflict and growth in Africa, Volume 1: The Sahel*, OECD, Paris, p. 35.
8. People's Republic of China Ministry of Foreign Affairs, 2006, *Mali*, viewed 3 August 2015, http://www.china.org.cn/english/features/focac/183436.htm
9. Ibid.
10. People's Republic of China Ministry of Commerce 2011, *China-Mali bilateral relations*, viewed 3 August 2015, http://english.mofcom.gov.cn/article/zt_fuva/lanmub/201104/20110407524784.shtml
11. People's Republic of China Ministry of Foreign Affairs, 2006, *Mali*, viewed 3 August 2015, http://www.china.org.cn/english/features/focac/183436.htm
12. 'Chinese, Malian presidents meet on bilateral ties', *Xinhua*, 13 February 2009, viewed 9 July 2016, available at: http://news.xinhuanet.com/english/2009-02/13/content_10810437.htm
13. Anda, MO 2000, *International relations in contemporary Africa*, University Press of America, Lanham, p. 218.
14. Zhang, E & Lu, B 2016, 'Terror in Mali and new Chinese perspectives', *Caixin*, 27 January, viewed 19 March 2016, http://english.caixin.com/2016-01-27/100904502.html
15. Shinn, DH 2013, 'China's response to the Islamist threat in Mali', *China-US Focus*, 21 June, viewed 3 February 2016, http://www.chinausfocus.com/peace-security/chinas-response-to-the-islamist-threat-in-mali/
16. Wing, SD 2013, 'Briefing Mali: Politics of a crisis', *African Affairs*, vol. 112, no. 448, p. 476; Boko, SH 2002, *Decentralization and reform in Africa*, Springer, New York, p. 12.
17. Sako, S 2014, *Crisis in Mali: Lessons from an ongoing democratic transition*, Legatum Institute, London, p. 1, 5.

18. Roberto, WM, Closs, MB, & Ronconi, GBA 2013, 'The situation in Mali', *UFRGS Model United Nations Journal*, vol. 1, p. 75.
19. Whitehouse, B 2012, 'The force of action: Legitimizing the coup in Bamako, Mali', *Africa Spectrum*, vol. 47, no. 2–3, p. 94.
20. 'Ibrahim Boubacar Keita wins Mali presidential election', 2013, *BBC*, 13 August, viewed 13 July 2016, http://www.bbc.com/news/world-africa-23677124
21. Small Arms Survey 2013, *Rebel forces in Northern Mali: Documented weapons, ammunition and related materiel*, viewed 6 August 2015, http://www.smallarmssurvey.org/fileadmin/docs/E-Co-Publications/SAS-SANA-Conflict-Armament-Research-Rebel-Forces-in-Northern-Mali.pdf
22. Lunn, J 2012, *Mali in crisis: A political and security overview*, House of Commons, International Affairs and Defence Section, p. 2.
23. Luntumbue, M 2013, 'Crises maliennes: enjeux et défis d'un dialogue national', *Diplomatie*, pp. 80–84.
24. Ogunsanwo, A 1974, *China's policy in Africa: 1958–71*, Cambridge University Press, Cambridge, p. 219.
25. People's Republic of China Ministry of Foreign Affairs 2012, *Foreign Ministry Spokesperson Hong Lei's Regular Press Conference on March 22, 2012*, viewed 8 September 2015, http://www.china-un.org/eng/fyrth/t917058.htm
26. Nuland, V 2012, *Situation in Mali, Press Statement*, United States State Department, viewed 18 September 2015, http://www.state.gov/r/pa/prs/ps/2012/03/186633.htm
27. Hirsch, A 2012, 'The international response to Mali's crisis has been woefully inadequate', *The Guardian*, 13 July, viewed 1 June 2015, http://www.theguardian.com/commentisfree/2012/jul/13/international-response-mali-inadequate
28. Kimani, S 2012, 'SA closes embassy in Mali after coup', *South Africa Broadcasting Corporation (SABC)*, 22 March, viewed 1 June 2015, http://www.sabc.co.za/news/a/7dbb11004a9b656ebdb4ffde3293b68e/SA-closes-embassy-in-Mali-after-coup-20122203
29. People's Republic of China Ministry of Foreign Affairs 2012, *Foreign Ministry Spokesperson Hong Lei's Regular Press Conference on March 23, 2012*, viewed 1 June 2015, http://www.china-embassy.org/eng/fyrth/t921893.htm
30. Shinn, DH 2013, 'China's response to the Islamist threat in Mali', *China-US Focus*, 21 June, viewed 3 February 2016, http://www.chinausfocus.com/peace-security/chinas-response-to-the-islamist-threat-in-mali/
31. People's Republic of China Ministry of Foreign Affairs 2012, *Foreign Ministry Spokesperson Hong Lei's Regular Press Conference on March 23,*

2012, 1 June 2015, http://www.china-embassy.org/eng/fyrth/t921893.htm; 'China condemns Mali coup' 2012, *AFP*, 23 March, viewed 1 June 2015, https://sg.finance.yahoo.com/news/china-condemns-mali-coup-093022233.html

32. People's Republic of China Ministry of Foreign Affairs 2012, *Foreign Ministry Spokesperson Liu Weimin's Regular Press Conference on May 3, 2012*, viewed 1 June 2015, http://www.fmcoprc.gov.hk/eng//zgwjsw/t929329.htm
33. Lando, B 2013, 'Intervention in Mali: Another free ride for China?' *The World Post*, 13 January 2013, viewed 15 January 2016,http://www.huffingtonpost.com/barry-lando/china-business-africa_b_2468659.html
34. Medeiros, E S & Fravel, MT 2003, 'China's new diplomacy', *Foreign Affairs*, Nov/Dec. Issue, viewed 7 April 2014, https://www.foreignaffairs.com/articles/asia/2003-11-01/chinas-new-diplomacy
35. Haenle, P 2013, 'China misses a golden opportunity in Syria', *Financial Times*, 8 October 2013, viewed 8 October 2013, http://carnegietsinghua.org/2013/10/08/china-misses-golden-opportunity-in-syria
36. People's Republic of China Ministry of Foreign Affairs 2012, *Foreign Ministry Spokesperson Hong Lei's Regular Press Conference on March 23, 2012*, viewed 1 June 2015, http://www.china-embassy.org/eng/fyrth/t921893.htm
37. 'China calls for resolution of Mali crisis via dialogue' 2012, *Xinhua*, 29 March, viewed 3 June 2015, http://en.people.cn/90883/7772785.html
38. People's Republic of China Ministry of Foreign Affairs 2012, *Foreign Ministry Spokesperson Hong Lei's Regular Press Conference on March 30, 2012*, viewed 1 June 2015, http://mn.chineseembassy.org/eng/fyrth/t919318.htm
39. Okeke, VOS & Oji, RO 2014, 'United Nations-ECOWAS intervention in Mali-Guinea Bissau: Geo-economic and strategic analysis', *Global Journal of Human-Social Science Research*, vol. 14, no. 3, p. 6.
40. 'Towards intervention in Mali' 2012, *IRIN News*, 2 October, viewed 3 June 2015, http://www.irinnews.org/report/96436/analysis-towards-intervention-mali
41. Okemuo, G 2013, 'The EU or France? The CSDP mission in Mali the consistency of the EU Africa policy', *Liverpool Law Review*, vol. 34, no. 3, pp. 219, 235.
42. Irish, J 2012, 'Mali asks U.N. for "immediate" action on force to recapture north', *Reuters*, 24 September, viewed 6 June 2015, http://www.reuters.com/article/us-un-assembly-mali-idUSBRE88N14B20120924; Dembele, D 2012, 'China offers support to Mali military in fight against Islamists', *Bloomberg*, 26 September, viewed 6 June 2015, http://www.bloomberg.com/news/articles/2012-09-26/china-offers-support-to-mali-military-in-fight-against-islamists

43. UN Security Council 2012, *Resolution 2085, S/RES/2085 (2012)*, 20 December, viewed 6 June 2015, http://www.securitycouncilreport.org/atf/cf/%7B65BFCF9B-6D27-4E9C-8CD3-CF6E4FF96FF9%7D/s_res_2085.pdf
44. United Nations Security Council 2013, *Security Council Press Statement on Mali, SC/10878 AFR/2502*, 10 January, viewed 6 June 2015, http://www.un.org/press/en/2013/sc10878.doc.htm
45. Martin, P & Cohen, D 2011, 'Through Chinese eyes: He Wenping (part 3)', *The Interpreter*, 2 December, viewed 12 June 2015, http://www.lowyinterpreter.org/post/2011/12/02/Through-Chinese-eyes-He-Wenping-%28Part-3%29.aspx
46. He, W 2013, 'Hollande has set alarming precedent for intervention', *Global Times*, 22 January, viewed 12 June 2015, http://www.globaltimes.cn/content/757501.shtml
47. 'Mali's PM calls for foreign intervention' 2012, *Al Jazeera*, 27 September, viewed 16 June 2015, http://www.aljazeera.com/news/africa/2012/09/201292755022310928.html
48. ECOWAS 2013, *Resolution A/RES.MSC.1/01/13 Expressing gratitude to the Republic of France and other ECOWAS partners for their interventions towards the Resolution of the crisis in Mali*, 19 January, viewed 9 June 2015, http://documentation.ecowas.int/download/en/reports/communiques/extraordinary_summit_of_ecowas_heads_of_state_and_government/Gratitude%20to%20France%20on%20Mali.pdf
49. Charbonneau, B & Sears, JM 2014, 'Fighting for liberal peace in Mali? The limits of international military intervention', *Journal of Intervention and Statebuilding*, vol. 8, no. 2–3, p. 7.
50. Sun, Y 2013, 'How China views France's intervention in Mali: An analysis', *Brookings Institution*, 23 January, viewed 9 June 2015, http://www.brookings.edu/research/opinions/2013/01/23-china-france-intervention-mali-sun
51. Musakwa, T 2013, 'Leading Africa expert in China: French military intervention in Mali 'was necessary', *China-Africa Project*, 30 January, viewed 9 June 2015, http://www.chinaafricaproject.com/france-china-mali-he-wenping-cass-beijing/
52. Ibid.
53. Hollis, J 2012, 'China offers military aid to Mali in fight against Islamists rebels', *Atlanta Blackstar*, 26 September, viewed 9 June 2015, http://atlantablackstar.com/2012/09/26/china-offers-aid-to-mali-in-fight-against-islamists-rebels/
54. Li, J & Jin, J 2013, 'China will neither send troops to Mali, nor will it give money: Military says it may help with peacekeeping efforts after the war [中国在马里不出兵也不出钱 军方称战后可以维和]', *SOHU*, 22 January, viewed 9 June 2015, http://mil.sohu.com/20130122/n364250702.shtml

55. United Nations Security Council 2015, *Resolution 2227 (2015)*, 29 June, viewed 5 August 2015, http://www.un.org/en/ga/search/view_doc.asp?symbol=S/RES/2227(2015)
56. United Nations Security Council 2013, *Resolution 2100 (2013)*, 25 April, viewed 5 August 2015, http://www.un.org/en/peacekeeping/missions/minusma/documents/mali%20_2100_E_.pdf
57. United Nations Security Council 2015, *Resolution 2227 (2015)*, 29 June, viewed 5 August 2015, http://www.un.org/en/ga/search/view_doc.asp?symbol=S/RES/2227(2015)
58. People's Republic of China Ministry of Foreign Affairs 2014, *Foreign Ministry Spokesperson Hua Chunying's Regular Press Conference on June 26*, viewed 4 August 2015, http://www.fmprc.gov.cn/mfa_eng/xwfw_665399/s2510_665401/t1169049.shtml
59. Chan, M 2014, 'China's growing peacekeeping commitment to UN shows shift in foreign policy', *South China Morning Post*, 30 May, viewed 30 May 2014, http://www.scmp.com/news/china/article/1521454/chinas-growing-peacekeeping-commitment-un-shows-shift-foreign-policy
60. Hanauer, L. & Morris, LJ 2014, *Chinese engagement in Africa: Drivers, reactions, and implications for U.S. policy*, RAND Corporation, California, p. 44.
61. Netherlands Institute of International Relations, n.d., *China's role in peacekeeping and counter terrorism in Mali*, Clingendael, The Hague, viewed 9 January 2016, http://www.clingendael.nl/event/chinas-role-peacekeeping-and-counter-terrorism-and-counter-violent-extremism-mali
62. Chan, M 2014, 'China's growing peacekeeping commitment to UN shows shift in foreign policy', *South China Morning Post*, 30 May, viewed 30 May 2014, http://www.scmp.com/news/china/article/1521454/chinas-growing-peacekeeping-commitment-un-shows-shift-foreign-policy

Bibliography

Alden, C., & Zheng, Y. (2018). China's changing role in peace and security in Africa. In C. Alden, A. Alao, C. Zhang, & L. Barber (Eds.), *China and Africa: Building peace and security cooperation on the continent* (pp. 39–66). New York: Palgrave Macmillan.

Anda, M. O. (2000). *International relations in contemporary Africa* (p. 218). Lanham: University Press of America.

Bove, V., Gleditsch, K. S., & Sekeris, P. G. (2015). "Oil above water": Economic interdependence and third-party intervention. *Journal of Conflict Resolution*, 1–27. https://doi.org/10.1177/0022002714567952.

Chivvis, C. S. (2016). *The French war on Al Qa'ida in Africa*. Cambridge: Cambridge University Press.

Conteh-Morgan, E. (2001). International intervention: Conflict, economic dislocation, and the hegemonic role of dominant actors. *International Journal of Peace Studies, 6*(2), 33–52.

Duggan, N. (2018). China's new intervention policy: China's peacekeeping mission in Mali. In C. Alden, A. Alao, C. Zhang, & L. Barber (Eds.), *China and Africa: Building peace and security cooperation on the continent* (pp. 209–223). New York: Palgrave Macmillan.

Francis, D. J. (2013). *The regional impact of the armed conflict and French intervention in Mali.* Norwegian Peacebuilding Resource Centre, Oslo. Retrieved July 13, 2016, from http://www.peacebuilding.no/var/ezflow_site/storage/original/application/f18726c3338e39049bd4d554d4a22c36.pdf

Guelke, A. (1974). Force, intervention and internal conflict. In F. S. Northedge (Ed.), *The use of force in international relations* (pp. 99–123). London: Faber.

Hanauer, L., & Morris, L. J. (2014). *Chinese engagement in Africa: Drivers, reactions, and implications for U.S. policy.* California: RAND Corporation.

Kleine-Ahlbrandt, S. T. (2009). Beijing, global free-rider. *Foreign Policy*, 12 November. Retrieved September 3, from https://foreignpolicy.com/2009/11/12/beijing-global-free-rider/

Lecocq, B. (2005). The Bellah question: Slave emancipation, race, and social categories in late twentieth-century Northern Mali. *Canadian Journal of African Studies/Revue canadienne des Ãctudes africaines, 39*(1), 42–68.

Ogunsanwo, A. (1974). *China's policy in Africa: 1958–71.* Cambridge: Cambridge University Press.

Okemuo, G. (2013). The EU or France? The CSDP mission in Mali the consistency of the EU Africa policy. *Liverpool Law Review, 34*(3), 217–240.

Ping, J. (2014). The crisis in Mali. *Harvard International Review*, 22 March. Retrieved September 3, 2018, from http://hir.harvard.edu/article/?a=6033

Roberto, W. M., Closs, M. B., & Ronconi, G. B. A. (2013). The situation in Mali. *UFRGS Model United Nations Journal, 1*, 71–97.

Shaw, S. (2013). Fallout in the Sahel: The geographic spread of conflict from Libya to Mali. *Canadian Foreign Policy Journal, 19*(2), 199–210.

Shinn, D. H. (2013). China's response to the Islamist threat in Mali. *China-US Focus*, 21 June. Retrieved February 3, 2016, from http://www.chinausfocus.com/peace-security/chinas-response-to-the-islamist-threat-in-mali/

Soto-Viruet, Y. (2012). The mineral industries of Mali and Niger. In *U.S geological survey yearbook 2010* (pp. 28.1–28.4). Retrieved September 3, from https://minerals.usgs.gov/minerals/pubs/country/2010/myb3-2010-ml-ng.pdf

Zeng, A. (2014). Strong foundations of friendship. *China Daily*, 7 May. Retrieved September 3, 2018, from http://usa.chinadaily.com.cn/opinion/2014-05/07/content_17489828_2.htm

CHAPTER 6

South Sudan

6.1 Introduction

Still reeling from the devastating effects of Libya's intrastate armed conflict—the loss of billions of dollars' worth of projects and assets, and the biggest evacuation of overseas citizens in its recent history—China found itself confronted by yet another intrastate armed conflict. This time, hardly two years after the Libyan armed conflict and a year after the coup d'état in Mali, the conflict was in South Sudan, Africa's newest nation. To China, South Sudan had been a challenge even before it existed as a sovereign state. The complexity of its war of independence from the Sudan, the subsequent split and then the war between South Sudan and Sudan over oil transit fees and revenue sharing all contributed to making the South Sudan intrastate armed conflict more devastating to China's interests in that country. Chinese oil companies were also still coming to terms with the complexities of working with the two antagonistic Sudans in their interdependent oil sector. Already they had suffered extensive losses due to oil production disruptions during the Juba-Khartoum war hardly a year before. On top of that problem, the intrastate armed conflict between the government of South Sudan and forces loyal to the country's former vice-president Riek Machar threatened to wipe out what was left of the country's oil industry—which is largely dominated by China's own state-owned enterprise CNPC.

O. Hodzi, *The End of China's Non-Intervention Policy in Africa*,
Critical Studies of the Asia-Pacific,
https://doi.org/10.1007/978-3-319-97349-4_6

Apart from economic losses, the crises in Libya and Mali had already exposed the inadequacies of Beijing's foreign policy strategies, especially the efficacy of its non-intervention principle when faced with intrastate armed conflicts in Africa. The stakes were therefore high for Beijing when the South Sudan intrastate armed conflict broke out in December 2013. Just as in Libya, China had invested billions in the South Sudan oil sector. Furthermore, it had to show its citizens as well as other global powers that it was able to handle such situations as a responsible global power. It is upon this background that this chapter explores China's intervention in South Sudan's intrastate armed conflict. This chapter starts by tracing historical relations between China and southern Sudan actors since Sudan's independence in 1956. It then examines China's pragmatic foreign policy strategies, first in transforming its antagonistic relationship with the Sudan People's Liberation Movement (SPLM) into an amiable one, and then in balancing its triangulated relationship with Khartoum and Juba. All in all, the argument advanced in this chapter is that, unlike in the case of Libya and Mali, China's intervention in South Sudan's armed conflict was proactive, deliberate and assertive, suggesting that its perception of African intrastate armed conflicts as threatening to its external economic interests is evolving.

6.2 Background of China-South Sudan Relations

Relations between China and South Sudan are a case of "enemies turning to friends."[1] Antagonism between the two started in 1955 when the southern rebellion against the Khartoum government broke out. The antagonism then ended in 2005 with formation of a government of national unity under the Comprehensive Peace Agreement (CPA)[2] framework. In the course of that 40-year period, two civil wars were fought—with a decade-long peace period (1972–1983) in-between. The first civil war, from 1955 to 1972, was between the government of Sudan and the *Anya-Nya* movement, which represented people of the southern Sudan. After a ten-year-long armistice, in 1983 the second civil war (1983–2005), pitting the government of Sudan against the SPLM, started. In the second civil war, the *Anya-Nya* movement was succeeded by the SPLM in its struggle for greater autonomy and subsequent independence of southern Sudan. That period of southern Sudan's war for self-determination is what Daniel Large refers to as the inimical period of China-South Sudan relations. The amiable period followed the gaining of independence by South

Sudan in 2011, while the period between signing of the CPA in 2005 and South Sudan becoming an independent sovereign state in 2011 marked the transitional period of their relationship from being "enemies to friends." What this long and convoluted historical background of China-South Sudan relations means is that in order to gain a comprehensive understanding of China's intervention in South Sudan's intrastate armed conflict, it is critical to first explore relations between China and southern Sudan's liberation war movements—the *Anya-Nya* and SPLM—within the context of China-Khartoum relations.

On 18 August 1955, four months before independence of the Sudan, the Equatorial Corps, a southern military garrison composed of mainly southern Sudanese soldiers, mutinied against the government of Sudan in protest to what it saw as overconcentration of power in the North, and disenfranchisement of the South. That mutiny marked the beginning of Sudan's first civil war. Southern soldiers who rebelled were joined by others forming a southern Sudan rebel group known as the *Anya-Nya* movement. For 17 years the group fought for greater autonomy and independence of the Christian-animist black Africans in southern Sudan from the "Arab" Muslims in the north. Politically, culturally, and religiously the North identified with the Middle Eastern and North African countries while Southerners were predominantly black Africans identifying with sub-Saharan Africa, particularly their East African neighbours.

Between 1960 and 1972, the North-South intrastate armed conflict became more internationalised. Arab states, and communist countries such as the Soviet Union, East Germany and Yugoslavia, including China, provided the government of Sudan with military weapons. Their support for Sudan was based on two considerations: General Jaafar Mohammed Numayri's communist ideology, and Cold War geopolitical considerations. Britain, being the former colonial power and architect of the political structure that had largely resulted in political and economic alienation of southerners, also supported the government. As foreign powers flocked to render support to Khartoum, the *Anya-Nya* movement struggled to get backing, even from China which at that time supported national wars and liberation war movements in Africa. It was only after the Six-Day war between Israel and Arab countries that the *Anya-Nya* movement started getting meaningful military and administrative assistance from the Israeli government and the Israeli Defence Forces.[3]

China's response to southern Sudan's *Anya-Nya* movement was at odds with its actions in other parts of Africa where it supported liberation war movements fighting for self-determination. Citing constraints from its foreign policy of non-intervention in the internal affairs of other countries, Beijing "never advanced any rhetorical or material support to *Anya-Nya* rebels"[4] even though their struggle met the criteria for a "people's war" similar to what China supported in other African countries.[5] To China, the intrastate armed conflict between the *Anya-Nya* and the government of Sudan was an internal issue that it could not interfere with. Be that as it may, China's actions in other countries negate the "non-intervention in the internal affairs of other states" argument. For example, during the Nigerian civil war, China supported rebels who sought secession of eastern Nigeria ("Biafra") from the Federal Republic of Nigeria.[6] Short of according them diplomatic recognition, the People's Republic of China gave various forms of support and aid to the secessionists,[7] and urged them "to persevere in the struggle and wage a people's war till victory was achieved" (Ogunsanwo 1974, p. 235). Similarly, in Zaire, now known as the Democratic Republic of Congo, China supported opposition groups that fought against the Congolese government following the ouster of Patrice Lumumba in September 1960.[8] Accordingly, Beijing's argument that it was constrained from supporting the *Anya-Nya* by its non-intervention principle was not convincing to southerners.

In addition, "even if China had wanted to support the guerrilla fighters in the south, a rational calculation of interests involved in other areas would have weighed against such support, especially as there was no guarantee of success for the fighters" (Ogunsanwo 1974, p. 174). With no reasonable prospects of success for the *Anya-Nya* rebellion, China was not willing to risk its friendly diplomatic relations with Sudan. But prospects of *Anya-Nya*'s success were by no means the only reason Beijing never extended any assistance to them. The essential reason was that geopolitical considerations and national interests played a critical role in Beijing's selection of which African liberation war movements to support, particularly with regard to Sudan. Its main geopolitical concern was dissipating the Soviet Union's influence in newly independent African countries and undermining Taiwan by increasing the number of African countries it had diplomatic relations with. The *Anya-Nya* movement and its struggle against the Sudanese government were in no way going to assist China in achieving those geopolitical objectives.

In that respect, having established diplomatic relations with China in 1959, and as one of the first four independent African countries to have recognised the People's Republic of China, Sudan was strategic to China's ambitions of increasing its influence in the Middle East and North Africa (MENA) region. Moreover, Sudan's geographical location, as well as its religious and political leaning towards the "Arab-Muslim" MENA countries made it even more instrumental to China's geopolitical expansion objective. Accordingly, supporting a secessionist movement against the Sudanese government would have jeopardised their friendly diplomatic relations and put at risk China's interests in the newly independent North African Arab states of Egypt, Morocco, Algeria and the Arab world in general.[9] So seriously did China take its geopolitical interests and relations with Sudan that when the Democratic Republic of Congo (DRC) threatened to support the southern Sudan rebels, the Chinese government expressed grave concern and "announced *its readiness to help the Sudan* against any foreign intervention aiming at undermining it" (Ogunsanwo 1974, p. 174).

Notwithstanding, the first Sudan civil war ended in 1972 when the *Anya-Nya* movement and the government of Sudan signed the Addis Ababa Agreement. Among other things, the agreement granted regional autonomy to southern Sudan, and incorporated *Anya-Nya* forces into the Sudan Armed Forces (SAF) and government bureaucracy. However, in the late 1970s, President Numayri declared Sudan an Islamic State and introduced Islamic law even in the South—effectively withdrawing southern Sudan's autonomy over its own internal affairs. In addition, when oil and other mineral discoveries were made in areas bordering North and South Sudan, Numayri unilaterally attempted to "redefine the boundaries between North and South, so that the oil rich area around Bentiu, the fertile lands of Renk, together with the nickel and uranium deposits all fall into northern territory" (Scott 1985, p. 69). As it became obvious to southerners and other foreign parties interested in investing in Sudan's mining and energy sector that the major oil and mineral deposits were located in southern Sudan, "oil and its exploration became a burning political issue" (Scott 1985, p. 70). The result was another revolt by southern army officers in May 1983. This time the struggle against the Sudanese government was led by the Sudan People's Liberation Movement/Army (SPLM/A) under the leadership of the charismatic Colonel John Garang de Mobar.[10]

China's policy regarding SPLM/A in the second civil war the same as it was with the *Anya-Nya* in the first civil war. However, the discovery of oil and other valuable mineral resources increased the strategic importance of Sudan to China, further endearing Khartoum to Beijing, and diminishing any possibilities of positive relations between Beijing and SPLM. Chances of Beijing even considering assisting the SPLM were dealt a heavy blow when China's National Oil Companies (NOCs) took advantage of the departure of Western oil companies such as Chevron, Talisman, Lundin and OMV from Sudan due to pressure from their governments and global human rights activists. Chinese NOCs were not bothered by Khartoum's bad human rights record, support for terrorism and perpetration of war crimes and genocide in Darfur, so they quickly grabbed the opportunity and dominated Sudan's oil sector. In fact, Sudan became China's leading foreign oil project; and, as put by Chen Fengying of the China Contemporary International Relations Institute in Beijing, Sudan represented in practice China's strategy of going for oil in places where American and European companies were not present.[11]

As Chinese oil companies expanded their investments in Sudan's oil sector, oil revenue surged. In turn, Khartoum increased its military budget, enabling the SAF to purchase more arms to fight the SPLM. "Prior to the increase in oil revenues in the late 1990s and early 2000s, the Sudan Armed Forces (SAF) had consistently complained about its lack of financial and material means to wage war effectively against the Sudan Peoples' Liberation Movement/Army (SPLM/A)" (Large 2007, p. 4). But with the oil revenue from Chinese oil fields flowing in, China assisted the government of Sudan to set up and operate three military weapon factories near the Sudanese capital city of Khartoum.[12] In addition, China also became Sudan's major weapons supplier. From the early 1990s, China had been supplying Sudan with Scud missiles, ammunition, tanks, helicopters and fighter aircraft.[13] As alleged by the Human Rights First not only did it increase its weapons supply, it also breached an international arms embargo against Sudan by supplying it with light weapons in the years that Khartoum's war against the SPLM intensified.[14] Refuting allegations that China had breached the arms embargo against Sudan, Foreign Ministry spokesman Qin Gang maintained that conventional weapons exported from China to Sudan were of a very limited quantity, constituting a small portion of Sudan's military import.[15] However, the implication was that the growth of Sudan's oil sector as a result of Chinese oil investments became deeply entwined with patterns of violence in South Sudan.[16]

The apparent symbiotic relationship between Chinese oil companies and the government of Sudan made Beijing's claims of non-intervention in Sudan's intrastate armed conflict implausible. As put by Irene Panozzo, "China's foreign tenets of state sovereignty, territorial integrity and non-interference in internal affairs had translated into the defence of Khartoum's position against the southern struggle for self-determination and possible independence" (2015, p. 177). Making things even more complicated for China to profess non-intervention in Sudan is that the SAF often used air strips at the Greater Nile Petroleum Operating Company's (GNPOC) oil installations to launch attacks against the SPLM/A. The Sudanese army, as well as army-backed militias, also provided security to Chinese workers and oil installations located in southern Sudan, where SPLM/A and other groups operated. As a result, the prevailing opinion among ordinary southern Sudanese, SPLM/A and other rebel groups was that China was part of the conflict but fighting on the side of the government of Sudan. Lam Akol, a rebel commander in the Sudan People's Liberation Movement United, who had previously served as Sudan's transportation minister from 1998 to 2002, encapsulated that perception when he said: "the Chinese have every reason not to lose these oil fields, and that is why they are committed to fighting the war by supplying the Sudan government the wherewithal."[17] In concurrence, Deng Awou, a former commander in SPLA, said: "the suffering of the [South Sudan] people is on the hands of the Chinese" (Kline 2010, p. 64).

Southern Sudanese perceptions that China was an active participant in their conflict against the government of Sudan were confirmed by the director of Middle East and North African Studies at Shanghai International Studies University, Professor Zhu Weilie. Professor Zhu argued that in Sudan, China had to balance its interests in order to protect the supply of oil from Sudan, and that meant militarily supporting Sudan's war against the SPLM. The implication was that "during the last ten years of the north-south civil war, China had been considered in the south as the enemy's best friend and financier because of Beijing's investments in Sudan's oil sector, its arms sales to Khartoum and its political backing of the NCP's rule" (Panozzo 2015, p. 177). In light of the above, prior to 2005, China-SPLM relations were as the proverbial "a friend of an enemy is an enemy."

Up until signing of the CPA between SPLM and the government of Sudan, China was unperturbed by SPLM's negative opinions regarding its relations with Khartoum. For Beijing, as long as the government of Sudan guaranteed the security of Chinese oil workers and installations, and as long as the oil was flowing with little or no interruption from SPLM, it did not matter what SPLM or southerners thought. Basically, its strategy was to ignore the Sudanese civil war for as long as it did not interfere with its oil operations—separating, as alluded to by China's deputy foreign minister Zhou Wenzhong, business from politics. In that respect, Beijing considered the SPLM-Khartoum civil war as an internal affair with which it was not in a position to interfere (Kurlantzick 2007, p. 222). In like manner, Zhang Dong, China's ambassador to Sudan, asserted: "China never interferes in Sudan's internal affairs."[18] That exactly is what Khartoum had hoped for from Beijing, especially considering its isolation by Western countries. So, in an interview, Sudan's mining minister Awad Ahmed Al-Jaz said: "[The] Chinese are very nice, they don't have anything to do with any politics or problems. Things move smoothly, successfully. They are very hard workers looking for business, not politics" (Goodman 2004). It was therefore under those circumstances that China consolidated its position as the foremost investor in Sudan's oil industry despite the majority of the oil reserves being in southern Sudan.

6.3 The Genesis of Beijing-SPLM Relations

In 2005, there was a paradigm shift in SPLM and government of Sudan relations, which compelled China to recalibrate its relations with the SPLM. On 9 January 2005, representatives of the two parties appended their signatures to the CPA—not only ending two decades of North-South conflict, but also ushering a new Juba-Beijing-Khartoum triangular political, economic and diplomatic dispensation. As a compilation of several agreements signed between the antagonists from 2002, the CPA covered issues ranging from the sharing of oil wealth between North and South, to setting up of a Government of National Unity comprising the Sudan's Islamist National Congress Party (NCP) and the SPLM. But, most importantly, the agreement made provision for southerners to decide at the end of a six-year transitional period whether to remain united with the North or secede into an independent state. It was the referendum that jolted China into considering establishing contacts with SPLM while maintaining ties with Khartoum.

Although it appeared obvious that southerners would choose secession, the NCP, China and some SPLM leaders hoped for unity of the two Sudans. Considering 70% of Sudan's oil fields were located in southern Sudan and that China had invested in oil fields located in oil-rich Muglad and Melut basins straddling the North-South border,[19] it was mostly out of economic interests that Khartoum and China preferred the *status quo*—that is, one-Sudan-two-systems under NCP's dominance. In particular, as noted by Anne Itto, SPLM's deputy secretary general, following her visit to China in August 2009, Chinese government officials feared that if southern Sudan seceded, there would be insecurity and that their assets in the form of pipelines and billions worth of other oil investments would go to waste.[20] Apart from oil interests, secession of southern Sudan risked putting "China's foreign policy tenets under strain" (Panozzo 2015, p. 179)—it threatened to plunge Beijing into a quagmire of how to strategically court SPLM after so many years of hostilities between them.

On the other hand, driven by a nationalist agenda, John Garang, leader of SPLM and First Vice-President in Sudan's Government of National Unity, advocated an all-inclusive united Sudan[21] under the "one-country-two-systems model, whereby the people of southern Sudan would decide after six years whether to remain within the Sudan or to opt for independence."[22] Although he appeared to have given the responsibility of choosing either secession or unity to southerners, Garang was as unapologetic in his support for a united Sudan as he was in his opposition to secession. In one of his passionate speeches he declared in 1992 that "if anybody wants to separate even in the North, we will fight him because the Sudan must be one. It should not be allowed to disintegrate or fragment itself."[23] On that, Garang was on the same page with China because in meetings with SPLM, Chinese government officials emphasised continued support for "Sudan's peace, unification and development."[24] However, the vision of a "one-country-two-systems" model in Sudan that John Garang propelled gradually faded[25] with his death in a helicopter crash on 30 July 2005. Salva Kiir Mayardit, the man who succeeded him as both SPLM leader and Sudan's First Vice-President in the Government of National Unity, was pro-secessionist, and therefore the campaign for southern Sudan independence gained momentum.[26]

6.4 China-SPLM Courtship: Building Relations for a Mutually Beneficial Future?

Prior to the CPA, SPLM and China had no known official contact. Official relations between China and the Sudan had all along been north-centric and focused on Khartoum-Beijing engagement. "Khartoum tightly controlled relations with China from the centre, largely preventing its ally from having contact with the Southern rebels" (International Crisis Group 2012, p. 2). Conceivably for economic and geopolitical considerations, Beijing reciprocated by exclusively dealing with the Khartoum government (Large 2011b, p. 54). The second reason is that China claimed to have been precluded from making official contact with the SPLM because its relations with Sudan were dictated by the Five Principles on Peaceful Co-existence, in particular the non-interference principle which prohibits China from making contact with opposition political parties in other countries. What China's leaders could not acknowledge publicly is that its dominant position in Sudan's energy sector was necessitated by their support for the Khartoum government in its fight against the SPLM. It was also because China chose to be indifferent to atrocities committed against southerners and Darfurians by Sudan on the basis "that business should not be mixed with politics."[27] The third reason, as put by China's Defence Minister Cao Guangchuan, is that China's PLA attached greater significance to developing relations and cooperating with the Sudanese army on various issues.[28] To that end, China supplied Khartoum with heavy military weapons that in turn were used to fight SPLM in the south. Because of that, there existed a sense of animosity and distrust between China and SPLM as they begun to forge official relations after signing of the CPA.

Be that as it may, the CPA had two major enablement elements that fostered relations between Beijing and the SPLM. The foremost factor is that it "legitimised the SPLM and opened the door for the gradual expansion of SPLM-CPC political relations" (Shinn and Eisenman 2012, p. 80). The second factor is that the agreement enabled SPLM to transform itself from being a liberation movement into a political party, able and "willing to consider engagement with all potential external partners, including China" (Large 2011a, p. 165). On the basis of these two factors, it was almost obvious to Beijing that under the CPA framework, the autonomous government of southern Sudan could become a direct partner "without obliging China to formally deny sovereignty and territorial integrity tenets or alter its warm relations with Khartoum" (Panozzo 2015, p. 177). Accordingly, as soon as the CPA came into effect, Beijing initiated "a 'dual-track' diplomatic policy, allowing the establishment of warm 'quasi-diplomatic' relations with Juba well before the south's independence" (Panozzo 2015, p. 179).

The first official contact between Beijing and SPLM occurred in March 2005, two months after NCP and SPLM signed the CPA. John Garang, leader of southern Sudan and First Vice-President in the central unity government, delegated Salva Kiir, his deputy, to lead an SPLM delegation that included the head of SPLM economic section Akwal Manak, chairman of the SPLM external relations Niyal Dheng, and SPLM spokesmen Samson Kwaje and Pagan Amum to visit China.[29] In Beijing, they discussed possible economic cooperation between Beijing and Juba. Perhaps due to the untimely death of John Garang, the next official visit by SPLM bureaucrats to China happened two years after the first one. President Hu Jintao, who was on a state visit to Khartoum in February 2007, met with and invited Salva Kiir to visit China.[30] Five months later, in July 2007, the Chinese Foreign Ministry spokesperson Qin Gang announced the arrival in Beijing of Salva Kiir in his capacity as First Vice-President of the Government of Sudan.[31] It turned out to be a watershed moment in Beijing-SPLM relations. In a subtle but unyielding warning to the Chinese to take relations with SPLM seriously, Salva Kiir, during his meetings with Chinese government officials in Beijing, emphasised the concentration of Sudan's oil reserves in southern Sudan territory and the high probability of its secession from northern Sudan. The veiled warning worked because thereafter there was a re-orientation in China's policy regarding the SPLM, leading to more contact and interaction between the two.[32] In the following year, 2008, the special envoy of the Chinese government and Assistant Foreign Minister Zhai Jun visited Juba and opened China's first Consulate in southern Sudan,[33] which according to China's first ambassador in South Sudan, Li Zhiguo, played "an important role in strengthening close exchanges and enhancing cooperation."[34] Thus, as put by Daniel Large, the CPA was "turning enemies into friends" (Large 2011a, p. 165).

Despite several official visits between SPLM and Chinese government and Chinese Communist Party (CCP) officials, Beijing remained hesitant to fully engage SPLM before the independence of southern Sudan. The hesitancy continued even after China was given several assurances by SPLM that in terms of the CPA, Juba "was entitled to establish its own relations with external actors for purposes of developing economic relations in support of development programs in Southern Sudan" (Schumann 2010, p. 111). Substantive political relations still remained slow in coming. Instead, it was private Chinese businesses and state-owned oil companies already in southern Sudan that took the lead in developing economic and trade relations with Juba. The situation, however, changed when China recognised the inevitability of a split of the two Sudans as the referendum date drew closer. In October 2010, less than three months before the January 2011 South Sudan referendum, a CCP delegation visited Juba to gather more information about South Sudan, but clearly China was preparing for a new phase of relations between China and an SPLM-led South Sudan.

In subsequent meetings between the SPLM and China, several Chinese government officials including Du Yanling, director-general in the International Department of the Communist Party of China Central Committee, assured the SPLM that China stood "ready to provide help to the south within its capacity, no matter what changes will be in the situation" (Boswell 2010). Considering China's investments in southern oil fields, the future South Sudan government's dependence on oil revenue from Chinese-operated oil fields, and the latent capacity of China to use its veto against South Sudan's independence, SPLM officials were delighted to get China's re-assurance just before the referendum. In return for Beijing's re-assurance, Anne Itto, SPLM's deputy secretary general and South Sudan's minister of agriculture, promised Beijing that "southern Sudan will continue to respect China's interests in the region."[35] According to the *Sudan Tribune*, the SPLM secretary general Pagan Amum also weighed in, saying, "the largest investment in southern Sudan today is Chinese… They have invested billions of dollars in the oil sector, and have a large number of Chinese workers in the oil fields… We have given assurances to the Chinese leadership delegation to protect the Chinese investments in southern Sudan, and are desirous to see more investment in the future."[36]

Notwithstanding the mutual assurances, there was no telling what the populist government of South Sudan would do if there was public pressure to punish China for supporting Khartoum regimes during their struggle for independence. Although the CPA guaranteed security of existing oil contracts, senior SPLM officials and commanders commonly made reference to re-negotiation and revocation of contracts held by Chinese companies as punishment for its role in disenfranchisement of southerners and lack of support for SPLM's struggle for independence. One of those senior figures was Anne Itto. In an interview with the *Sudan Tribune*, she claimed to have warned the Chinese government that "if they want to protect their assets, the only way is to develop a very strong relationship with the government of Southern Sudan, respect the outcome of the referendum, and then we will be doing business." She then added: "the role of China [is] to support peace in Sudan, especially to prevail on the NCP not to take the country back to war again."[37] With the intention of protecting its investments in the South, the Chinese government intensified engagements with SPLM in the run-up to the referendum, pledging to respect its choice for self-determination.

What all this meant is that China's attention to and recognition of the SPLM was necessitated by an overwhelming need to hedge against risk of losing its oil investments in South Sudan. Thus, as aptly put by Daniel Large, "in engaging the Government of Southern Sudan… Beijing responded to political imperatives flowing from investment protection concerns produced by established interests as part of an apparent hedging strategy geared toward the possibility of Southern secession" (2009, p. 624). In concurrence, Ben Simpfendorfer suggests that in engaging the SPLM, China reflected "a growing recognition that political regimes can and do change, and so opening dialogue with opposition movements in conflict with the state is a pragmatic means of hedging against this risk" (Simpfendorfer 2015, p. 211). Meanwhile, even though SPLM would have wanted to take revenge against Beijing, it was precluded from doing so by its overwhelming need for oil revenue from Chinese-operated oil fields to finance the new state. Hence, "the fact that China already had invested heavily in oil infrastructure made China an attractive partner" (Antony and Jiang 2014, p. 80). For that reason, South Sudan found it imperative to cultivate normal diplomatic relations with China in order not to disrupt the flow of oil revenue. All things considered, both the SPLM and Beijing's responses to the political imperatives occasioned by independence of South Sudan were linked to mutual concerns about investment projections and hedging against risk rather than political considerations.

6.5 China in Independent South Sudan

By the time South Sudan gained independence on 9 July 2011, China had made significant strides in strengthening bilateral relations.[38] Together with the United States, Britain and Russia, it was one of the first major powers to recognise the new country as an independent sovereign state. To confirm Beijing's position regarding South Sudan's statehood, its foreign minister Yang Jiechi announced China's official recognition and setting up of diplomatic relations with South Sudan at the ambassadorial level on the basis of the Five Principles of Peaceful Coexistence.[39] The Joint Communique on the Establishment of Diplomatic Relations between the two countries was signed by Jiang Weixin, China's minister of housing and urban-rural development, on behalf of the Chinese government; on that same day, the Chinese embassy in South Sudan was opened.[40] To consummate the new diplomatic relations, Foreign Minister Yang Jiechi paid his first official visit to independent South Sudan barely a month after South Sudan's independence; speaking to the South Sudanese press, he re-stated China's commitment to "step-up friendly exchanges with South Sudan at all levels, particularly at the high-level, to cement political mutual trust."[41]

Beside state-to-state relations, SPLM-CPC party-to-party relations assumed critical importance in dissipating past antagonistic misgivings and in fostering "mutual political trust" between Juba and Beijing. Before South Sudan's independence, party-to-party ties were restricted and took place within the confines of the Sudanese government of national unity and in the ambit of the CPA framework. In essence, China had been restricted from expanding relations with SPLM due to domestic political tensions between SPLM and NCP, which compelled it to prefer expanding relations with the NCP.[42] Starting from 2005, several SPLM delegations had visited China initially in their capacity as officials of the government of national unity, and then after independence as SPLM officials. In 2009, Riek Machar, deputy chairman of SPLM and vice-president of the government of South Sudan, met Zhou Yongkang, a member of the Standing Committee of the CPC Central Committee Political Bureau, to discuss strengthening of ties between SPLM and CPC.[43] After independence, the two political parties signed a memorandum of understanding to strengthen friendship and cooperation, enabling the Communist Party of China to "receive up to three delegations from SPLM each year to learn about China's experiences in various areas."[44]

The first SPLM delegation to visit China under the SPLM-CPC memorandum of understanding left for China in April 2011. Comprising ten SPLM officials on a study tour aimed at understanding CPC's experiences in party building, the delegation was led by Antipas Nyok, SPLM's Secretary for Political Affairs and Mobilization. In China, the delegation met several officials of the CPC, including Chao Weidong, deputy-director at the International Department of the Central Committee of the CPC.[45] Six months later, another SPLM delegation led by its SecretaryGeneral Pagan Amum visited China in October 2011. During their visit, they met with Wang Jiarui, head of the International Department of the Communist Party of China. At the meeting, Pagan Amum emphasised the importance his country placed on developing friendly ties with China, and he reiterated South Sudan's commitment to promoting "bilateral pragmatic cooperation in areas such as oil, agriculture, minerals, housing construction, telecommunications, water conservation and transportation."[46] Speaking of the SPLM-CPC relations, Li Changchun, a Standing Committee member of the Political Bureau of the Communist Party of China, underscored the significance of building and consolidating relations between SPLM and CPC to suit the new circumstances, that is, the independence of SPLM-led South Sudan.[47]

The third SPLM delegation was funded by the CPC to visit China and learn about its financial management systems. Accordingly, a ten-member delegation comprising ten finance ministers from ten states of South Sudan as well as high-ranking SPLM officials such as Atem Garang, the party's chief whip in the National Legislative Assembly, visited China on the study tour.[48] The final SPLM delegation to visit China in 2012 was led by Political Bureau members Mark Nyipouch and Akol Paul and was comprised of 14 members of the SPLM National Liberation Council and the SPLM General Secretariat. The ten-day study tour was aimed at learning various aspects of CPC governance, and the delegates attended lectures at the China Executive Leadership Academy Pudong and met Vice-Minister of the International Department of the CPC Li Jinjun as well as Director-General of the North Africa Bureau of the International Department of the CPC Central Committee, Du Yanling. They also visited leading Chinese firms such as Huawei, Sinohydro and the Export-Import Bank of China.[49]

Despite the party-to-party and state-to-state exchanges, it was not long before China and South Sudan's commitment to cementing mutual political trust was tested. The first major test was a dispute between Juba and Khartoum over oil transit fees, which quickly escalated into an interstate armed conflict resulting in South Sudan shutting down oil production, cutting its oil supplies to Beijing and effectively jeopardising billions of dollars in Chinese investments.[50] Within that context, President Salva Kiir honoured an earlier invitation to visit President Hu Jintao in Beijing.[51] In his meeting with President Hu as well as other "Chinese leaders, including Chairman of the Standing Committee of the National People's Congress Wu Bangguo, and Vice Premier, member of the Standing Committee of the Political bureau of the CPC Central Committee Li Keqiang"[52] Kiir urged China to rein in Khartoum and assist in resolving the conflict to ensure continued flow of oil revenue that South Sudan desperately needed.

In addition to seeking China's intervention in resolving the conflict with Khartoum, President Kiir conveniently used the Beijing trip to send President Omar al-Bashir a veiled message that Khartoum no longer had monopoly over relations with Beijing as before—Juba was also getting closer to Beijing.[53] As put by South Sudan's Information Minister Barnaba Marial Benjamin, relations between China and the two Sudans were like "a case of a husband with two wives… [So] there must be some sort of relationship where China can play a positive role, even in this war" (Raghavan 2012). In response, President Hu confirmed China's role in taking concrete action to resolve the conflict. Trying not to play into the Khartoum-Juba feud, President Hu stated that for China, "the top priority is to actively cooperate with the mediation efforts of the international community and halt armed conflict in the border areas."[54] On balance, it appeared President Kiir's visit to Beijing in the midst of Juba's interstate armed conflict with Khartoum reflected a new confidence in South Sudan's bilateral relations with China and the strategic importance he placed on China and its ability to resolve conflicts with Sudan, but that situation was soon tested when South Sudan descended into an intrastate armed conflict of its own.

6.6 China and the South Sudan Intrastate Armed Conflict

As the Khartoum-Juba intrastate armed conflict subsided, on 15 December 2013 South Sudan plunged into an intrastate armed conflict of its own, pitting the government of South Sudan led by President Salva Kiir against forces loyal to the country's former Vice-President Riek Machar. What started as a political power struggle between President Salva Kiir and his deputy Riek Machar soon took on an ethnic character—dividing the new country's two largest ethnic groups—the Dinka and the Nuer—as well as the Sudan People's Liberation Army (SPLA). The subsequent suspension and arrest of senior SPLM officials[55] on charges of an attempted coup split the SPLM into two main factions and escalated the conflict further. Having escaped arrest in Juba, Riek Machar declared himself leader of what then became known as the Sudan People's Liberation Movement in Opposition (SPLM-IO), and his forces soon took over control of major parts of Jonglei, Upper Nile and Unity States.

As the armed conflict gained momentum, the targeting of oil installations in the Unity State and Upper Nile State dragged China, South Sudan's major oil investor and leading importer, into the conflict. At the time of independence, oil revenue had represented 98% of South Sudan's government revenue, the majority of which came from Chinese-operated oil fields. With 3.5 billion barrels of proven oil reserves as of 1 January 2014, three times more than Sudan's oil reserves, CNPC had a major stake in both Dar Petroleum Operating Company (DPOC), 41% share, and 40% stake in GNPOC, both of which were the major oil companies operating in South Sudan. Sinopec, another Chinese oil company, had a 6% stake in DPOC.[56] As the conflict raged on, oil fields in Unity and Upper Nile States were forced to shut down, and the Adar Yale oilfield came under attack on several occasions. Some of the shutdown was too sudden and done so hurriedly that machinery was damaged and oil leakages were severe, causing both economic losses and damage to the environment. Apart from the loss of 45,000 bbl/day of oil produced at fields in Unity State, "satellite images taken by the U.S.-funded Satellite Sentinel Project show[ed] that key oil infrastructure was severely damaged, including oil storage tanks and manifolds" (EIA 2014, p. 11). As a result, production dropped by almost 20%,[57] a further decline from an already reduced percentage of South Sudan's oil to China's total imports when it split from the Sudan and when it voluntarily shut down oil production during the interstate armed conflict with Sudan. To enhance oil production and also avoid further disruption due to conflicts with Khartoum, CNPC had reluctantly agreed to partner with the government of South Sudan to construct refineries at Bentiu, located in Unity State, and in "South Sudan's second planned 10,000-bbl/day refinery in the Upper Nile near Blocks 3 and 7,"[58] but that too was forced to stop due to the armed conflict—causing innumerable financial and production loses to the Chinese oil companies.

Besides oil companies, Chinese private and state-owned construction and telecommunication companies that were active in South Sudan found their operations threatened by the armed conflict as well. Media reports suggested that more than 100 Chinese companies were operating in South Sudan in sectors related mainly to petroleum, construction and communications as of December 2013. Chinese companies with major projects in South Sudan at the time of the armed conflict included Zhong Hao Overseas, a privately owned construction firm in Beijing that built water and sanitation facilities, housing for government officials, a hospital and roads in South Sudan. State-owned Sinohydro Corporation dominated South Sudan's engineering and infrastructure sector; it also "provided a water plant in Western Equatorial, a thirty-seven kilometer road in Malakal and high-way construction linking the North and the South" (Antony and

Jiang 2014, p. 81). China Harbour Engineering Corporation also won the tender to renovate Juba International Airport, estimated to cost US$1.6 billion. ZTE set up the Sudan Telecommunication Network through a 200 million euro loan from China's Exim Bank.[59] Although some of these companies had completed their projects at the time of the intrastate armed conflict, the majority were forced to either suspend operations or scale down operations.

In what also turned out to be a repeat of the Libyan experience for Chinese workers, several Chinese companies had to evacuate their workers. For example, CNPC "evacuated 97 of its staff in December 2013 because of the conflict."[60] Its main oilfields located in the Unity State and Upper Nile State regions under the control of Riek Machar's rebel fighters were forced to shut down.[61] Not wanting to endanger its workers, in December 2013 the CNPC announced that it was arranging for the orderly evacuation of its workers from the affected oil fields to Juba, the capital city of South Sudan.[62] As put by Luke Patey, the evacuation of CNPC workers from the Palogue oilfield, South Sudan's largest oilfield, led to extensive loses in production, affecting both the South Sudanese government and the CNPC because, as he puts it, "without Chinese and other foreign staff, a limited number of South Sudanese technicians … struggled to keep production levels high."[63]

Aside from economic implications of the intrastate armed conflict in South Sudan on China's interests, the conflict tested President Hu's commitment to upholding peace and security in Africa. At the Fifth Ministerial Conference of the Forum on China-Africa Cooperation China had presented the Beijing Action Plan (2013–2015), underscoring for the first time the importance of China-Africa cooperation in the fields of peace and security. A specific clause in the Beijing Action Plan had acknowledged efforts of the Chinese government's Special Representative for African Affairs, who actively engaged in mediation efforts in Africa's hotspots, and "welcomed his continued constructive role in peace and security endeavors."[64] It is not a coincidence that the commitment was made hardly a year after the Libyan crisis that resulted in loss of significant Chinese investments. In many respects the commitment to peace and security in Africa signified a growing recognition in China that intrastate armed conflicts threatened its economic interests on the continent. The South Sudan intrastate armed conflict was therefore the first test to China's commitment to assist in resolving peace and security issues in Africa.

6.7 Unilateral and Multilateral Mediation

In comparison with its ambivalent intervention in the Libyan intrastate armed conflict, China's intervention in South Sudan was multidimensional, assertive and definite in its character. But it also set it on collision with its non-intervention principle which precluded it from having contact with opposition parties in other countries, especially in warring situations. Soon after the South Sudan armed conflict broke out on 15 December 2013, China's ambassador to Ethiopia convened a clandestine meeting at an Addis Ababa hotel with representatives of rebel forces led by Riek Machar. To support claims that the meeting was supposed to be off the record, Zhong Jianhua, China's special envoy to South Sudan, claimed in a CCTV interview on 1 March 2014 that China had not made direct contact with the rebels. He said, "we also sent messages to the rebels indirectly, telling them we are willing to help achieve peace… I'm now trying to establish direct contact with the rebels to express our will and help achieve a ceasefire."[65] An IGAD official privy to that meeting questioned its motive especially considering the timing, absence of South Sudan government officials and, of course, China's non-intervention principle.[66] He then opined that from his assessment China wanted to gather information and intelligence on the goings on in South Sudan in order to determine its course of action rather than mediate the conflict. But still that might not have been the reason to meet only rebel forces in Ethiopia rather than officials of the government of South Sudan. In fact, China wanted to get assurances from Riek Machar that Chinese assets located in oilfields his forces had captured on the onset of the conflict were going to be secure. In concurrence with that assessment, the International Crisis Group notes that China circumvented IGAD in order to protect its oil infrastructure, which was its main priority.

The IGAD official was not far from the truth because it was not coincidental that the Addis Ababa hotel meeting was convened soon after President Kiir publicly admitted losing control of Unity State and Jonglei amidst claims by Riek Machar that his forces had taken over control of oil fields in Unity and Upper Nile States.[67] The Upper Nile and Unity State oilfields were strategic to China, the government of Sudan and Riek Machar rebel forces because, as put by Luke Patey, these fields represented 80% and 20% of oil production, respectively. It is those considerations that propelled the Chinese ambassador in Ethiopia to convene an urgent meeting with Riek Machar's representatives. For Riek Machar, capturing those oilfields, and announcing that he was going to divert oil revenue from Juba and deal directly with Sudan in implementing the cooperation agreements[68] which China helped broker between Juba and Khartoum in 2012, increased his bargaining leverage, weakened President Salva Kiir's government by cutting its main source of revenue and attracted the attention of the Chinese government.[69] A report published by the International Crisis Group alleges that because of the strategic importance of Unity State and Upper Nile State oil fields to China and Khartoum, "their security was the subject of an independent agreement between Sudan, China and the SPLM/A-IO" (International Crisis Group 2015, p. 11). If this is true, then by its own definition, China intervened in South Sudan's war by entering into an agreement with a rebel force for protection of its oil fields there.

In less than two weeks of the intrastate armed conflict, China announced the arrival of its official special envoy in South Sudan. Zhong Jianhua, a diplomat considered to have extensive knowledge of Sudan and South Sudan, was appointed China's special envoy to South Sudan. In a statement, Foreign Ministry spokeswoman Hua Chunying said, "on behalf of the Chinese government, special envoy Zhong Jianhua is currently visiting South Sudan and neighboring countries, and actively carrying out mediation efforts. China is willing to continuously enhance communication and coordination with all the relevant parties and jointly push for restoration of stability in South Sudan."[70] After wide consultations with parties to the conflict and other relevant stakeholders such as the Khartoum government, Zhong Jianhua, China's Special Representative on African Affairs, participated in talks held in January 2014. As a result of the negotiations, a ceasefire agreement between South Sudan's warring parties was signed. In fact, Harry Verhoeven maintains that "Chinese diplomats took unprecedented steps in publicly pressuring belligerents Salva Kiir and his former vice-president, Riek Machar, to sign a ceasefire agreement" (2014, p. 64). Thrilled by the role Beijing had played in brokering the ceasefire agreement, Zhong Jianhua confirmed the role Chinese diplomats from embassies in Ethiopia and South Sudan had played in early attempts towards ceasefire monitoring. He then proudly acknowledged the emerging engagement of China in peace and security initiatives in Africa, admitting that though it was a new experience for China, it was indeed "a new chapter for Chinese foreign affairs,"[71] seemingly implying that starting with South Sudan, China was ready to take on the challenge of actively resolving African conflicts.

No sooner than the ink was dry on the ceasefire agreement, fighting resumed. Riding on its ceasefire-brokering experience, China offered to continue mediating between the warring parties, risking a further departure from its non-interference principle.[72] But this time, partly in response to queries that China was departing from its non-intervention tradition due to its engagement with rebel forces in South Sudan, Beijing creatively fitted its South Sudan mediation within its foreign policy objective of sustaining its economic development and protecting overseas citizens and national interests from external threats, of which the intrastate armed conflict in South Sudan was one. The explanation was sufficient to silence dissenting voices in China, assured Chinese citizens worried that the Libyan experience was going to be repeated in South Sudan and, most importantly, pre-empted concerns in Africa that China was moving towards unilateral intervention in African countries' internal affairs. Nevertheless, in pursuit of the above national core objectives, Foreign Minister Wang Yi visited Addis Ababa, where the fighting parties were holding peace negotiations and urged both parties to cease fighting and resolve the conflict amicably. BBC reported that he even offered to mediate personally between the warring sides.[73]

The swiftness with which China's ambassador to Ethiopia organised the meeting with Riek Machar's representatives, and with which Beijing dispatched its special envoy to Juba, suggests a rising concern in Beijing that "challenges confronting peace and security in Africa are increasing"[74] and that the increase in conflict and insecurity was detrimental to its economic interests. Given that China now considered the emerging intrastate armed conflict in South Sudan as threatening its economic interests in that country, it was increasingly prepared to take rapid and decisive intervention even though the action would violate its own non-intervention principle. Secondly, the sending of a special Chinese envoy to South Sudan reflected a new perception within China's foreign policy elites that it was imperative to engage all parties in a conflict, whether government or opposition, in order to mitigate losses. This meant even engaging opposition forces first, particularly in cases where they controlled areas with strategic Chinese assets and investments. In many respects this policy implied a substantial shift in how China perceived intrastate armed conflicts in African countries—from a perception that they were non-threatening, as was the case in early stages of the Libyan armed conflict, to a perception that they threatened its core national interests in foreign countries, thus requiring assertive intervention.

6.8 China as the "Go-Between"

Leaving nothing to chance, China convened several meetings with parties to the South Sudan conflict. In July 2014, South Sudan's Vice-President and Deputy Chairman of SPLM, James Wani Igga, requested a meeting with China's foreign minister Wang Yi in Beijing. From their discussions at that meeting, it emerged that the South Sudanese vice-president intended on giving assurances to Beijing that "the government of South Sudan will do its utmost to ensure the safety of the Chinese personnel and agencies in the country"—a concern which Foreign Minister Wang Yi had also raised in their meeting. In response, Foreign Minister Wang Yi expressed China's willingness to continue playing a positive role in resolving the conflict in South Sudan.[75] Following on to that meeting, Foreign Minister Wang Yi met members of the SPLM-IO in Beijing in September 2014, before meeting South Sudan government representatives in Khartoum.

In January 2015, China, working with IGAD, facilitated a meeting of foreign ministers and representatives of the warring parties in Khartoum. Although the meeting was held under the "Special Consultation in Support of South Sudan Peace Process" led by IGAD, and was attended by foreign ministers of China, Sudan, South Sudan and Ethiopia, as well as representatives of Riek Machar, China was praised for facilitating the meeting. South Sudan's foreign minister Barnaba Benjamin said: "we welcome the Chinese role which we believe is constructive and seeks to resolve the conflict in South Sudan. We hope these consultations, under China's patronage, would put the IGAD-led negotiations on the right track."[76] Seyoum Mesfin, Ethiopia's former foreign minister, said that "we have no objection toward what China is doing and we believe the Chinese role is in the interest of the initiative of the IGAD which is patronizing the negotiations between the two conflicting parties in South Sudan."[77] The same sentiments were echoed by Sudan's foreign minister Ali Karti, who pointed out that "China, as a permanent member state in the UN Security Council, is working seriously and sincerely to end the conflict in South Sudan. It is acting on the base of its international responsibility and not to achieve any other purposes."[78]

A common feature in China's mediation efforts and bilateral talks with South Sudan's government officials and rebel forces was a persistent demand that they guarantee protection of Chinese assets and economic investments and ensure security of Chinese nationals in South Sudan. For instance, following reports of rebel attacks on oil facilities, the SPLA announced on 16 January 2015 that "oil fields have never been under control of anybody. They have been under full control of the SPLA and the general command assured the oil companies in Adar and Faluj that their protection is 100%."[79] That announcement was a response to pressure from China, which requested assurances at a meeting held in Khartoum between China's minister of foreign affairs, Wang Yi, and his South Sudan counterpart, Barnaba Mariel Benjamin, that South Sudan was committed to protecting Chinese oil workers and assets. According to the South Sudanese minister of information, Michael Makuei Leuth, the meeting was initiated by China and was attended by members of the opposition faction led by former president Riek Machar. After the meeting, Barnaba Mariel Benjamin told the media that "I think it is a very, very important thing—that they (the Chinese) wanted the assurance that these institutions are properly protected and not to be destroyed in any form."[80] This statement corroborates an African Union (AU) diplomat's suspicions that this "supposedly IGAD-led" meeting was a parallel meeting organised and designed by China to protect its oil investments in South Sudan.[81]

The assurances were a confirmation of earlier commitments made in a telephone conversation on 14 April 2014 when the foreign minister of South Sudan, Barnaba Marial Benjamin, and China's minister of commerce, Gao Hucheng, stated that Chinese enterprises were still operating in South Sudan and that the "government of South Sudan could take forceful measures to protect the safety of lives and properties of Chinese people and enterprises, and render more facilitation and guarantee for business production and operation, material transportation and personnel entry and exit."[82] The use of language that seemed to imply a command to South Sudan's government to "take forceful measures to protect" Chinese citizens and property in South Sudan suggests a more assertive China confident in its ability to pressure the Juba government into protecting its economic interests.

As noted by Luke Patey, the author of *The New Kings of Crude: China, India and the Global Struggle for Oil in Sudan and South Sudan*, "China's concern regarding South Sudan is not energy per se but rather a corporate investment from a major Chinese national oil company in jeopardy."[83] Luke Patey's argument is supported by Zhong Jianhua, who reiterated several times in an interview with CCTV that both the South Sudanese government and the rebels should "ensure the safety of Chinese citizens and firms," adding that "we [China] told them to try to avoid damaging the property of Chinese firms, and ensure the safety of Chinese citizens under any circumstances."[84] Foreign Minister Wang Yi had refuted that notion, arguing that "China's mediation of South Sudan issues is completely the responsibility and duty of a responsible power, and not because of China's own interests."[85] While that might have been part of the reason, the major one was, as he had admitted earlier, that "war and conflicts hurt the oil industry…, an area in which China, Sudan and South Sudan have worked closely together."[86] He had then argued that the mediation was not meant for China to benefit alone—it was a mutually beneficial intervention aimed at getting a win-win solution to the conflict. It was therefore apparent that China's efforts towards direct mediation in the South Sudan civil war "runs parallel with its interest in ensuring billions of oil investments in South Sudan stay out of harm's way."[87] This policy was confirmed by Ma Qiang, the Chinese ambassador to South Sudan, who told Reuters that "we have huge interests in South Sudan so we have to make a greater effort to persuade the two sides to stop fighting and agree to a ceasefire."[88]

To force the belligerents in South Sudan to cease fire, and in a marked departure from its "business is business, no politics involved" precept that it had used to defend selling weapons to Khartoum in its war against the SPLM before South Sudan's independence, China took a more assertive but firm position. It halted the sale of US$38 million worth of arms to the South Sudan government by its state-owned arms manufacturer China North Industries Group Corporation. According to Lan Kun, an attaché at the Chinese embassy in Juba, the Chinese government decided it was not appropriate to deliver the consignment of weapons to South Sudan; therefore, "No more weapons are heading to South Sudan… There are some media reports that were alleging that the Chinese government was behind this business operation and wants to undermine this peace process. That is totally untrue."[89] The Chief of the Political Section in the Embassy of China in South Sudan reiterated that since the beginning of the armed conflict, the Chinese government ordered all relevant Chinese companies to halt weapons trade with South Sudan (Gridneff 2014). The *South China Morning Post* described China's embargo on sale of weapons to Juba by Chinese companies as indicative of a swap of "its reserved diplomacy for a hands-on approach to help resolve a … rebellion in South Sudan that threatens Beijing's oil investments."[90]

6.9 Multilateral Intervention: Leveraging on IGAD

To legitimise its bilateral engagements and mediation efforts, China leveraged its participation in the IGAD mediation processes. Chinese ambassador to the AU Xie Xiaoyan worked with the US, Norwegian and UK diplomats within the IGAD-PLUS plus framework to resolve the conflict. As reported in the *South China Morning Post* in June 2014, "the permanent Chinese presence at the Addis Ababa talks and their frequent lobby chats and closed-door consultations with diplomats from the United States, Britain and Norway—the main Western backers of newly independent South Sudan—show China's more proactive approach."[91] The coming in of China to renewed IGAD-PLUS[92] mediation talks following breach of the Cessation of Hostilities Agreement between Salva Kiir forces and Riek Machar's "will provide as well the much-needed role of China as it has strategic economic interest in South Sudan" (Deng 2015).

According to an official at IGAD, China has been actively involved in the mediation process in South Sudan in different capacities and to a varying extent, but not always to the satisfaction of other IGAD-PLUS members, that is, the United States, Norway and Britain. A Norwegian diplomat in Addis Ababa who had extensively participated in the IGAD meetings on South Sudan dismissed China's presence in IGAD as a nuisance, arguing that it never meaningfully contributed to the peace deliberations. He suspected China came to the meetings only to gather information and keep abreast with latest developments in South Sudan's conflict. The same remarks were recounted by several IGAD officials and diplomats from Uganda. For instance, in an interview, an IGAD high-ranking official complained that although China was heavily involved in the mediation process and peace monitoring mechanism and had seconded some Chinese officials to be part of the peace monitoring mechanism, it provided funds off the record to rebels to protect its investments. Her argument was that China was in IGAD simply to protect its oil investments. However, she quickly added that Kenya, Ethiopia, Sudan and Uganda also had interests in South Sudan. Nevertheless, as admitted by Zhong Jianhua, mediation of African intrastate armed conflicts in multilateral frameworks was still a new experience for China, and therefore it often could not balance its interests with the common objective of bringing peace to South Sudan.

6.10 Multilateral Intervention: UN Peacekeeping as a Platform

To complement its mediation and bilateral engagements with South Sudan belligerents, China used its position in the UNSC to leverage its influence on multilateral interventions. Previously, China had sent engineers, doctors and other non-combat personnel as part of the United Nations Advance Mission in the Sudan, and the UN Mission in South Sudan (UNMISS) as from 9 July 2011. But an announcement that China had agreed to send battalion troops under the auspices of the UN was probably the most significant intervention made by China in South Sudan's civil war. The PRC minister of foreign affairs, Wang Yi, reported at the High-Level Meeting on U.N. Peacekeeping that:

> China will send a 700-strong infantry battalion to the UN Mission in South Sudan (UNMISS). This will be the first Chinese infantry battalion to participate in a peacekeeping mission. China is considering sending helicopters to the UN Peacekeeping Operation. This would be the first-ever involvement of Chinese airmen in a peacekeeping mission. China is ready to send more civilian policemen, including forensic experts and criminal detectives, to peacekeeping operations. China will continue to support, to the extent of its ability, efforts to strengthen peacekeeping capacity building of African countries, including the establishment of African Capacity for Immediate Response to Crises (ACIRC).[93]

According to the PRC Defence Commander Wang Zhen, the battalion deployed to South Sudan in 2014 was "equipped with drones, armored infantry carriers, antitank missiles, mortars, light self-defense weapons, bulletproof uniforms and helmets, among other weapons."[94] Several media reports suggested that the deployment was meant to protect Chinese oil workers and facilities in South Sudan. This was probably true because the UN Security Council Resolution extended the mandate of UNMISS to include protecting and deterring violence against civilians, including foreign nationals and oil installations. However, as reported in *The Wall Street Journal*, Chinese troops under the UNMISS peacekeeping "are now concentrated not in oil rich states, but in Wau of Western Bahr el Gazel state" (Zhou 2014). Notwithstanding this fact, threats to its economic interests and citizens in South Sudan were a dominant motivation for China's deployment of the combat troops under the United Nations Peacekeeping Mission.

6.11 Conclusion

The case of South Sudan suggests that China's foreign policy strategy, non-interference principle and perception of African intrastate armed conflicts as threatening to its national interests are evolving. In addition, its ability to transform hostile relations with South Sudan during the struggle for its independence since 1955 into friendly or at least workable relations in 2005 and its intervention in South Sudan's intrastate armed conflict reflect two essential points regarding the non-intervention principle: Foremost, the non-intervention principle is designed to protect China from foreigners meddling in its internal affairs; and secondly, it is meant to enable China to gain competitive advantage against rival powers[95] and woo potential partners, particularly in the developing world. China's relations with South Sudan reflect the efficacy of that strategy when it is applied with pragmatism. As stated earlier, China's intervention behaviour in South Sudan was guided by "a distilled pragmatism that serves the country's direct interests."[96] Together with the mutual benefit and win-win rhetoric, the non-interference principle in the case of South Sudan was a "little more than a camouflage concealing China's private interests and the pursuit of profoundly different goals."[97] In this context, it would be simplistic to talk of China's foreign policy being guided by the principle of non-interference, when in effect "it has never remained a passive on-looker when its interests are at stake"[98]; furthermore as noted by Ma Qiang, the Chinese ambassador to South Sudan, in an Al Jazeera interview in June 2014, "non-interference does not mean standing by when people of a country are facing disaster."[99] For that reason, the question that should pre-occupy scholars is not whether China interferes in the domestic affairs of African states or not, but when it does and what forms interference takes and with what consequences. This is a critical departure from the current dominant discourse on China's non-interference principle vis-à-vis its external behaviour in Africa.

Earlier on, it was argued that China takes a pragmatic approach to protecting its national interests abroad. It was suggested that the approach is wrapped up in abstract and ambiguous statements of policy that are aimed at enhancing its foreign behaviour manoeuvrability and "ability to maintain the policy of noninterference which facilitated business with various countries."[100] By seeking to maintain its cordial relations with developing countries such as South Sudan that are riddled with political instability while at the same time safeguarding its national interests (Chinese nationals and companies operating in those countries), China's intervention is camouflaged in the non-interference rhetoric, which allows it to intervene in the internal armed conflict in South Sudan in a non-threatening manner. It should be noted that SPLM has in the past been suspicious of China and Chinese oil companies whom they regarded as accomplices of the Khartoum government; for instance, in February 2012, South Sudan deported an official of CNPC for failing to abide by its regulations. China thus had to tread carefully.

Undeniably, as security threats faced by Chinese companies and nationals working in politically volatile countries became grave, China is being compelled to devise more strategies of protecting its foreign interests. That does not mean that China's non-interference principle is evolving; rather, it suggests that it is becoming more useful in securing China's direct interests vis-à-vis the contemporary risks threatening China's national interests. As noted by Zhong Jianhua, there has been "no change of policy as Beijing had now realised that tackling conflicts had become necessary for advancing Beijing's historical policy of promoting African development."[101] In employing the non-interference principle as a tool for securing its interests abroad, the actual security strategies of intervention are the ones that are evolving. Compared to the security strategies of Africa's traditional partners such as the United States and the European Union, China's strategies are still "comparatively far less developed."[102] Furthermore, the extent of China's engagement in peace and security in Africa is still unclear.[103] Consequently, there is need to "examine the challenges that both policies face, in terms of the need to adjust to the ever-changing national, continental and global environments"[104] and to explore the motivations and objectives for China's non-interference principle in Africa.

Responding to questions raised by readers of the *China Daily* newspaper, Li Shaye, Director-General of African Affairs in the Chinese Ministry of Foreign Affairs, on 27 February 2013 admitted that "with the expanding cooperation between China and Africa, China's interests in Africa are growing bigger and bigger, so political unrest in Africa will be affecting China to a much bigger extent."[105] The cumulative effect is that despite a strong official adherence to non-intervention, China's stance on intervention in foreign countries is undergoing a process of softening (Kassim 2014, p. 35). A major responsibility of a great power is, according to Yan Xuetong, the ability to protect its national interests and citizens in foreign countries. The conflict that China was confronted with in Libya was the mounting need to protect its foreign interests and nationals with its emphasis on adherence to the principle of non-intervention in the Libyan conflict. But because protecting one's interests and citizens in another country entails intervening in the affairs of that country, there was a dilemma in China's "direct involvement in, and responses to, international crises, conflicts and their resolutions" (Kassim 2014, p. 32). Hence, as China recalibrates its perception of threats emanating from intrastate armed conflicts in its African partners, it is also re-thinking how it should best respond to crises in those countries.

Notes

1. Large, D 2011, 'Southern Sudan and China: Enemies into friends?' in D Large & LA Patey (eds.), *Sudan looks east: China, India and the politics of Asian alternatives*, James Currey, New York, pp. 157–175.
2. The Comprehensive Peace Agreement was an amalgamation of six agreements signed between 2002 and 2004 by the Government of Sudan and the Sudan People's Liberation Movement/Army. The following constituted the CPA: (1) The Protocol of Machakos (20 September 2002); (2) The Protocol of Security Arrangements (25 September 2003); (3) The Protocol of Wealth Sharing (7 January 2004); (4) The Protocol of Power-Sharing (26 May 2004); (5) The Protocol of the Resolution of Conflict in Southern Kordofan/Nuba Mountains and the Blue Nile States (26 May 2004); (6) The Protocol on the Resolution of Conflict in Abyei (26 May 2004). Source: United Nations Mission in Sudan n.d., *The background of Sudan's Comprehensive Peace Agreement*, viewed 23 January 2016, https://unmis.unmissions.org/Default.aspx?tabid=515
3. Poggo, SS 2009, *The first Sudanese civil war: Africans, Arabs, and Israelis in Southern Sudan, 1955–1972*, Palgrave Macmillan, London, p. 1.
4. Large, D 2011, 'Southern Sudan and China: Enemies into friends?' in D Large & LA Patey (eds.), *Sudan looks east: China, India and the politics of Asian alternatives*, James Currey, New York, p. 159.
5. Ogunsanwo, A 1974, *China's policy in Africa: 1958–71*, Cambridge University Press, Cambridge, p. 72.
6. Larkin, BD 1973, *China and Africa, 1949–1970: The foreign policy of the People's Republic of China*, University of California Press, California, p. 178.
7. Porter, BD 1986, *The USSR in Third World conflicts: Soviet arms and diplomacy in local wars 1945–1980,* Cambridge University Press, Cambridge, p. 91.
8. Larkin, BD 1973, *China and Africa, 1949–1970: The foreign policy of the People's Republic of China*, University of California Press, California, p. 180.

9. Ogunsanwo, A 1974, *China's policy in Africa: 1958–71*, Cambridge University Press, Cambridge, pp. 236–237.
10. Biel, MR 2003, 'The civil war in Southern Sudan and its effect on youth and children', *Social Work & Society,* vol. 1, no. 1, pp. 119–127.
11. Goodman, PS 2004, 'China invests heavily in Sudan's oil industry; Beijing supplies arms used on villagers,' *Washington Post*, 23 December, viewed 7 February 2016, http://www.washingtonpost.com/wp-dyn/articles/A21143-2004Dec22.html
12. Kline, J 2010, *Ethics for international business: Decision-making in a global political economy,* Routledge, London, p. 64.
13. Human Rights Watch 1998, 'Sudan: Global trade, local impact—Arms transfer to all sides in the civil war in Sudan', *Human Rights Watch*, vol. 10, no. 4 (A), p. 37, viewed 7 February 2016, https://www.hrw.org/sites/default/files/reports/sudan0898%20Report.pdf
14. Human Rights First 2008, *Investing in tragedy: China's money, arms, and politics in Sudan*, viewed 18 February 2016, https://www.ciaonet.org/attachments/14585/uploads
15. Consulate-General of China in San Francisco 2008, *Foreign ministry spokesperson Qin Gang's remarks on the accusation of China as the largest light weapons provider to Sudan*, viewed 10 February 2016, http://www.chinaconsulatesf.org/eng/xw/t416292.htm
16. Large, D 2007, 'Arms, oil and Darfur: The evolution of relations between China and Sudan', *Small Arms Survey,* no. 7, p. 4.
17. Goodman, P.S 2004, 'China invests heavily in Sudan's oil industry; Beijing supplies arms used on villagers,' *Washington Post*, 23 December, viewed 7 February 2016, http://www.washingtonpost.com/wp-dyn/articles/A21143-2004Dec22.html
18. 'Chinese Ambassador: Sino-Sudanese cooperation in full swing' 2007, *Xinhua*, 1 February, viewed 10 February 2016, http://www.china.org.cn/english/infernational/198553.htm
19. Anthony, R & Jiang, H 2014, 'Forum: Security and engagement: the case of China and South Sudan', *African East-Asian Affairs,* no. 4, p. 80.
20. 'SPLM gives assurances on Chinese oil investments in South Sudan' 2010, *Sudan Tribune*, 15 October, viewed 11 February 2016, http://www.sudantribune.com/spip.php?article36612
21. 'Text: Garang's speech at the signing ceremony of S. Sudan peace deal' 2005, *Sudan Tribune*, 10 January, viewed 11 February 2016, http://www.sudantribune.com/spip.php?article7476; Idris, A 2013, *Identity, citizenship, and violence in two Sudans: Reimagining a common future,* Palgrave Macmillan, London, p. 98; Malwal, B 2015, *Sudan and South Sudan: From one to two*, Palgrave Macmillan, London, p.xi.

22. United Nations Security Council 2005, *Sudan Peace Agreement signed 9 January 2005 historic opportunity, Security Council told*, UN Security Council Press Release, 8 February, viewed 11 February 2016, http://www.un.org/press/en/2005/sc8306.doc.htm
23. Garang, J 1992, 'Speech by John Garang, 9 April 1985, following downfall of Nimeiri', in M Khalid (ed.), *The call for democracy in Sudan*, Kegan Paul International, Cardiff, p. 137.
24. 'Sudan expects China's continued support' 2007, *Xinhua*, 19 July, viewed 10 February 2016, http://www.china.org.cn/english/international/217629.htm
25. Patey, L 2014, *The new kings of crude: China, India, and the global struggle for oil in Sudan and South Sudan*, Hurst, London, p. 217.
26. Brosché, J 2008, 'CPA – New Sudan, old Sudan or two Sudans? – A review of the implementation of the Comprehensive Peace Agreement' in UJ Dahre (ed.), *Post-conflict peace-building in the Horn of Africa*, Lund University, Lund, p. 235.
27. Whalley, J 2011, *China's integration into the world economy*, World Scientific, New Jersey, p. 235.
28. Kitissou, M, McGarrah, J & Kablan, PG 2010, 'Ethics in foreign-policy making: US and China's approach to the crisis in Darfur, Sudan', in M Ndulo & M Grieco (eds.), *Failed and failing states: The challenges to African reconstruction*, Cambridge Scholars Publishing, Newcastle, p. 48; 'Chinese, Sudanese senior military leaders hold talks' 2007, *Xinhua*, 5 April, viewed 12 February 2016, http://www.china.org.cn/english/international/206101.htm
29. 'High ranking SPLM delegation visits China' 2005, *Sudan Tribune*, 18 March, viewed 29 January 2016, http://www.sudantribune.com/spip.php?article8613
30. 'President Hu invites Sudan's Salva Kiir to visit China' 2007, *Sudan Tribune*, 3 February, viewed 14 February 2016, http://www.sudantribune.com/spip.php?article20078
31. Consulate-General of the People's Republic of China in San Francisco 2007, *Sudanese First Vice President to visit China*, 12 July, viewed 16 January 2016, http://www.chinaconsulatesf.org/eng/xw/t339574.htm
32. Large, D 2012, 'Between the CPA and southern independence: China's post-conflict engagement in Sudan', *South African Institute of International Affairs*, Occasional Paper No. 115, p. 15.
33. People's Republic of China Ministry of Foreign Affairs 2008, *Special envoy of the Chinese government and Assistant Foreign Minister Zhai Jun visits Sudan successfully*, 4 September, viewed 16 January 2016, http://www.fmprc.gov.cn/mfa_eng/wjdt_665385/wshd_665389/t511195.shtml

34. Embassy of China in South Sudan 2011, *Sino-South Sudan relation opens a new chapter, bilateral cooperation benefits the two peoples*, viewed 16 January 2016, http://ss.chineseembassy.org/eng/sbjw/t864347.htm
35. Boswell, A 2010, 'China pledges to boost southern Sudan ties after secession vote', *Bloomberg*, 14 October, 15 January 2016, http://www.bloomberg.com/news/articles/2010-10-14/china-pledges-to-boost-southern-sudan-ties-after-january-vote-on-secession
36. 'SPLM gives assurances on Chinese oil investments in South Sudan' 2010, *Sudan Tribune*, 15 October, viewed 13 February 2016, http://www.sudantribune.com/spip.php?article36612
37. Ibid.
38. According to a report by International Crisis Group, between September 2011 and May 2011, there were eight high-level bilateral exchanges between Beijing and CCP officials and SPLM leaders in the South Sudan government (see: International Crisis Group 2012, *China's new courtship in South Sudan*, Africa Report No. 186, p. 6., viewed 30 May 2015, http://www.crisisgroup.org/~/media/Files/africa/horn-of-africa/sudan/186-chinas-new-courtship-in-south-sudan.pdf).
39. Embassy of People's Republic of China in South Sudan 2011, *China recognizes independence of South Sudan*, viewed 6 March 2015, http://ss.chineseembassy.org/eng/sbjw/t838441.htm
40. Embassy of People's Republic of China in South Sudan 2012, *Sino-Sudan political exchanges*, 23 November, viewed 6 March 2015, http://ss.chineseembassy.org/eng/sbgx/zjjw/
41. China's Foreign Ministry in Hong Kong 2011, *Foreign Minister Yang Jiechi's written interview with South Sudan press*, 9 August, viewed 6 March 2015, http://www.fmcoprc.gov.hk/eng/zgwjsw/t847127.htm
42. Shinn, DH & Eisenman, J 2012, *China and Africa: A century of engagement,* University of Pennsylvania Press, Philadelphia, p. 81.
43. 'Senior CPC official hails China-Sudan relations' 2009, *Xinhua News Agency*, 18 November, viewed 10 February 2016, http://en.people.cn/90001/90776/90883/6817075.html
44. 'SPLM officials, finance chiefs in China' 2012, *SPLM Today*, 6 September, viewed 11 February 2016, http://www.splmtoday.com/index.php/news-mainmenu-2/691-splm-officials-finance-chiefs-in-china
45. 'SPLM delegation visits China' 2011, *SPLM Today*, 20 April, viewed 11 February 2016, http://phpmyadmin.splmtoday.com/index.php/component/index.php?option=com_content&view=article&id=606:splm-delegation-visits-china&catid=1:latest&Itemid=2
46. 'China, South Sudan vow to advance bilateral ties' 2011, *Xinhua*, 20 October, viewed 11 February 2016, http://ss.chineseembassy.org/eng/sbjw/t869369.htm

47. 'CPC to forge stronger bonds with South Sudan's ruling party, says CPC senior leader', *Xinhua* 21 October, viewed 11 February 2016http://ss.chineseembassy.org/eng/sbjw/t869768.htm
48. 'SPLM officials, finance chiefs in China' 2012, *SPLM Today*, 6 September, viewed 11 February 2016, http://www.splmtoday.com/index.php/news-mainmenu-2/691-splm-officials-finance-chiefs-in-china
49. 'SPLM leaders complete study tour of China' 2012, *SPLM Today*, 12 December, viewed 8 February 2016, http://www.splmtoday.com/index.php/news-mainmenu-2/700-splm-leaders-complete-study-tour-of-china
50. Raghavan, S 2012, 'South Sudan's president visits China during crisis', *The Washington Post*, 24 April, viewed 1 March 2016, https://www.washingtonpost.com/world/africa/south-sudans-president-visits-china-during-crisis/2012/04/24/gIQAowXKfT_story.html
51. China's Foreign Ministry in Hong Kong 2011, *Foreign Minister Yang Jiechi's written interview with South Sudan press*, 9 August, viewed 6 March 2015, http://www.fmcoprc.gov.hk/eng/zgwjsw/t847127.htm
52. Embassy of People's Republic of China in South Sudan 2012, *Sino-Sudan political exchanges*, 23 November, viewed 6 March 2015, http://ss.chineseembassy.org/eng/sbgx/zjjw/
53. Raghavan, S 2012, 'South Sudan's president visits China during crisis', *The Washington Post*, 24 April, viewed 1 March 2016, https://www.washingtonpost.com/world/africa/south-sudans-president-visits-china-during-crisis/2012/04/24/gIQAowXKfT_story.html
54. Saiget, R 2012, 'S. Sudanese President Kiir accuses Khartoum gov't of declaring 'war'', *The China Post*, 25 April, viewed 19 November 2014, http://www.chinapost.com.tw/international/africa/2012/04/25/338993/S-Sudanese.htm
55. The suspended SPLM leaders included the following: SPLM secretary general Pagan Amum Okech and several former ministers, including Oyay Deng Ajak (investment); Gier Choung Aloung (internal affairs); Majak D'Agoot (deputy defence); John Luk Jok (justice); Cirino Hiteng (culture); Deng Alor Koul (foreign affairs); Madut Biar (telecommunications) and Kosti Manibe (finance); as well as the former ambassador to the United States Ezekiel Lol Gatkuoth and former Lakes state Governor Chol Tong Mayay.
56. Energy Information Administration 2014, *Country analysis brief: Sudan and South Sudan*, U.S. Energy Information Administration, 3 September, viewed 6 September 2014, https://www.eia.gov/beta/international/analysis_includes/countries_long/Sudan_and_South_Sudan/sudan.pdf
57. Wu, Y 2014, 'China's oil fears over South Sudan fighting', *BBC Chinese*, 8 January, viewed 8 January 2014, http://www.bbc.co.uk/news/world-africa-25654155

58. Energy Information Administration 2014, *Country analysis brief: Sudan and South Sudan*, U.S. Energy Information Administration, 3 September, viewed 6 September 2014, https://www.eia.gov/beta/international/analysis_includes/countries_long/Sudan_and_South_Sudan/sudan.pdf
59. Wang, X & Lu, X 2014, 'Investment in South Sudan: The opportunity and the challenge coexist', *People's Daily*, April 16, viewed 24 July 2015, http://en.people.cn/102774/8599301.html; Embassy of People's Republic of China in the Republic of Zimbabwe 2011, *China announces diplomatic ties with South Sudan*, 9 July, viewed 6 March 2015, http://www.chinaembassy.org.zw/eng/xwdt/t841090.htm
60. '97 Chinese workers evacuated from South Sudan to Khartoum' 2013, *People Daily*, 25 December, viewed 27 December 2013, http://english.peopledaily.com.cn/90883/8495532.html
61. 'S. Sudan provides assurances for safety of Chinese oil workers' 2015, *Sudan Tribune*, 15 January, viewed 16 January 2015, http://www.sudantribune.com/spip.php?article53658
62. Rose, A & Chen, A 2013, 'China to evacuate South Sudan oil workers to capital', *Reuters,* December 20, viewed 20 December 2013, http://uk.reuters.com/article/2013/12/20/southsudan-unrest-china-idUKL3N0JZ24K20131220
63. Patey, L 2014, 'South Sudan: fighting could cripple oil industry for decades', *Sudan Tribune*, 28 January, viewed 29 January 2014, http://www.sudantribune.com/spip.php?article49741
64. FOCAC 2012, 'The Fifth Ministerial Conference of the Forum on China-Africa Cooperation Beijing Action Plan (2013–2015)', *FOCAC*, 23 July, viewed 10 October 2013, http://www.focac.org/eng/zxxx/t954620.htm
65. 'Chinese envoy urges protection of citizens & firms in S. Sudan' 2014, *CCTV*, 1 March, viewed 1 March 2014, http://english.cntv.cn/program/newsupdate/20140103/100797.shtml
66. Interview, IGAD Conflict Analyst, 28 August 2015. Addis Ababa, Ethiopia.
67. 'Salva Kiir: 'We lost control over Unity State and Jonglei' 2013, *Radio Tamazuj (Juba)*, December 23, viewed 24 December 2013, https://radiotamazuj.org/en/article/salva-kiir-%E2%80%98we-lost-control-over-unity-state-and-jonglei%E2%80%99
68. 'Ex-VP Machar says forces will divert oil revenues from Juba' 2013, *Sudan Tribune*, 23 December, viewed 24 December 2013, http://www.sudantribune.com/spip.php?article49298
69. Patey, L 2014, 'South Sudan: fighting could cripple oil industry for decades', *Sudan Tribune*, 28 January, viewed 29 January 2014, http://www.sudantribune.com/spip.php?article49741
70. 'China sends envoy to South Sudan to push peace talks' 2013, *Voice of America*, 27 December, viewed 28 December 2013, http://www.

voanews.com/content/reu-china-sends-envoy-south-sudan-push-peace-talks/1818388.html
71. Martina, M 2014, 'South Sudan marks new foreign policy chapter for China: Official', *Reuters*, 11 February, viewed 12 February 2014, http://www.reuters.com/article/us-china-southsudan-idUSBREA1A0HO20140211
72. Walker, B 2012, 'China's uncomfortable diplomacy keeps South Sudan's oil flowing', *China Dialogue*, November 26, viewed 25 May 2015, https://www.chinadialogue.net/article/show/single/en/5378-China-s-uncomfortable-diplomacy-keeps-South-Sudan-s-oil-flowing
73. Wu, Y 2014, 'China's oil fears over South Sudan fighting', *BBC Chinese*, 8 January, viewed 8 January 2014, http://www.bbc.co.uk/news/world-africa-25654155
74. FOCAC 2012, 'The Fifth Ministerial Conference of the Forum on China-Africa Cooperation Beijing Action Plan (2013–2015)', *FOCAC*, 23 July, viewed 10 October 2013, http://www.focac.org/eng/zxxx/t954620.htm
75. People's Republic of China Ministry of Foreign Affairs 2014, *Wang Yi: China and South Sudan enjoy relations of mutual trust, mutual support and mutual cooperation*, 3 July, viewed 3 July 2014, http://www.fmprc.gov.cn/mfa_eng/wjb_663304/zzjg_663340/xybfs_663590/xwlb_663592/t1171504.shtml
76. 'China-supported consultations reactivate peace process in S.Sudan' 2015, *China Daily*, 13 January, viewed 14 January 2015, http://usa.chinadaily.com.cn/world/2015-01/13/content_19304551_2.htm
77. Ibid.
78. 'China-supported consultations in Khartoum reactivate peace process in South Sudan', *Xinhua*, 13 January, viewed 13 January 2015, http://news.xinhuanet.com/english/china/2015-01/13/c_133915537.htm
79. 'South Sudan army says oil fields under full protection' 2015, *Sudan Tribune*, January 18, viewed 19 January 2015, http://www.sudantribune.com/spip.php?article53675
80. S. Sudan provides assurances for safety of Chinese oil workers' 2015, *Sudan Tribune*, 15 January, viewed 16 January 2015, http://www.sudantribune.com/spip.php?article53658
81. Interview with AU diplomat in Addis Ababa, Ethiopia.
82. People's Republic of China Ministry of Commerce 2014, *Minister Gao Hucheng holds telephone talks with South Sudan's Minister of Foreign Affairs and International Cooperation on bilateral ties and cooperation*, 6 April, viewed 9 April 2014, http://english.mofcom.gov.cn/article/newsrelease/significantnews/201404/20140400553492.shtml
83. Feng, B 2014, 'China to send its first infantry troops to U.N. Mission in South Sudan', *New York Times*, December 23, viewed 6 January 2015, http://sinosphere.blogs.nytimes.com/2014/12/23/china-to-send-its-first-infantry-troops-to-u-n-mission-in-south-sudan/?_r=0

84. 'Chinese envoy urges protection of citizens & firms in S. Sudan' 2014, *CCTV*, 1 March, viewed 1 March 2014, http://english.cntv.cn/program/newsupdate/20140103/100797.shtml
85. 'China's motive in South Sudan?' 2015, *Al Jazeera*, January 23, viewed 23 January 2015, http://www.aljazeera.com/programmes/insidestory/2015/01/china-motive-south-sudan-20151131954550 2114.html
86. 'Visit celebrates 'priceless' friendship' 2015, *China Daily*, February 16, viewed 16 February 2015, http://www.chinadaily.com.cn/m/touchroad/2015-01/22/content_19379710.htm
87. Porter, T 2014, 'Oil behind China's UN Peacekeeping troop deployment to South Sudan', *International Business Times,* 23 December, viewed 23 December 2014, http://www.ibtimes.co.uk/oil-behind-chinas-un-peacekeeping-troop-deployment-south-sudan-1480770
88. Jorgic, D 2014, 'China takes more assertive line in South Sudan diplomacy', *Reuters*, 5 June, viewed 5 June 2014, http://uk.reuters.com/article/2014/06/05/uk-southsudan-china-insight-idUKKBN0EG01Z20140605
89. Gridneff, I 2014, 'China halts arms sale to South Sudan after NORINCO shipment', *Bloomberg*, 30 September, viewed 16 October 2015, http://www.bloomberg.com/news/articles/2014-09-29/china-halts-weapons-sales-to-south-sudan-after-norinco-shipment
90. 'China adopts a more hands-on approach to the conflict in South Sudan' 2014, *South China Morning Post*, 10 June, viewed 16 October 2015, http://www.scmp.com/news/china/article/1528859/china-adopts-more-hands-approach-conflict-south-sudan
91. Ibid.
92. IGAD-PLUS members include the African Union (AU), United Nations (UN), European Union (EU), the Troika (the United States, the UK and Norway), China and the IGAD Partners Forum (IPF). The IPF includes major IGAD donors—Austria, Belgium, Canada, Denmark, France, Greece, Germany, Ireland, Italy, Japan, the Netherlands, Norway, Sweden, Switzerland, the UK, the United States, European Commission (EC), International Organisation for Migration (IOM), United Nations Development Program (UNDP) and the World Bank.
93. People's Republic of China Ministry of Foreign Affairs 2014, *Wang Yi: China firmly supports UN peacekeeping operations and has always taken an active part in them',* 27 September, viewed 3 July 2014, http://www.fmprc.gov.cn/mfa_eng/zxxx_662805/t1195527.shtml
94. 'China sends infantry battalion for UN peacekeeping', *Xinhua*, 22 December 2014, http://www.chinadailyasia.com/nation/2014-12/22/content_15205971.html
95. Gill, B, Huang, C, & Morrison, JS 2007, 'Assessing China's Growing Influence in Africa', *China Security*, vol. 3, no. 3, p. 7.

96. Halper, S 2012, *The Beijing Consensus: Legitimizing authoritarianism in our time*, Basic Books, New York, p.xvi.
97. Mohan, G & Power, M 2009, 'Africa, China and the 'new economic geography of development', *Singapore Journal of Tropical Geography*, vol. 30, no. 1, p. 25.
98. Adem, S 2010, 'The Paradox of Chinas Policy in Africa', *African and Asian Studies*, vol. 9, no. 3, p. 341.
99. 'China seeks bigger footprint in South Sudan' 2014, *Al Jazeera*, 22 June, viewed 23 January 2015, http://www.aljazeera.com/video/africa/2014/06/china-seeks-bigger-footprint-south-sudan-201462210433020240.html
100. Holslag, J 2009, 'China's new security strategy for Africa', *Parameters* vol. 39, no. 2, p. 25.
101. Fabricius, P 2014. 'Beijing's peacemaking efforts in South Sudan.' *Institute for Security Studies*, 6 November, viewed 21 December 2014, http://www.issafrica.org/iss-today/beijings-peacemaking-efforts-in-south-sudan
102. Kambudzi, AM 2013, 'Africa and China's non-interference policy: Towards peace enhancement in Africa', in MG Berhe and H Liu (eds.), *China-Africa Relations: Governance, Peace and Security*, Institute for Peace and Security Studies, Addis Ababa, p. 31.
103. Alden, C & Large, D 2013, 'China's Evolving Policy towards Peace and Security in Africa: Constructing a New Paradigm for Peace Building?', in MG Berhe and H Liu (eds.), *China-Africa Relations: Governance, Peace and Security*, Institute for Peace and Security Studies, Addis Ababa, p. 20.
104. Kambudzi, AM 2013, 'Africa and China's non-interference policy: Towards peace enhancement in Africa', in MG Berhe and H Liu (eds.), *China-Africa Relations: Governance, Peace and Security*, Institute for Peace and Security Studies, Addis Ababa, p. 29.
105. 'Lu talks with readers of China Daily website' 2013, *China Daily*, 27 February, viewed 21 October 2013, http://www.focac.org/eng/zxxx/t1017775.htm

Bibliography

Anthony, R., & Jiang, H. (2014). Forum: Security and engagement: The case of China and South Sudan. *African East-Asian Affairs*, No. 4, pp. 78–97.

Boswell, A. (2010). China pledges to boost southern Sudan ties after secession vote. *Bloomberg*, 14 October. Retrieved January 15, 2016, from http://www.bloomberg.com/news/articles/2010-10-14/china-pledges-to-boost-southern-sudan-ties-after-january-vote-on-secession

Deng, L. B. (2015). IGAD plus, SPLM-FD and prospects for peace in South Sudan. *Sudan Tribune*, 11 June. Retrieved June 13, 2015, from http://sudantribune.com/spip.php?article55309

EIA. (2014). *Country analysis brief: Sudan and South Sudan.* U.S. Energy Information Administration, 3 September. Retrieved September 6, 2014, from https://www.eia.gov/beta/international/analysis_includes/countries_long/Sudan_and_South_Sudan/sudan.pdf

Goodman, P. S. (2004). China invests heavily in Sudan's oil industry; Beijing supplies arms used on villagers. *Washington Post*, 23 December. Retrieved February 7, 2016, from http://www.washingtonpost.com/wp-dyn/articles/A21143-2004Dec22.html

Gridneff, I. (2014). China halts arms sale to South Sudan after NORINCO shipment. *Bloomberg*, 30 September. Retrieved October 16, 2015, from http://www.bloomberg.com/news/articles/2014-09-29/china-halts-weapons-sales-to-south-sudan-after-norinco-shipment

International Crisis Group. (2015). *South Sudan: Keeping faith with the IGAD peace process.* Africa Report No. 228, 27 July. Retrieved February 9, 2016, from http://www.crisisgroup.org/~/media/Files/africa/horn-of-africa/south%20sudan/228-south-sudan-keeping-faith-with-the-igad-peace-process.pdf

Kassim, Y. R. (2014). *The geopolitics of intervention: Asia and the responsibility to protect.* Singapore: Springer.

Kline, J. (2010). *Ethics for international business: Decision-making in a global political economy.* London: Routledge.

Kurlantzick, J. (2007). *Charm offensive: How China's soft power is transforming the world.* New Haven: Yale University Press.

Large, D. (2007). Arms, oil and Darfur: The evolution of relations between China and Sudan. *Small Arms Survey*, No. 7, pp. 1–12. Retrieved March 1, 2016, from http://www.smallarmssurveysudan.org/fileadmin/docs/issue-briefs/HSBA-IB-07-Arms.pdf

Large, D. (2009). China's Sudan engagement: Changing northern and southern political trajectories in peace and war. *The China Quarterly, 199*, 610–626.

Large, D. (2011a). Southern Sudan and China: Enemies into friends? In D. Large & L. A. Patey (Eds.), *Sudan looks east: China, India and the politics of Asian alternatives* (pp. 157–175). New York: James Currey.

Large, D. (2011b). South Sudan looks east: Between the CPA and independence. *Association of Concerned Africa Scholars*, no. 86, pp. 54–58.

Ogunsanwo, A. (1974). *China's policy in Africa: 1958–71.* Cambridge: Cambridge University Press.

Panozzo, I. (2015). Asian players in Sudan: Social and economic impacts of 'new-old' actors. In B. Casciarri, A. M. Munzoul, & F. Ireton (Eds.), *Multidimensional change in Sudan (1989–2011): Reshaping livelihoods, conflicts and identities* (pp. 163–181). New York: Berghahn.

Raghavan, S. (2012). South Sudan's president visits China during crisis. *The Washington Post*, 24 April. Retrieved March 1, 2016, from https://www.washingtonpost.com/world/africa/south-sudans-president-visits-china-during-crisis/2012/04/24/gIQAowXKfT_story.html

Schumann, P. (2010). International actors in Sudan: The politics of implementing comprehensive peace. In R. Furlong & B. Herrmann (Eds.), *Sudan – No easy ways ahead* (pp. 102–114). Berlin: Heinrich Böll Foundation.

Scott, P. (1985). The Sudan Peoples' liberation movement (SPLM) and liberation army (SPLA). *Review of African Political Economy, 33*, 69–82.

Shinn, D. H., & Eisenman, J. (2012). *China and Africa: A century of engagement.* Philadelphia: University of Pennsylvania Press.

Simpfendorfer, B. (2015). The impact of the Arab revolutions on China's foreign policy. In K. Brown (Ed.), *The EU-China relationship: European perspectives* (pp. 201–212). London: Imperial College Press.

Verhoeven, H. (2014). Is Beijing's non-interference policy history? How Africa is changing China. *The Washington Quarterly, 37*(2), 55–70.

Zhou, L. (2014). Chinese diplomats make exception to non-interference rule by meeting South Sudan opposition. *South China Morning Post*, 5 November. Retrieved November 5, 2014, from http://www.scmp.com/news/china/article/1632138/chinese-diplomats-make-exception-non-interference-rule-meeting south

CHAPTER 7

Conclusion: Trends and Patterns of China's Intervention in Africa

7.1 Introduction

This chapter assesses trends and patterns of China's intervention behaviour in African intrastate armed conflicts. The assessment is based on this book's discussion of the historical evolvement of China's intervention in foreign intrastate armed conflicts as its relative economic power and perception of threats to its overseas interests changed over time. The conclusion made in Chap. 3 is that the general trajectory of China's intervention behaviour can be explained by its position in the international system, measured by its relative economic power. This is because as China's relative economic power increased, it expanded its economic interests and political influence abroad; and when it decreased from the middle of the Ming dynasty to the end of the century of humiliation, and during the Cultural Revolution and Great Leap Forward, its overseas interests in Africa also decreased due to the inability to maintain and protect them. While that is useful for explaining China's intervention in African intrastate armed conflicts, increase or decrease of relative economic power does not in itself copiously explain specific variations in China's intervention behaviour. This is because as postulated by neoclassical realism, and as explained in Chap. 2, specific variations in a state's foreign policy can be explained only when systemic factors such as the increase in a state's relative economic power are translated through domestic-level variables.

O. Hodzi, *The End of China's Non-Intervention Policy in Africa*,
Critical Studies of the Asia-Pacific,
https://doi.org/10.1007/978-3-319-97349-4_7

Following onto that conclusion, Chaps. 4–6 examined China's specific interventions in intrastate armed conflicts that started between 2011 and 2013 in Libya (2011), Mali (2012) and South Sudan (2013)—in particular, the three chapters explored how changes in China's perception of intrastate armed conflicts as being threats to its interests there shaped its intervention behaviour. In the three chapters, the discussion of China's intervention in each of the three countries' armed conflicts began with a historical analysis of their political, economic and diplomatic relations with China since their respective independence. Having established those basic fundamentals of their bilateral relations with China, the impact of the intrastate armed conflicts that ensued in the three countries on China's economic interests there was examined. The general findings, which are discussed in detail below, are that China's main motivating factor in intervening in the three countries' internal conflicts is to protect its nationals and economic interests, which were affected by intrastate armed conflicts in the three countries. In all three cases, China's intervention was more pronounced when the intrastate armed conflicts threatened its interests, suggesting that the perception of intrastate armed conflicts as being a threat to its foreign interests was the domestic-level factor that influenced its intervention behaviour.

Based on conclusions made in Chaps. 4–6, the overall argument advanced in this book is that China's intervention behaviour in African intrastate armed conflicts is a result of the combined effect of an increase in its relative economic power, which compelled it to expand its interests into politically volatile countries in search for raw materials and markets to keep the engine of its economy on the trot, and changing perception that intrastate armed conflicts in Africa threatened its interests there. On the basis of this argument, this chapter assesses the trends and patterns of China's intervention in Africa drawing extensively from arguments made in the previous chapters. It then discusses how China's intervention behaviour in African intrastate armed conflicts challenges existing conventional understandings of intervention as a foreign policy tool used by Western great powers to safeguard their strategic interests abroad. It then concludes by making a case for an innovative (re-)definition of intervention in other states' internal affairs that enables an analytical assessment of the emerging intervention practices of non-Western rising global powers.

7.2 Emerging Trends and Patterns

China's intervention in civil wars in Libya, Mali and South Sudan reflect a gradualist approach to revision of its policy of non-intervention policy in other states' internal affairs. The incremental approach shows a transition from indifference to assertive intervention, from dismissing peacekeeping as intervention in the internal affairs of other states, to sending combat troops under the auspices of the United Nations Peacekeeping Operations and going on to becoming the biggest contributor of UN peacekeepers among the five permanent members of the UN Security Council. This gradualist approach betrays the internal contradictions within a China struggling to come to terms with extraordinary increases in its relative economic capabilities and expansion of national interests beyond its neighbourhood. It also reflects the contradictions of a power attempting to strike a balance between protecting overseas interests in countries in conflict with its non-intervention foreign policy. The result is that "where once non-interference and non-intervention were staunchly upheld as principles that China could not allow itself or others to transgress when discussing security matters relative to Africa, today it is becoming more commonplace to hear and expect the Chinese government to defy the odds" (Barton 2018, p. 38). If anything, the cases of China's intervention in Libya, Mali and South Sudan give a strong indication of an impending end of non-intervention of China in African civil wars.

Before the civil war in Libya, China placed the responsibility for protection of interests in African countries on the host. But with the gradual realisation that host countries were unable to fully protect their interests in cases of internal conflicts, China's approach has gradually gravitated towards assertive intervention. Abiodun Alao and Chris Alden concur that security threats to Chinese officials, businesses and investments combined with "the accompanying diplomatic conundrums these circumstances produced, provided the context for a reconsideration of China's involvement in some forms of bilateral and multilateral intervention in Africa. The result has been a gradualist engagement in selective areas of African security, induced by problems confronting it on the ground in particular African countries but shaped by Beijing's privileged global position in multilateral affairs" (Alao and Alden 2018, p. 29). The impending end of China's non-intervention in Africa takes a gradualist approach for several reasons.

The major reason is that non-intervention remains China's biggest competitive advantage in Africa, particularly in countries led by regimes wary of US and Europe's intervention in their internal affairs. A radical shift from non-intervention to intervention would be far more detrimental to China's reception by African countries. Simply, what would make China any different from France or the United States? Chinese leaders are well aware of this; hence the incremental approach to intervention—building a new rapport with African leaders. As discussed below, part of China's strategy is, for instance, insisting that its military base in Djibouti is a logistics naval base, that its combat troops in South Sudan and Mali are UN Peacekeepers with no combat mandate and that the use of smart power on South Sudan is not intervention but mediation. What China is doing is to entice or, in some sense, socialise African countries to accept the new role that it seeks to play in Africa. As put by a professor of international studies at Renmin University of China, China's non-intervention stance in Africa is a matter of "water turning into ice." His argument is that China's foreign policy remains non-interventionary. It is only the form in which the non-intervention is expressed that is changing in just the same way as water that has turned into ice is technically water in a different form. On that basis, China insists that it does not intervene in the internal affairs of other states, while taking actions that materially seek to influence the duration and outcome of civil wars in Libya, Mali and South Sudan.

7.2.1 Flexible Interpretation of the Non-intervention Principle

China is flexibly interpreting its non-intervention principle as its relative economic power increases and it expands its national interests abroad. That expansion is in turn exposing Chinese national interests to new forms of threats. In previous chapters, it was argued that due to the lateral pressure, as China's domestic economic grew exponentially, its relative economic power increased, enabling it to expand its economic interests abroad, including to some volatile countries such as South Sudan, Mali and Libya. As armed conflicts broke out in those countries China found itself entangled in their internal conflicts, compelling it to devise strategies to intervene and protect its interests. China's foreign affairs minister, Wang Yi, made a similar observation on 9 March 2016 when he said, "like any major country that is growing, China's overseas interests are expanding… So, it has become a pressing task for China's diplomacy to better protect our ever-growing overseas interests."[1] In seeking to protect those interests, which involves some degree of intervention, China has shown from the case of Libya, Mali and South Sudan that it is "willing to be more flexible on the questions of both host countries' consent and non-interference in other countries' internal affairs" (Mariani 2015, p. 258). The result is that Beijing is matching the increase in threats confronting its overseas interests with an expansion of its security forces' mandate to include safeguarding China's overseas interests.

While it is apparent that rising powers with expanding global interests will inevitably be compelled to protect those interests, and in the process intervene in other states' internal affairs, China is an exceptional rising power. The official Beijing policy is that China does not interfere in the internal affairs of other states. This creates a puzzle because protecting its economic interests or nationals abroad will invariably involve a degree of intervention in the internal affairs of the concerned state. Balancing those contradictory objectives is what has resulted in a mismatch between Beijing's foreign policy in theory and its foreign policy in practice. On the one hand, China claims that the non-intervention principle forms the cornerstone of its foreign policy, and is unchangeable, but as discussed in previous chapters, China is nevertheless intervening in conflicts that threaten its interests. The resultant effect is that there seem to be a concerted effort by Beijing to flexibly interpret the non-intervention principle in a manner that justifies its intervention behaviour in Africa, in order to maintain its "identity" as a non-interventionary power, distinct from Western powers.

What enables the vacillation of the interpretation of the non-intervention principle by China from strict and rigid to flexible is foremost the manner in which the principle is formulated and articulated by the PRC. Like most Chinese foreign policy principles, the principle of non-intervention is more of a maxim than something clearly expounded and articulated principle; hence there is no clarity on whether it is just a principle or a policy. The pervasiveness of the lack of clarity is such that Chinese foreign policy scholars refer to it as either a principle or a foreign policy, with some using the two terms interchangeably. This may seem inconsequential, but it has had a fundamental effect on the analysis of China's external intervention behaviour because principles are different from policies.

Sonia Lucarelli defines principles as "normative propositions that translate values into general 'constitutional' standards for policy action" (2006, p. 10). On the contrary, policy consists of the "development and conscious pursuit of some preferred goal or goals" by a government through selective political action.[2] The action may "include observable behaviors by countries..., or verbal pronouncements that do not necessarily lead to follow-up action" (Kaarbo et al. 2002, p. 4). The most notable distinction between principle and policy was given by the UK's former Prime Minister Neville Chamberlain when he said

> You can lay down sound and general propositions. You can say that your foreign policy is to maintain peace...; you can say that it is to use your influence, such as it is, on behalf of the right against wrong ... you can lay down all these general principles, but that is not policy. Surely, if you have a policy you must take the particular situations and consider what action or inaction is suitable for those particular situations. That is what I myself mean by policy, and it is quite clear that as the situations and conditions in foreign affairs continually change from day to day, your policy cannot be stated once and for all, it is to be applicable to every situation that arises. (Chamberlain 1937, p. 33)

As put by Chamberlain, there is a clear distinction between principles constituting the normative superstructure that guide statesmen in the exercise of foreign policy, and foreign policy which is political action that though related to, is not determined by such normative superstructures.

The implication is that in its current formulation, the Chinese government puts across non-intervention as both a foreign policy that can evolve based on particular situations, and as a principle that applies to all situations alike and is unchangeable. The Ministry of Foreign Affairs of the PRC collectively describes the Five Principles of Peaceful Co-existence as "the basic norms in developing state to state relations transcending social systems and ideology."[3] On the 60th Anniversary of the initiation of the Five Principles of Peaceful Coexistence, President Xi Jinping said: "In the new era today, the spirit of the Five Principles of Peaceful Coexistence, instead of being outdated, remains as relevant as ever; its significance, rather than diminishing, remains as important as ever; and its role, rather than being weakened, has continued to grow." He then reiterated the official PRC's rhetoric that "China neither interferes in other countries' internal affairs nor imposes its will on others"—declaring that the Five Principles are enshrined in China's Constitution and are the cornerstone of its foreign policy.[4] However, in contradiction to the supposed sanctity and unchangeable nature of the Five Principles of Peaceful Coexistence, he declared that "all good principles should adapt to changing times to remain relevant."[5] Yet, as put by Neville Chamberlain, principles do not change, policies do. So, while articulating it as a principle, Chinese leaders in actual effect take the non-intervention principle as a foreign policy that is adaptable to changing times—giving China subtle manoeuvrability in its implementation.

The manoeuvrability is reflected in arguments made by Chinese government officials in supporting their country's intervention or non-intervention in foreign intrastate armed conflicts. In the case of South Sudan where China, contrary to its policy of not meeting opposition groups or rebel forces in foreign countries, met Riek Machar, the leader of a rebel force fighting against the South Sudanese government, Zhong Jianhua said: "I think for the past two or three decades we were quite rigid about non-interference in the internal affairs of other countries... When you talk to a rebel force that means stepping into internal affairs" (Fabricius 2014). However, when a journalist referred to that as a change of policy, Zhong Jianhua's aide "pointed out that there had been no change in policy as Beijing had now simply realized that tackling conflicts had become necessary for advancing Beijing's historical policy of promoting African development" (Fabricius 2014). In that case, one would wonder whether China's newfound interest in tackling conflicts in Africa does not mean a change in policy that once precluded it from intervening in other states' internal affairs.

Regarding the intrastate armed conflict in Libya, China's Ambassador to the United Nations Li Baodong said: "China always opposes the use of force in international relations. During Security Council consultations on Resolution 1973, China and some other Council members raised some specific issue. Regrettably, however, there is no clarification or answer to many of these issues. China has serious concerns over some elements of the resolution."[6] Still, despite no clarification on the specific issues that it had raised, China still cast a vote of abstention on UNSC Resolution 1973 approving a 'No-Fly Zone' over Libya and authorising all necessary measures to protect civilians despite it being against its non-intervention principle. China's argument was that it was merely following the wishes of the African Union and the Arab league and that it was compelled by 'special circumstances in Libya.' However, when the Arab League supported a UN Security Council Resolution that sought to approve intervention in Syria, China vetoed it. "What this means is that China allows itself the greatest room to maneuver, free to endorse or oppose the actions of a regional grouping, depending on its interests" (Ching 2012).

In South Sudan and Mali, for the first time in its history, and in a radical shift to its policy against having the PLA troops operating in foreign lands, China sent combat troops under the United Nations Peacekeeping Mission instead of the usual non-military personnel. Retired Major General Xu Guangyu was at pains to explain that the dispatch of these forces was not a shift in Beijing's non-intervention principle. He was quoted in the *South China Morning Post* as saying, "China's combat troops will abide by the UN's peacekeeping regulations. Soldiers are allowed to open fire only for self-defence purposes, and never take positions to help either party during a civil war."[7]

Overall, the formulation of China's principle of non-intervention is such that its interpretation can be manipulated depending on China's position in the international system—enabling "China to semantically update its critique of the existing international order to resonate with evolving conceptions of the system" (Richardson 2012, p. 47). When it seeks to gain access into Africa, identify with the developing world or constrain intervention into its own internal affairs by other states, it extols the non-intervention principle, but when it best suits its interests, it flexibly interprets the principle, enabling it to justify its intervention in other states' internal affairs. Thus, as argued by Frank Ching, "China's principle of non-interference in another country's internal affairs is alive and well, subject to its own interpretation of whether a regional grouping's decision regarding a member country is in China's interests" (2012).

7.2.2 *As China's Relative Economic Power Increases, Its External Intervention Is Increasing*

China's intervention in foreign intrastate armed conflicts is historically first determined by its relative economic power—because as postulated by the lateral pressure theory, it expands its interests abroad in times when its relative economic power is on the increase as it searches for new markets and resources. The consequential pattern is that China tends to intervene in foreign intrastate armed conflicts when its relative economic power is higher, and vice versa. This pattern has been persistent since imperial China. In its heyday as the Middle Kingdom, superior in its technological advancement and economy, which contributed approximately 35% of the global economy, China was the centre of its own "global" tributary order. With such a grander relative economic power, Chinese emperors had the latent right of intervention in the internal affairs of other nations. Although the right to intervene was rarely exercised, the awareness of the right and a tendency to intervene when circumstances demanded it were notable.

When the relative economic power decreased, as other states developed at a faster pace than China, the latent right to intervene in the internal affairs of surrounding nations was lost. Instead, in times of inferior relative economic power it was China that became subject to external intervention in its internal affairs. This was the case during the century of humiliation when China was relegated to the peripheries of the global pecking order of states. Combined with the effects of being forcibly incorporated into the European-dominated Westphalian international system of states where relative economic and military capabilities mattered more than cultural supremacy, China lost its claim to the "Heavenly Mandate" and to being the Middle Kingdom at the core of its own global order, and, with it, the latent right of intervention in other states' internal affairs. Thus, the cyclic pattern: "when Chinese power prevailed, the empire was able to force its tribute system and its language of diplomatic discourse on surrounding peoples. When the empire was weak, the Chinese perception of the world had little effect on the course of events. The ultimate fact is the fact of power" (Schwartz 1968, p. 278).

Benjamin I. Schwartz's observation that the ultimate fact in China's foreign policy behaviour is relative power resonates with the trajectory of its external intervention behaviour in intrastate armed conflicts in Africa. Thus, in order to understand how China interprets its non-intervention principle, there is need to "review and compare several lists of historical intervention events to capture the phenomenon over time and to become aware of the variation in the way intervention is construed" (Feste 2003, p. 178). The descriptive historical analysis of China's intervention in foreign conflicts discussed in Chap. 4 suggested that China's intervention in other nations' internal affairs has always been commensurate with its relative economic power. This is because a state's interest in foreign affairs, particularly the internal affairs of other states, rises commensurately with growth in its global power.

From the imperial times of the Ming and Qing Dynasties, when China was at the centre of its global system, "it maintained order in the system and reserved the right to intervene in the internal affairs of its vassals" (Wang 2011, p. 145; see also Cohen 1973, p. 474). At the prime of its imperial power, and as the paramount leader of the tributary states, China possessed a latent right of intervention in their internal affairs, but that went only so far as its relative economic power enabled. The "Century of

Humiliation" was different—China was riddled by political instability and poverty. From being the most powerful nation in its known world, China found itself among the peripheral states in the European-dominated Westphalian international system—"out of step with its long former history as Asia's premier power and a major global trader" (Hough and Malik 2015, p. 362). Instead of being the one intervening in the affairs of other nations, it was the one being subjected to intervention by other states such as Japan, the Soviet Union, Britain, the United States, France, Portugal and the Netherlands. US overt military intervention in China stopped only at the end of the Chinese civil war and establishment of the communist regime in 1949 (Feste 2003, p. 180).

As discussed in Chap. 4, by the time Mao established the PRC in 1949, China's understanding of intervention was one of national humiliation, oppression and exploitation by powerful Western states that played active roles in its internal affairs. To protect itself from hegemonic global powers that sought to intervene in its internal affairs, Mao espoused the principles of state sovereignty, equality among states and respect for other states' territorial integrity. Non-intervention became the dominant principle upon which China's foreign policy was based. But as put by Peter Hough and Shahin Malik, what remained an overriding logic in Chinese collective mentality is that the century of humiliation was a result of China "falling behind the Europeans, Americans and Japanese economically in the nineteenth century when those nations industrialised" (2015, p. 362).

Emerging from the "almost-zero" per capita GDP growth China had from 1800 to 1950 (Zhu 2012, p. 103) China's understanding and experience of external intervention was as a victim of foreign subjugation. But under Mao, there was limited economic recovery in the highly unstable years of the mid-1950s and early 1960s. Xiaodong Zhu, Professor of Economics at the University of Toronto, suggests that from 1950 to 1978 "the average growth rate of real per capita GDP was a modest 3 percent a year, not much different from the growth rate in the United States though starting from a much lower base" (2012, p. 106). Consequently, China's relative economic power improved, albeit not to levels comparable with the economies of the United States, European states or the Soviet Union. But compared to countries in the developing world, especially Africa, China's relative economic power increased to levels that enabled it to expand its interests abroad, and exercise influence over them.

While it emphasised the Westphalian principles of respect for state sovereignty and non-intervention in internal affairs of other states mainly to protect itself from external intervention in its domestic affairs by superior global powers, China did intervene in intrastate armed conflicts for independence in Africa. Beyond supporting liberation movements, it also supported dissident armed groups fighting Soviet-aligned governments in independent African countries. That resulted in the suspension of diplomatic relations with several independent African countries. For, in Africa and the Third World, Mao's China had secured its position as leader of the Third World, and backed by an improving economy, it was confident of its geopolitical competitiveness in the struggle for influence over Africa and the rest of the Third World.

China's intervention in African intrastate armed conflicts receded when its economy faltered under the combined weight of the Great Leap Forward and the Cultural Revolution, and political squabbles that followed the subsequent death of Mao led China to increasingly abandon active support for liberation war movements and internationalisation of its revolutionary ideology in Africa. The economy that had been able to support internationalisation of the revolution to the Third World, albeit with great difficulties, was no longer able to do so, as it failed to rival economic and political support granted to African countries by the United States and the Soviet Union. Thus, from the mid-1960s onwards Chinese intervention in African intrastate armed conflicts slowed down until it was almost negligible when Deng Xiaoping took over leadership of the country.

The shift in China's national focus from revolution to economic production under Deng Xiaoping illustrates the importance and emphasis placed by post-Mao Chinese national leaders on strengthening China's relative economic power. As they replaced ideological considerations with economic interest considerations in the theory and practice of China's foreign policy, they argued that China's contributions to international affairs should be commensurate with its relative economic power. As discussed in Chap. 4, according to Deng Xiaoping, the disengagement from Africa and from playing a prominent role in its internal affairs was a tactical and strategic foreign policy action meant to give China an opportunity to improve its relative economic power to levels comparable with the United States. From then on, Deng Xiaoping argued that China's role and participation in international affairs were going to be commensurate with its economic power, suggesting that as its economic power increased so also would the role it plays in international affairs.

Sustained increases in China's domestic economic since 1978 massively increased its relative economic power. From having a GNI of US$213 billion in 1980, it reached US$5.752 trillion in 2010 before doubling to US$10.1 trillion in 2014, making it the second largest economy in the world. Also, in 2013, China became Africa's biggest trading partner, surpassing the United States. As was predicted by Deng Xiaoping in 1984, China is now a powerful state, playing a bigger role in international affairs as well as contributing more to the Third World. "We are seeing more of China flexing its muscles in Africa, exerting influence on African governments more than it did before … and that because China is now a big economic power"[8] is how a diplomat at the African Union reflected on the impact of increases in China's relative economic power. Another respondent working at IGAD in Addis Ababa concurred, but added that the "increase in China's global economic power explains its growing footprint in African civil wars, especially in South Sudan and Mali where it is getting entangled in regional geopolitical dynamics in its quest to protect its interests."[9] China is now "truly powerful, exerting a much greater influence in the world."[10] Accordingly, one can conclude that China's external intervention behaviour is commensurate with its relative economic power, and that as its economic interests expand in Africa, China is "putting a premium on strengthening the stability of African countries, irrespective of their political ideology, especially those that are major exporters of raw materials or have a significant Chinese presence" (Shinn 2016).

As enunciated by the lateral pressure theory discussed in Chap. 3, as China's relative economic power rises, it is increasingly expanding its economic interests in Africa, and its citizens are also settling and working in Africa. Gary Li concurringly states: "as Chinese investments abroad increase every year; overseas Chinese have found themselves caught up in conflicts which has required Beijing to expand substantial resources to extract them" (2015). Similarly, Irene Chan and Mingjiang Li also argue that "the expansion of Chinese presence throughout the world calls for more attention to protecting Chinese interests overseas" (2015, p. 266). The effect is that as some of the African countries plunge into intrastate armed conflicts, China is being compelled to intervene in order to protect its nationals and interests, while balancing that imperative with its identity as a non-interventionist power. The underlying factor is that "the growth of Chinese power and capability has certainly made it probable for China to adopt a more proactive stance in protecting its nationals and investments in other parts of the world" (Chan and Li 2015, p. 266). Thus, as put by Bernardo Mariani, "as befitting its global economic presence and place in the world, China can be expected to play a leading role in multilateral for a, constructively engaging with critical events beyond a rhetorical insistence on non-interference, and leading change in the peace and security agenda—not simply reacting to crises" (2015, p. 267).

7.2.3 Changes in Perception of Foreign Intrastate Armed Conflicts as Threats Are Leading to More Intervention

Based on the mutability of China's non-intervention principle, the emerging trend is that China is taking a liberal interpretation of the non-intervention principle and deepening its external intervention whenever its interests are affected by intrastate armed conflicts in Africa. With armed conflicts increasingly proving to be detrimental to China's economic interests in Africa, there is consensus among Chinese government officials, political leaders and scholars that those interests ought to be protected, suggesting that they now increasingly perceive intrastate armed conflicts in Africa to be a threat to their economic interests there. At the *Central Conference on Work Relating to Foreign Affairs*[11] held in Beijing in November 2014, President Xi underscored that "we should protect China's foreign interests and continue to improve our capacity to provide such protection."[12] Yan Xuetong, a leading international relations scholar in China, also suggested that China should "adopt active policies to protect its rapidly expanded national interests."[13] In concurrence, Zhongying Pang (2008), another renowned scholar, wrote: "China needs to carefully consider its right to intervene in humanitarian crises and severe attacks on Chinese interests or nationals." What, however, differs among them is how China ought to protect its foreign economic interests from intrastate armed conflicts in Africa.

Those who subscribe to self-help realist notions expect a rising power like China to back up its "economic forays with a projection of military might."[14] But President Xi, in keeping with the Five Principles of Peaceful Coexistence, in particular the principle of non-interference in other countries' internal affairs, contends that China should "promote peaceful resolution of differences and disputes between countries through dialogue and consultation, and oppose the wilful use or threat of force."[15] The official rhetorical opposition to militant approaches to protecting its foreign interests is what is mostly construed as China's adherence to the non-intervention principle, yet for those who keep an eye on China's historical and contemporary intervention patterns in Africa since the 1950s, the question has never been whether China intervenes or not, but when does it intervene and how, especially when "Chinese nationals and investments in the region [Africa] are threatened or there are interruptions in the flow from Africa of critical raw materials that support China's economy" (Shinn 2016).

7.2.4 *No Opposition to Intervention by Western Global Powers*

Based on the above patterns, one of related emerging trends is that China is gradually relaxing its opposition to intervention in African intrastate armed conflicts by Western global powers such as the United States, France and NATO. According to Kjell Engelbrekt Beijing is demonstrating "flexibility and an acceptance of the notion that handling of challenges to peace and security may be 'delegated' to authoritative transnational bodies in the regions concerned" (2014, p. 51). David Shinn (2013) concurs: "as threats to Chinese interests in Africa increase, there has been a steady strengthening of its willingness to cooperate with others" Furthermore, "while it still adheres to the principle of non-interference, China no longer opposes international intervention organised by the West, as long as the intervention is legitimate and justifiable" (Pang 2008). Yang Razali Kassim agrees that "since the late 1990s China's attitude to international intervention entered a process of change ... China no longer simply challenges or opposes international intervention initiated by the West" (2014, p. 33). The shift is typified in China's consent to adoption of the doctrine of the responsibility to protect, allowing the international community to take all means necessary, including military intervention, to protect civilians in countries were the state is unable to. Since then China has supported, directly and indirectly, unilateral intervention and multilateral intervention led by Western powers in countries such as Sudan, Mali and Libya.

In the case of Libya, China allowed the UNSC to impose sanctions, asset freezes and a no-fly zone against the Gaddafi regime. The no-fly zone in Libya was heavily lobbied for by France, in order to decapitate Gaddafi's air force which gave it strategic advantage over the NTC. As discussed in Chap. 5, Chinese foreign policy makers and diplomats at the United Nations were aware of the intended objective of the no-fly zone, and, as put by Li Baodong, in deliberations leading to adoption of Resolution 1973, China had raised those concerns. But, regardless of its concerns against military intervention in Libya not being addressed, China abstained from voting, giving its tacit approval to the NATO-led military intervention in Libya. As argued in Chap. 5, the main reason for Chinese support of the multilateral intervention in Libya is that the Gaddafi regime had rebuffed all attempts towards a political settlement of the armed conflict, further endangering Chinese businesses, assets and nationals in Libya.

In Mali, China supported France's unilateral intervention in Mali because as put by He Wenping, "the situation in Mali was urgent."[16] What made "the situation urgent" is that the Tuareg and the Islamists were overrunning Bamako as political bickering in the Transitional Government continued. The implication of the Islamists taking over Mali is that China was likely to lose significant investments in the Malian agriculture, and construction sector which it dominated. Furthermore, French military intervention to retain Malian control of Northern Mali protected China's interests in Niger because there was high probability of the Tuareg rebellion spreading into Niger, where other Tuareg people are. In Niger, China's state-owned SINO-U had invested US$300 million in a uranium mine at Azelik; CNPC had invested over US$5 billion to develop oil reserves and to build a refinery and pipeline in eastern Niger (Shinn and Eisenman 2012, p. 246). Both Azelik and eastern Niger are adjacent to Northern Mali which was under the control of Islamists and is believed to have significant oil reserves (Boeke and Schuurman 2015, p. 806). By supporting French intervention in Mali, China sought to have its interests protected at minimal cost to itself, and thus it found it pragmatic to support the intervention.

Another emerging trend is that China is using multilateral institutions to intervene in African intrastate armed conflicts. As argued above, until the 1990s China had a general mistrust of international organisations such as the United Nations which it considered extensions of US hegemony. "Until the early 1970s, the Chinese government often criticized the UN as a faced and instrument of Western domination of the world" (Wang and Rosenau 2009, p. 14). But with the increase in its position in the international system as its relative economic power increased, China is increasingly embracing these institutions and exploiting them to its advantage. Its actions in the three intrastate armed conflicts in Libya, Mali and South Sudan suggest a trend that China is increasingly using its position in the UNSC to protect its interests against armed conflicts in Africa, which entails intervention in the countries' internal affairs. Through the UN Security Council, China is taking deliberate actions that attempt "to influence designated behaviour of individuals in another nation without engaging in a continuing contest of violence" (Feste 2003, p. 191). This strategy fits into its objective of seeking to influence the outcome of intrastate armed conflicts in target countries through influence rather than force. Furthermore, in the camouflage of multilateral interventions, China maintains its legitimacy and identity as a power that does not intervene in the internal affairs of other states.

China's gradual relaxing of its opposition to intervention in African intrastate armed conflicts by Western global powers such as the United States, France and NATO is motivated by two factors: Beijing's perceived global power status, and pragmatism. The increase in China's relative economic power has effectively boosted Beijing's self-awareness as a global power. Combined with the expansion of its interests abroad, China is also simultaneously realising the limitations to its unilateral capabilities to protect those interests. This is where its pragmatism comes in. If it is not able to fully protect its foreign interests alone, then when Western powers, multilateral institutions and the United Nations take the initiative to resolve armed conflicts in areas where China's interests are threatened, there is little or no reason to object. Thus, as argued in the case of Mali, Libya and South Sudan, as long as China's foreign interests are secured through action taken by Western governments, the United Nations or other multilateral organisations, China is increasingly supporting such action because it serves its interests. In addition, intervention by multilateral institutions and the United Nations, although instigated and led by Western powers, is often considered legitimate intervention. Because of that veneer of legitimacy, China is increasingly supporting their intervention since its foreign interests will be secured at minimal cost to Beijing. At the same time, if there is backlash against intervention by Western powers as was the case in Libya, China will simply abdicate responsibility and exonerate itself. Either way, China stands to benefit from Western intervention in African intrastate armed conflicts that threaten Beijing's interests there.

7.2.5 China Is Increasingly Using UN Peacekeeping Operations to Intervene in Africa

In line with the trend of using multilateral institutions to intervene in the internal affairs of other states, China is also increasingly using non-threatening multilateral intervention methods to protect its interests abroad. This change is partly in line with the country's "larger foreign policy strategy, during the past two decades, of supporting multilateral solutions rather than unilateral actions to address strategic threats" (Hirono and Lanteigne 2012, p. 1). One such method is the contribution of peacekeeping and peace monitoring forces to United Nations Peacekeeping Operations in Africa. In the past China was opposed to peacekeeping operations, which it considered intervention in other states' internal affairs. Shogo Suzuki notes that China "viewed PKOs with the utmost suspicion, frequently denouncing them as tools of US or Soviet imperialism and refusing to make any financial or human contributions" (2012, p. 29). Yet since its first civilian observers' contribution to the UN Peacekeeping mission in Namibia in 1989, China has risen to become the highest personnel contributor among the UN Security Council members, and the eighth largest contributor of police, UN Military Experts on Mission and troops (3042 in total) to UN peacekeeping operations as of 30 April 2016,[17] demonstrating "how far its foreign policy in this regard has shifted and changed in a relatively short period of time" (Huang 2012, p. 16).

Its financial contributions to UN peacekeeping operations also increased from 4% in 2012 to 6.64% in the 2014–2015 period,[18] making China the sixth largest financial contributor to UN peacekeeping operations. The highest five are: the United States (28.38%); Japan (10.83%); France (7.22%); Germany (7.14%) and the UK (6.68%).[19] In December 2015, Wang Min, China's deputy permanent representative to the United Nations, announced that China's contributions for the 2016–2018 period will increase to 7.9%, and will be expected to further increase to 10.2% in the following next three years.[20] In a major surprise, during his UN General Assembly speech on September 2015 President Xi Jinping announced:

> China's decision to establish a 10-year, US1 billion Chin-UN peace and development fund to support the UN's work, advance multilateral cooperation and contribute more to world peace and development... China will join the new UN Peacekeeping Capability Readiness System and thus has decided to take the lead in setting up a permanent peacekeeping police squad and build a peacekeeping standby force of 8,000 troops... China will provide a total of US$100 million of free military assistance to the African Union in the next five years to support establishment of the African Standby Force and the African Capacity for Immediate Response to Crisis.[21]

In May 2016, barely a year after President Xi made that announcement, China's permanent representative to the UN, Liu Jieyi, signed an agreement with Edmond Mulet, UN Secretary-General's *chef de cabinet,* regarding a multiyear US$200 million contribution by China towards the UN Peace and Development Trust Fund. As reported in Chinese press, the two parties agreed that the US$200 million will be hosted at the UN, which will set up a committee made up of personnel from China and the UN.[22] When fully implemented, these initiatives will make China one of the largest human and financial contributors to UN peacekeeping operations, and, as put by Wang Min, "the increase is an objective reflection of China's national strength in the international system."[23]

Zhongying Pang asserts that China's participation in UN peacekeeping operations reflects a shift in its foreign policy of non-intervention in other states. Wang (2013) describes it as a drastic shift "from ardent opposition in the 1970s to avid support in the 2000s." Marc Lanteigne attributes the shift to "China's growing global diplomatic, strategic and economic interests, as well as the country's increasing acceptance of 'responsibility to protect' (or R2P, known in Chinese as *baohu de zeren*) principles, [which] all prompted a revisiting of the robust peacekeeping question…, including whether China would be in a position to send combat forces in addition to support and engineering personnel" (2014, p. 8). China is therefore embracing "the current constellation of international institutions, rules, and norms as a means to promote its national interests,"[24] such that "the growth of Beijing's peacekeeping role seems, however, to have been accompanied by a subtle shift in China's position on state sovereignty" (Tardy and Wyss 2014, p. 9), putting "it in a position to help protect Chinese interests in Africa" (Shinn 2016).

With the exception of Libya, in addition to non-military personnel, China contributed combat or security troops with peace enforcement responsibilities to MINUSMA in Mali, and UNMISS in South Sudan. Previously, China had been content with sending engineers, doctors and other non-military personnel. Both Missions are "multidimensional and integrated" UN missions that take place in unstable situations characterised by ongoing armed conflicts where they have a mandate to use force. Unlike peacekeeping operations that normally require the consent of the target state, peace enforcement operations "are not based on consent and are deployed to create—rather than maintain peace" (Heldt and Wallensteen 2007, p. 10). Furthermore, because they are aimed at rebuilding a state, which includes holding of elections and reform and restructuring of the legal, judiciary and security sectors, these "multidimensional and integrated" UN missions "are nothing short of attempts at nation-building, that seek to remake a state's political institutions, security forces, and economic arrangements" (Bertran 1995, p. 389). They invariably "entail a substantial degree of top-down social engineering..., [they] are problematic in that they may constitute a violation of the sovereignty of the host state" (Suzuki 2012, p. 32). Accordingly, China's peacekeeping operations in Mali and South Sudan are as defined by Birger Heldt and Peter Wallensteen as "third-party state interventions that involves the deployment of military troops and/or military observers and/or civilian police in a target state... Is neutral towards the conflict parties, but not necessarily impartial towards their behaviour" (Heldt and Wallensteen 2007, p. 11).

The puzzle is that China portrays itself as a "responsible global power" that respects state sovereignty and non-intervention in the internal affairs of other states. But, as put by Shogo Suzuki, "China's decision to get involved in various PKOs since the end of the Cold War contradicts these self-professed principles ... [because] they entail a considerable erosion of the host state's sovereignty" (2012, p. 32). The use of force and the "use of all means necessary" in some PKOs in fulfillment of their mandate gnaw at other states' sovereignty and territorial integrity—by supporting and actively participating in such non-traditional peacekeeping operations, China adulterates its non-intervention policy. The deployment of the PLA soldiers under the UN missions in Mali and South Sudan demonstrates, as already noted by Marc Lanteigne, that "China continues to make use of its support for UN peacekeeping operations not only to advance its strategic agenda but to offer an alternative approach to traditional intervention by great powers" (2014, p. 9). In the case of South Sudan, a diplomat at the African Union suggested that China had vigorously attempted to have the UN troops assigned to protect oil refineries and other Chinese assets in South Sudan. Although they eventually were stationed elsewhere, what the Chinese lobby meant is that it viewed the UN Peacekeeping mission in South Sudan as a tool to protect its interests there rather than as an altruistic attempt at maintaining peace.

In concurrence, Zhongying Pang states: "China has gradually realized that peacekeeping missions can help to secure a peaceful international environment, which works in China's national interests as the country begins to build a sound external environment for its long-term economic growth and social development" (2005, p. 81). Although arguing that Chinese peacekeepers are not always deployed in resource-rich countries, or that they are a "strategic prerequisite to resource access," Bernardo Mariani agrees that "broadly, China's involvement in peacekeeping stems from the recognition that China's plans for economic growth and modernization are increasingly linked to a stable, secure and peaceful world, and that UN peacekeeping operations work in China's national interest" (2015, p. 256). UN peacekeeping operations are therefore a convenient balance and pragmatic tool for expanding its influence over the duration and effect of intrastate armed conflicts in Africa. "These operations suggest ... a move towards a new model which bridges the gap between more traditional UN peacekeeping and the more forceful Western-led humanitarian interventions" (Cottey and Bikin-Kita 2006, p. 29); as "China aligns its foreign policy with its expanding global interests" (Hille 2013).

7.2.6 From Passive and Inactive to Assertive and Proactive Intervention Approach

Another emerging trend is that China's approach to intrastate armed conflicts in Africa has cautiously, selectively and incrementally evolved from being inactive and passive, to being proactive and assertive in defence of its economic interests. The passive and inactive approach in Libya is to a greater extent related to the perception in Beijing that armed conflicts in Africa did not affect its interests there. But with the impact that the Libyan conflict had on its nationals and investments there, there has been a radical shift towards a more proactive and assertive approach, which was the case in Mali, but more so in South Sudan. This is also because China realises, unlike before the Libyan case, that its economic development requires energy and primary commodities in Africa, and that its ability to access those resources and sustain its economic growth is tied to stability in those African countries. Accordingly, "peace and security in Africa is suddenly China's interest too" (Allison 2015).

The shift towards assertive and proactive intervention is also because as China's relative economic power increases, and as its interests in Africa become entrenched, it is assuming greater global responsibilities in order to create a conducive international environment for its advancement. Since 2010, China overtook the United States to become Africa's biggest trading partner. With the second largest economy in the world, and with interests and influence extended beyond its borders and immediate Asian region, there is also an expectation that it should play a major role in global governance. Although it denies it is a major global power, choosing instead to describe itself as a developing country, there is global consensus, and consensus within China as well, that it is a major global power. The pursuance of "major-power diplomacy" by China especially under

President Xi Jinping suggests a growing confidence and acceptance among China's leadership of its new global power status[25] and it "is increasingly confident in casting itself as a great power" (Yang 2009, p. 31). That acceptance of China's "status as one of the only two major powers and its attendant responsibilities (and the responsibilities of other states to China) is clear and being translated into China's foreign policy actions and intentions" (Cook 2015, p. 114). Accordingly, there is increased domestic and international consensus on the "impracticability of keeping a low profile and non-interference, as China faces the inevitable need to protect its overseas interests either in a proactive or passive way" (Chan and Li 2015, pp. 258–259).

Another factor contributing to the shift towards assertive and proactive intervention is that China's relations with African countries are transitioning from being influenced by ideology and the Sino-Soviet rivalry over geopolitical influence in independent Africa to being influenced by economic interests. This "shift on foreign policy orientation is also tied to larger systemic processes that affect the nation's proclivity for foreign engagement and its capability for such activity. This allows the question of national interests and capabilities to be separately examined rather than take them as given characteristics of autonomous agents" (Feste 2003, p. 186). Unlike in the past when it did not interfere with conflicts in Mali and South Sudan due to ideological and geopolitical considerations, the burgeoning of economic and trade relations with these countries compels it to intervene in cases where its interests are threatened. In such cases, as illustrated in Libya, Mali and South Sudan, China takes a liberal interpretation of the non-intervention principle, justifying its intervention in those countries' internal armed conflicts and allowing other global powers and multilateral organisations to intervene.

In most African countries, the protection of China's economic interests and nationals is guaranteed by the host African government. In many respects this fact absolved China of the responsibility to protect its interests in cases of political instability and armed conflicts erupting, as long as the host state remained intact. This explains why China delayed intervention in Libya and was historically indifferent to insurrections and coup d'états in Mali—it considered the regimes in the two countries to be strong enough to guarantee the safety of its citizens and assets there. The emerging transition from passivity to proactive intervention in African intrastate armed conflicts that are discussed in this book is therefore motivated by the failure of African governments to protect Chinese interests and nationals in the event of intrastate armed conflicts breaking out. So, even though China demanded that the governments of Mali and Libya protect its economic interests there, they still failed to force China to take action to protect them. The case was different in South Sudan. In hindsight, given the failures of the Malian and Libyan governments to protect Chinese economic interests, in South Sudan China was both assertive and proactive in intervening in the conflict and protecting its nationals and economic interests.

From the above discussion it has been argued that as shown from the cases of Libya, Mali and South Sudan, China has moved from ambivalent intervention to reactive multilateral intervention and to proactive bilateral intervention. What, however, remains scope for further research is whether China will remain proactive and assertive in its intervention in African intrastate armed conflicts. If it remains on the above intervention trajectory, it can be argued that China's future intervention in African intrastate armed conflicts will remain influenced by Beijing perception of the threat imposed by the armed conflict on its interests abroad. Where its interests are affected materially, China will be more proactive and assertive in its bilateral and multilateral intervention, but where its interests are not significantly affected, it may be passive and reactionary because, as shown in this book, Beijing's intervention is mainly motivated by its perception of threat caused by some foreign intrastate armed conflicts on its interests.

7.3 Implications for Understandings of Intervention

In sum, there is no doubt that in practice China is incrementally, but materially, re-interpreting its non-intervention policy. The gradualist approach has so far worked because, unlike interventions by France, the United States and NATO in African civil wars, China's veiled interventions have attracted little or no objection from African countries. In fact, political leaders in South Sudan, Mali, Zimbabwe and Ethiopia argue that China's "interventions" in African conflicts are not intervention in those countries' internal affairs but constructive assistance to manage and resolve the conflicts. That justification of Chinese intervention and demonisation of same acts by the United States or European powers by Africa leaders reflect, in some sense, the cosy relationship between China and most African countries. Or perhaps the agency of African leaders in determining what is described as intervention or not. More importantly, it shows the utility of China's propaganda, that is, using terms such as "win-win solution" and "mutually beneficial" to describe what is otherwise intervention in African conflicts and internal affairs.

The challenge for China may not, however, emerge from Africa but from its geopolitical contestation over influence in Africa with the United States. Rex Tillerson, the former US Secretary of State, urged African countries to be wary of their dealings with China because they risked ceding their state sovereignty to Beijing. In attempting to cast doubt on China's adherence to its foreign policy principle of "respect for other states" sovereignty, Rex Tillerson sought to delegitimise Beijing in Africa by casting aspersions on the very foundational basis of China-Africa relations. China's entrance into Africa is based on its insistence on respecting African countries' sovereignty; an accusation that it was doing the opposite is a grave indictment on China. If "in international discourse, the basic element in a violation of sovereignty is intervention" (Lu 2006, p. 4), then a global contestation over the boundaries of state sovereignty makes intervention a contested concept, not only in academic terms but in its practice. Accordingly, intervention is likely to remain intervention, a contested concept, as its boundaries shift with swings in the distribution of global power, understanding of sovereignty and geopolitical interests of the United States and Europe vis-à-vis rising non-Western global powers.

In addition, what will make intervention in practice even more complex is the dominant perception that China is an illiberal, authoritarian power that might seek to mould the world into its own image. With intervention regarded by the United States and its allies as a tool for conflict management and resolution, that is largely underpinned by a set of liberal norms such as democratisation, human rights and liberal state building, the emergence of China as an intervening power is a challenge to the liberal peace agenda. This concern in Washington DC and Brussels is the reason why Zoellick and Tillerson think China should be socialised first before it can play a responsible role in global governance. But, as China becomes more assertive in global affairs, and the United States under the Trump administration recoils and antagonises its allies, there is no foreseeable reason why China should conform. The emergent puzzle of the twenty-first century is: what then happens when there are historic shifts in global power distribution, say, from the West to the East as Fareed Zakaria puts it? Or, to put it more bluntly in Martin Jacques' words, "When China rules the world" will the understanding and reasoning about intervention also shift in a manner that impacts its practice in the "real world"?

Notes

1. People's Republic of China Ministry of Foreign Affairs 2016, *Foreign Minister Wang Yi meets the press*, 9 March, viewed 22 May 2016, http://www.fmprc.gov.cn/mfa_eng/zxxx_662805/t1346238.shtml
2. Herman, CF 1983, 'Foreign Policy', in S Nagel (ed.), *Encyclopedia of Policy Studies*, Dekker, New York, p. 274.
3. Ministry of Foreign Affairs of the People's Republic of China n.d., *China's initiation of the Five Principles of Peaceful Co-Existence*, viewed 3 October 2013, http://www.fmprc.gov.cn/mfa_eng/ziliao_665539/3602_665543/3604_665547/t18053.shtml
4. Xi, J 2014, 'Carry forward the Five Principles of Peaceful Coexistence to build a better world through win-win cooperation,' Speech presented at meeting marking the 60th anniversary of the initiation of the Five Principles of Peaceful Coexistence, Jakarta, Indonesia, 28 June, viewed 30 June 2014, http://www.china.org.cn/world/2014-07/07/content_32876905.htm; http://www.fmprc.gov.cn/mfa_eng/wjdt_665385/zyjh_665391/t1170143.shtml
5. Ibid.
6. Permanent Mission of the People's Republic of China to the UN 2011, *Explanation of vote by Ambassador Li Baodong after adoption of Security Council Resolution on Libya*, 17 March, viewed 10 February 2015, http://www.china-un.org/eng/gdxw/t807544.htm
7. Chan, M 2014, 'China's growing peacekeeping commitment to UN shows shift in foreign policy', *South China Morning Post*, 30 May, viewed 30 May 2014, http://www.scmp.com/news/china/article/1521454/chinas-growing-peacekeeping-commitment-un-shows-shift-foreign-policy
8. Interview with AU diplomat, Addis Ababa, Ethiopia.
9. Interview, IGAD Analyst, Addis Ababa, Ethiopia.
10. Deng, X. 1984, 'Speech at the Third Plenary Session of the Central Advisory Commission of the Communist Party of China', 22 October 1984, in Deng, X 1994, *Selected Works of Deng Xiaoping: Volume III*, Beijing: Foreign Language Press.
11. "The conference was attended by members of the Political Bureau of the CPC Central Committee, members of the Secretariat of the CPC Central Committee, officials of the Standing Committee of the National People's Congress, State Councilors, President of the Supreme People's Court, Procurator-General of the Supreme People's Procuratorate, leading officials of the Chinese People's Political Consultative Conference and members of the Central Military Commission; leading officials from provinces, autonomous regions and municipalities under direct jurisdiction of the central government as well as the Xinjiang Production and Construction Corps, cities separately listed in the state

plan, government and military departments and some enterprises and financial institutions under the direct management of the central government, as well as Chinese ambassadors and consuls-general with ambassadorial rank posted overseas, Chinese representatives to international organizations and commissioners of the Foreign Ministry to the Hong Kong Special Administrative Region and the Macao Special Administrative Region." (See: 'Xi eyes more enabling int'l environment for China's peaceful development' 2014, *Xinhua*, 29 November, viewed 29 November 2014, http://news.xinhuanet.com/english/china/2014-11/30/c_133822694_5.htm)

12. 'Xi eyes more enabling int'l environment for China's peaceful development' 2014, *Xinhua*, 29 November, viewed 29 November 2014, http://news.xinhuanet.com/english/china/2014-11/30/c_133822694_5.htm
13. Yan, X 2006, 'The rise of China and its power status', *The Chinese journal of international politics*, vol. 1, no. 1, p. 33.
14. Holslag, J 2009, 'China's new security strategy for Africa', *Parameters,* vol. 39, no. 2, p. 23.
15. 'Xi eyes more enabling int'l environment for China's peaceful development' 2014, *Xinhua*, 29 November, viewed 29 November 2014, http://news.xinhuanet.com/english/china/2014-11/30/c_133822694_5.htm
16. Musakwa, T 2013, 'Leading Africa expert in China: French military intervention in Mali 'was necessary', *China-Africa Project*, 30 January, viewed 9 June 2015, http://www.chinaafricaproject.com/france-china-mali-he-wenping-cass-beijing/
17. United Nations 2016, *Ranking of military and police contributions to UN Operations*, viewed 15 May 2016, http://www.un.org/en/peacekeeping/contributors/2016/apr16_2.pdf; see also: http://www.un.org/en/peacekeeping/contributors/2016/apr16_1.pdf
18. United Nations 2016, *Scale of assessments for the apportionment of the expenses of the United Nations peacekeeping operations*, viewed 15 May 2016, http://www.un.org/en/ga/search/view_doc.asp?symbol=A/67/224/Add.1
19. United Nations 2016, *Financing peacekeeping,* viewed 15 May 2016, http://www.un.org/en/peacekeeping/operations/financing.shtml
20. Guan, X 2015, 'China becomes second largest contributor to UN peacekeeping funds', *China Daily*, 24 December, viewed 30 August 2019, http://www.chinadaily.com.cn/world/2015-12/24/content_22797970.htm
21. Xi, J 2015, Speech at General Debate of the 70th Session of the UN General Assembly, 28 September, viewed 30 September 2015, http://gadebate.un.org/sites/default/files/gastatements/70/70_ZH_en.pdf
22. 'China signs agreement with UN to finance peace, security, development activities' 2016, *Xinhua*, 7 May, viewed 7 May 2016, http://news.xinhuanet.com/english/2016-05/07/c_135340457.htm

23. 'China to become third-largest contributor to UN regular budget: Chinese envoy' 2015, *Xinhua*, 24 December, viewed 6 January 2016, http://news.xinhuanet.com/english/2015-12/24/c_134948572.htm
24. Medeiros, E S & Fravel, MT 2003, 'China's new diplomacy', *Foreign Affairs*, Nov/Dec. Issue, viewed 7 April 2014, https://www.foreignaffairs.com/articles/asia/2003-11-01/chinas-new-diplomacy
25. Li, C & Xu, L 2014, 'Chinese enthusiasm and American cynicism: The 'new type of great power relations'', *China-US Focus*, 4 December, viewed 5 December 2014, http://www.chinausfocus.com/foreign-policy/chinese-enthusiasm-and-american-cynicism-over-the-new-type-of-great-power-relations/

Bibliography

Alao, A., & Alden, C. (2018). Africa's security challenges and China's evolving approach to Africa's peace and security architecture. In C. Alden, A. Alao, C. Zhang, & L. Barber (Eds.), *China and Africa: Building peace and security cooperation on the continent* (pp. 13–38). New York: Palgrave Macmillan.

Allison, S. (2015). Peacekeeping in South Sudan: Is this the end for China's non-intervention policy? *Daily Maverick*, 2 March. Retrieved March 14, 2015, from http://www.dailymaverick.co.za/article/2014-06-02-peacekeeping-in-south-sudan-is-thisthe-end-for-chinas-non-intervention-policy/#.VQIEZY6UegY

Barton, B. (2018). *Political trust and the politics of security engagement: China and the European Union in Africa*. New York: Routledge.

Bertran, E. (1995). Reinventing governments: The promise and perils of United Nations peacebuilding. *Journal of Conflict Resolution, 39*(3), 387–418.

Boeke, S., & Schuurman, B. (2015). Operation 'Serval': A strategic analysis of the French intervention in Mali, 2013–2014. *Journal of Strategic Studies, 38*(6), 801–825.

Chamberlain, N. (1937). *The struggle for peace*. Camberley: Hutchinson and Company.

Chan, I., & Li, M. (2015). Going assertive: Chinese foreign policy under the new leadership. In Y. Zheng & L. L. P. Gore (Eds.), *China entering the Xi Jinping era* (pp. 258–269). London: Routledge.

Ching, F. (2012). China uses non-interference when and where it chooses. *The China Post*, 4 April. Retrieved February 12, 2014, from http://www.chinapost.com.tw/commentary/china-post/frank-ching/2012/04/04/336729/p2/China-uses.htm

Cohen, J. A. (1973). China and intervention: Theory and practice. *University of Pennsylvania Law Review, 121*(471), 471–505.

Cook, M. (2015). China's power status change: East Asian challenges for Xi Jinping's foreign policy. *China Quarterly of International Strategic Studies, 1*(01), 105–131.

Cottey, A., & Bikin-Kita, T. (2006). The military and humanitarianism: Emerging patterns of intervention and engagement. In V. Wheeler & A. Harmer (Eds.), *Resetting the rules of engagement: Trends and issues in military-humanitarian relations* (pp. 21–38). London: Overseas Development Institute.

Engelbrekt, K. (2014). Why Libya? Security Council Resolution 1973 and the politics of justification. In K. Engelbrekt, M. Mohlin, & C. Wagnsson (Eds.), *The NATO intervention in Libya: Lessons learned from the campaign* (pp. 41–62). London: Routledge.

Fabricius, P. (2014). Beijing's peacemaking efforts in South Sudan. *Institute for Security Studies*, 6 November. Retrieved December 21, 2014, from http://www.issafrica.org/iss-today/beijings-peacemaking-efforts-in-south-sudan

Feste, K. A. (2003). *Intervention: Shaping the global order*. Westport, CT: Praeger.

Heldt, B., & Wallensteen, P. (2007). *Peacekeeping operations: Global patterns of intervention and success, 1948–2004*. Stockholm: Folke Bernadotte Academy. Retrieved May 12, 2016, from http://papers.ssrn.com/sol3/papers.cfm?abstract_id=1899505

Hille, K. (2013). China commits combat troops to Mali. *Financial Times*, 27 June. Retrieved May 1, 2015, from http://www.ft.com/intl/cms/s/0/e46f3e42-defe-11e2-881f-00144feab7de.html#axzz48zjIGHJY

Hirono, M., & Lanteigne, M. (2012). Introduction: China and UN peacekeeping. In M. Lanteigne & M. Hirono (Eds.), *China's evolving approach to peacekeeping* (pp. 1–14). London: Routledge.

Hough, P., & Malik, S. (2015). China: Security and threat perceptions. In P. Hough, S. Malik, A. Moran, & B. Pilbeam (Eds.), *International security studies: Theory and practice* (pp. 358–365). New York: Routledge.

Huang, C. (2012). Principles and praxis of China's peacekeeping. In M. Lanteigne & M. Hirono (Eds.), *China's evolving approach to peacekeeping* (pp. 15–28). London: Routledge.

Kaarbo, J., Lantis, J. S., & Beasley, R. K. (2002). The analysis of foreign policy in comparative perspective. In R. K. Beasley, J. Kaarbo, J. S. Lantis, & M. T. Snarr (Eds.), *Foreign policy in comparative perspective: Domestic and international influences on state behaviour* (pp. 1–23). Washington, DC: CQ Press.

Kassim, Y. R. (2014). *The geopolitics of intervention: Asia and the responsibility to protect*. Singapore: Springer.

Lanteigne, M. (2014). *China's peacekeeping policies in Mali: New security thinking or balancing Europe?* NFG Working Paper No. 11/2014, Berlin. Retrieved April 12, 2016, from http://www.diss.fu-berlin.de/docs/servlets/MCRFileNodeServlet/FUDOCS_derivate_000000004251/wp1114-china-peacekeeping-policies-mali.pdf

Li, G. (2015). Xi's blue helmets: Chinese peacekeeping in context. *China Brief*, Vol. 15, No. 21. Retrieved May 18, 2016, from http://www.jamestown.org/programs/chinabrief/single/?tx_ttnews%5Btt_news%5D=44558&cHash=d348f26929a27218408abf17b59a157c#.Vzl39PlcSko

Lu, C. (2006). *Just and unjust interventions in world politics: Public and private.* New York: Palgrave Macmillan.

Lucarelli, S. (2006). Introduction. In S. Lucarelli & I. Manners (Eds.), *Values and principles in European Union foreign policy* (pp. 1–18). New York: Routledge.

Mariani, B. (2015). China's role in UN peacekeeping operations. In C. P. Freeman (Ed.), *Handbook on China and developing countries* (pp. 252–271). Northampton: Elgar.

Pang, Z. (2005). China's changing attitude to UN peacekeeping. *International Peacekeeping, 12*(1), 87–104.

Pang, Z. (2008). Playing by 'the rules': Is China a partner or ward? *Spiegel*, 17 October. Retrieved May 18, 2016, from http://www.spiegel.de/international/world/playing-by-the-rules-is-china-a-partner-or-ward-a-584758.html

Richardson, C. J. (2012). A responsible power? China and the UN peacekeeping regime. In M. Lanteigne & M. Hirono (Eds.), *China's evolving approach to peacekeeping* (pp. 44–56). London: Routledge.

Schwartz, B. I. (1968). The Chinese perception of the world order, past and present. In J. K. Fairbank (Ed.), *The Chinese world order: Traditional China's foreign relations* (pp. 276–288). Cambridge: Harvard University Press.

Shinn, D. H. (2013). China confronts terrorism in Africa. *China-US Focus*, 18 November. Retrieved February 3, 2016, from http://www.chinausfocus.com/peace-security/china-confronts-terrorism-in-africa/

Shinn, D. H. (2016). China's security policy in Africa and the Western Indian Ocean. *International Affairs Forum*. Retrieved May 16, 2016, from http://www.ia-forum.org/Content/ViewInternalDocument.cfm?ContentID=7925

Shinn, D. H., & Eisenman, J. (2012). *China and Africa: A century of engagement.* Philadelphia: University of Pennsylvania Press.

Suzuki, S. (2012). Why does China participate in intrusive peacekeeping? Understanding paternalistic Chinese discourse on development and intervention. In M. Lanteigne & M. Hirono (Eds.), *China's evolving approach to peacekeeping* (pp. 29–43). London: Routledge.

Tardy, T., & Wyss, M. (2014). Introduction: Africa – The peacekeeping laboratory. In T. Tardy & M. Wyss (Eds.), *Peacekeeping in Africa: The evolving security architecture* (pp. 1–14). London: Routledge.

Wang, B. W. (2013). The Dragon brings peace? Why China became a major contributor to United Nations peacekeeping. *Stimson Center Spotlight*, 12 July. Retrieved July 24, 2015, from http://www.stimson.org/spotlight/the-dragon-bringspeace-why-china-became-a-major-contributor-to-united-nationspeacekeeping-/

Wang, H., & Rosenau, J. N. (2009). China and global governance. *Asian Perspective, 33*(3), 5–39.

Wang, Y. K. (2011). *Harmony and war: Confucian culture and Chinese power politics*. New York: Columbia University Press.

Yang, J. (2009). The rise of China: Chinese perspectives. In K. J. Cooney & Y. Sato (Eds.), *The rise of China and international security: America and Asia respond* (pp. 13–37). London: Routledge.

Zhu, X. (2012). Understanding China's growth: Past, present, and future. *Journal of Economic Perspectives, 26*(4), 103–124.

Bibliography

Adem, S. (2010). The paradox of Chinas policy in Africa. *African and Asian Studies, 9*(3), 334–355.

Aidoo, R., & Hess, S. (2015). Non-interference 2.0: China's evolving foreign policy towards a changing Africa. *Journal of Current Chinese Affairs, 44*(1), 107–139.

Alao, A., & Alden, C. (2018). Africa's security challenges and China's evolving approach to Africa's peace and security architecture. In C. Alden, A. Alao, C. Zhang, & L. Barber (Eds.), *China and Africa: Building peace and security cooperation on the continent* (pp. 13–38). New York: Palgrave Macmillan.

Alden, C. (2005). China in Africa. *Survival, 47*(3), 147–164.

Alden, C., & Large, D. (2013). China's evolving policy towards peace and security in Africa: Constructing a new paradigm for peace building? In M. G. Berhe & H. Liu (Eds.), *China-Africa relations: Governance, peace and security* (pp. 16–28). Addis Ababa: Institute for Peace and Security Studies.

Alden, C., & Zheng, Y. (2018). China's changing role in peace and security in Africa. In C. Alden, A. Alao, C. Zhang, & L. Barber (Eds.), *China and Africa: Building peace and security cooperation on the continent* (pp. 39–66). New York: Palgrave Macmillan.

Alessi, C., & Xu, B. (2015). *China in Africa*. Council on Foreign Relations, Washington, DC. Retrieved March 14, 2016, from http://www.cfr.org/china/china-africa/p9557

Alexandroff, A. S., & Cooper, A. F. (2010). *Rising states, rising institutions: Challenges for global governance*. Washington, DC: Brookings Institution Press.

O. Hodzi, *The End of China's Non-Intervention Policy in Africa*, Critical Studies of the Asia-Pacific,
https://doi.org/10.1007/978-3-319-97349-4

Allison, S. (2015). Peacekeeping in South Sudan: Is this the end for China's non-intervention policy? *Daily Maverick*, 2 March. Retrieved March 14, 2015, from http://www.dailymaverick.co.za/article/2014-06-02-peacekeeping-in-south-sudan-is-thisthe-end-for-chinas-non-intervention-policy/#.VQIEZY6UegY

Altfeld, M. F., & Bueno de Mesquita, B. (1979). Choosing sides in war. *International Studies Quarterly, 23*(1), 87–112.

Anda, M. O. (2000). *International relations in contemporary Africa* (p. 218). Lanham: University Press of America.

Anthony, R., & Jiang, H. (2014). Forum: Security and engagement: The case of China and South Sudan. *African East-Asian Affairs*, No. 4, pp. 78–97.

Armijo, L. E. (2007). The BRICs countries (Brazil, Russia, India, and China) as analytical category: Mirage or insight? *Asian Perspective-Seoul, 31*(4), 7–42.

Armijo, L. E., & Katada, S. N. (2014). New kids on the block: Rising multipolarity, more financial statecraft. In L. E. Armijo & S. N. Katada (Eds.), *The financial statecraft of emerging powers: Shield and sword in Asia and Latin America* (pp. 1–20). Basingstoke: Palgrave Macmillan.

Armijo, L. E., & Roberts, C. (2014). The emerging powers and global governance: Why the BRICS matter. In R. E. Looney (Ed.), *Handbook of emerging economies* (pp. 503–524). New York: Routledge.

Aubone, A. (2013). Explaining US unilateral military intervention in civil conflicts: A review of the literature. *International Politics, 50*(2), 278–302.

Aybet, G. (2011). Turkey and the ambivalent, reluctant military intervention over Libya. *Today's Zaman*, 24 March. Retrieved March 14, 2014, from http://www.todayszaman.com/op-ed_turkey-and-the-ambivalent-reluctant-military-intervention-over-libya-by-gulnur-aybet_239022.html

Aydin, A. (2012). *Foreign powers and intervention in armed conflicts.* Stanford: Stanford University.

Aydin, A. (2008). Choosing sides: Economic interdependence and interstate disputes. *The Journal of Politics, 70*(4), 1098–1108.

Baldwin, D. A. (1971). Thinking about threats. *Journal of Conflict Resolution, 15*(1), 71–78.

Barkin, J. S., & Cronin, B. (1994). The state and the nation: Changing norms and the rules of sovereignty in international relations. *International Organisation, 48*(1), 107–130.

Barton, B. (2018). *Political trust and the politics of security engagement: China and the European Union in Africa.* New York: Routledge.

Bayart, J. (2000). Africa in the world: A history of extraversion. *African Affairs, 99*(395), 217–267.

Bercovitch, J. (1997). Mediation in international conflict: An overview of theory, a review of practice. In W. I. Zartman & J. L. Rasmussen (Eds.), *Peacemaking in international conflict: Methods and techniques* (pp. 125–153). Washington, DC: United States Institute of Peace.

Bertran, E. (1995). Reinventing governments: The promise and perils of United Nations peacebuilding. *Journal of Conflict Resolution, 39*(3), 387–418.

Bilgin, P. (2008). Thinking past 'western' IR? *Third World Quarterly, 29*(1), 5–23.

Blanchard, C. M. (2010). *Libya: Background and US relations*. DIANE Publishing.

Blanchard, L. P. (2014). *The crisis in South Sudan*. Congressional Research Service, Washington, DC. Retrieved March 14, 2014, from https://www.fas.org/sgp/crs/row/R43344.pdf

Boeke, S., & Schuurman, B. (2015). Operation 'Serval': A strategic analysis of the French intervention in Mali, 2013–2014. *Journal of Strategic Studies, 38*(6), 801–825.

Boskin, M. J. (1986). Macroeconomics, technology, and economic growth: An introduction to some important issues. In R. Landau & N. Rosenberg (Eds.), *The positive sum strategy: Harnessing technology for economic growth* (pp. 33–56). Washington, DC: National Academy Press.

Boswell, A. (2010). China pledges to boost southern Sudan ties after secession vote. *Bloomberg*, 14 October. Retrieved January 15, 2016, from http://www.bloomberg.com/news/articles/2010-10-14/china-pledges-to-boost-southern-sudan-ties-after-january-vote-on-secession

Boulden, J. (2013). The United Nations Security Council and conflict in Africa. In J. Boulden (Ed.), *Responding to conflict in Africa: The United Nations and regional organizations* (pp. 13–32). New York: Palgrave Macmillan.

Bove, V., Gleditsch, K. S., & Sekeris, P. G. (2015). "Oil above water": Economic interdependence and third-party intervention. *Journal of Conflict Resolution*, 1–27. https://doi.org/10.1177/0022002714567952.

Brosché, J. (2008). CPA – New Sudan, old Sudan or two Sudans? – A review of the implementation of the Comprehensive Peace Agreement. In U. J. Dahre (Ed.), *Post-conflict peace-building in the Horn of Africa* (pp. 230–251). Lund: Lund University.

Bull, H. (1986). *Intervention in world politics*. Oxfordshire: Clarendon.

Bull, H. (1984). *Intervention in world politics*. Oxford: Oxford University Press.

Burchill, S. (2005). *The national interest in international relations theory*. New York: Springer.

Burton, G. (2013). *Emerging powers and the Israeli-Palestinian conflict*. Working Paper 15, Issam Fares Institute for Public Policy and International Affairs, American University of Beirut. Retrieved February 12, 2014, from http://www.aub.edu.lb/ifi/international_affairs/unaw/Documents/working_paper_series/20130515ifi_UN_wp_Burton.pdf

Calabrese, J. (2013). China and the Arab awakening: The cost of doing business. *China Report, 49*(1), 5–23.

Campbell, H. (2013a). *NATO's failure in Libya: Lessons for Africa*. Pretoria: Africa Institute of South Africa.

Campbell, H. (2013b). *Global NATO and the catastrophic failure in Libya: Lessons for Africa in the forging of African unity*. Monthly Review Press, New York.

Campbell, I., Wheeler, T., Attree, L., Butler, D., & Mariani, B. (2012). *China and conflict-affected states: Between principle and pragmatism*. London: SaferWorld.

Campos, I., & Vines, A. (2008). Angola and China: A pragmatic partnership. In J. Cooke (Ed.), *US and Chinese engagement in Africa: Prospects for improving US-China-Africa cooperation*. Washington, DC: Center for Strategic and International Studies (CSIS). Retrieved April 5, 2014, from http://csis.org/files/media/csis/pubs/080711_cooke_us_chineseengagement_web.pdf.

Carlson, A. (2004). Helping to keep the peace (albeit reluctantly): China's recent stance on sovereignty and multilateral intervention. *Pacific Affairs, 77*(1), 9–27.

Carpenter, T. G. (2014). *Beijing's nervous ambivalence about Crimea*. China-US Focus, 31 March. Retrieved from http://www.chinausfocus.com/foreign-policy/beijings-nervous-ambivalence-about-crimea/

Chamberlain, N. (1937). *The struggle for peace*. Camberley: Hutchinson and Company.

Chan, S. (2012). *Looking for balance: China, the United States, and power balancing in East Asia*. Stanford: Stanford University Press.

Chan, W. T. (1973). *A source book in Chinese philosophy*. Princeton: Princeton University Press.

Chan, I., & Li, M. (2015). Going assertive: Chinese foreign policy under the new leadership. In Y. Zheng & L. L. P. Gore (Eds.), *China entering the Xi Jinping era* (pp. 258–269). London: Routledge.

Cheng, C. (2014). *China's economic development, 1950–2014: Fundamental changes and long-term prospects*. London: Lexington Books.

Ching, F. (2012). China uses non-interference when and where it chooses. *The China Post*, 4 April. Retrieved February 12, 2014, from http://www.chinapost.com.tw/commentary/china-post/frank-ching/2012/04/04/336729/p2/China-uses.htm

Ching, J. (2004). Confucianism and weapons of mass destruction. In S. H. Hashimi & S. P. Lee (Eds.), *Ethics and weapons of mass destruction: Religious and secular perspectives* (pp. 246–269). Cambridge: Cambridge University Press.

Chivvis, C. S. (2016). *The French war on Al Qa'ida in Africa*. Cambridge: Cambridge University Press.

Choucri, N., & North, R. C. (1975). *Nations in conflict: National growth and international violence*. San Francisco: WH Freeman.

Chow, G. C., & Li, K. (2002). China's economic growth: 1952–2010. *Economic Development and Cultural Change, 51*(1), 247–256.

Cilliers, J., & Schuenemann, J. (2013). *The future of intrastate conflict in Africa more violence or greater peace?* Institute for Security Studies Paper 246, p. 2. Retrieved January 3, 2014, from https://www.issafrica.org/uploads/Paper246.pdf

Cohen, J. A. (1973). China and intervention: Theory and practice. *University of Pennsylvania Law Review, 121*(471), 471–505.

Cohen, R. (1978). Threat perception in international crisis. *Political Science Quarterly, 93*(1), 93–107.

Collier, P., & Hoeffler, A. (2004). Conflicts. In B. Lomborg (Ed.), *Global crises, global solutions* (pp. 129–150). Cambridge: Cambridge University Press.

Collier, P., & Hoeffler, A. (2007). Civil war. In T. Sandler & K. Hartley (Eds.), *Handbook of defense economics: Defense in a globalized world* (Vol. 2, pp. 711–739). Amsterdam: North-Holland Publications.

Conteh-Morgan, E. (2001). International intervention: Conflict, economic dislocation, and the hegemonic role of dominant actors. *International Journal of Peace Studies, 6*(2), 33–52.

Cook, M. (2015). China's power status change: East Asian challenges for Xi Jinping's foreign policy. *China Quarterly of International Strategic Studies, 1*(01), 105–131.

Cooper, A. F., & Flemes, D. (2013). Foreign policy strategies of emerging powers in a multipolar world: An introductory review. *Third World Quarterly, 34*(6), 943–962.

Corkin, L. (2013). *Uncovering African agency: Angola's management of China's credit lines.* Surrey: Ashgate.

Cottam, R. W. (1977). *Foreign policy motivation: A general theory and a case study.* Pittsburgh: University of Pittsburgh Press.

Cottey, A., & Bikin-Kita, T. (2006). The military and humanitarianism: Emerging patterns of intervention and engagement. In V. Wheeler & A. Harmer (Eds.), *Resetting the rules of engagement: Trends and issues in military-humanitarian relations* (pp. 21–38). London: Overseas Development Institute.

Cox, W. R. (1992). Towards a post-hegemonic conceptualization of world order: Reflections on the relevancy of Ibn Khaldun. In J. N. Rosenau & E. O. Czempiel (Eds.), *Governance without government: Order and change in world politics* (pp. 132–159). Cambridge: Cambridge University Press.

Dadush, U. (2014). Key trends in the world economy. In R. E. Looney (Ed.), *Handbook of emerging economies* (pp. 13–29). New York: Routledge.

Dai, Y. (2004). A disguised defeat: The Myanmar campaign of the Qing dynasty. *Modern Asian Studies, 38*(01), 145–189.

Danilovic, V. (2002). *When the stakes are high: Deterrence and conflict among major powers.* Michigan: The University of Michigan Press.

Deng, L. B. (2015). IGAD plus, SPLM-FD and prospects for peace in South Sudan. *Sudan Tribune*, 11 June. Retrieved June 13, 2015, from http://sudantribune.com/spip.php?article55309

Deng, X. (1983). *Deng Xiaoping wenxuan 1975–1982 (Selected works of Deng Xiaoping 1975–1982).* Beijing: Renminchubanshe. Retrieved January 7, 2016, from https://archive.org/stream/SelectedWorksOfDengXiaopingVol.1/Deng02#page/n0/mode/2up

Deng, X. (1994). *Selected works of Deng Xiaoping: Volume III*. Beijing: Foreign Language Press. Retrieved January 7, 2016, from https://archive.org/stream/SelectedWorksOfDengXiaopingVol.3/Deng03#page/n1/mode/2up

Deng, Y., & Wang, F. (1999). Introduction: Toward an understanding of China's world view. In Y. Deng & F. Wang (Eds.), *In the eyes of the Dragon. China views the world* (pp. 1–19). Lanham: Rowman & Littlefield.

Dixon, J. (2003). *Suggested changes to the COW civil war dataset 3.0*. Paper presented at the annual meeting of the International Studies Association, Portland, Oregon, February 25–March 1.

Dreyer, J. T. (2015). The 'Tianxia Trope': Will China change the international system? *Journal of Contemporary China, 24*(96), 1015–1031.

Duggan, N. (2018). China's new intervention policy: China's peacekeeping mission in Mali. In C. Alden, A. Alao, C. Zhang, & L. Barber (Eds.), *China and Africa: Building peace and security cooperation on the continent* (pp. 209–223). New York: Palgrave Macmillan.

EIA. (2014). *Country analysis brief: Sudan and South Sudan*. U.S. Energy Information Administration, 3 September. Retrieved September 6, 2014, from https://www.eia.gov/beta/international/analysis_includes/countries_long/Sudan_and_South_Sudan/sudan.pdf

Eisenman, J., Heginbotham, E., & Mitchell, D. (2007). *China and the developing world: Beijing's strategy for the twenty-first century*. New York: ME Sharpe.

Elman, C., & Elman, M. F. (2003). *Progress in international relations theory: Appraising the field*. Cambridge: MIT Press.

Engelbrekt, K. (2014). Why Libya? Security Council Resolution 1973 and the politics of justification. In K. Engelbrekt, M. Mohlin, & C. Wagnsson (Eds.), *The NATO intervention in Libya: Lessons learned from the campaign* (pp. 41–62). London: Routledge.

Engelbrekt, K., & Wagnsson, C. (2014). Introduction. In K. Engelbrekt, M. Mohlin, & C. Wagnsson (Eds.), *The NATO intervention in Libya: Lessons learned from the campaign* (pp. 1–14). New York: Routledge.

Evron, Y. (2014). Sino-Israeli defense relations: In search of common strategic ground. In D. C. Chau & T. M. Kane (Eds.), *China and international security: History, strategy, and 21st-century policy* (pp. 239–257). Santa Barbara: Praeger.

Fabricius, P. (2014). Beijing's peacemaking efforts in South Sudan. *Institute for Security Studies*, 6 November. Retrieved December 21, 2014, from http://www.issafrica.org/iss-today/beijings-peacemaking-efforts-in-south-sudan

Fairbank, J. K. (1968). A preliminary framework. In J. K. Fairbank (Ed.), *The Chinese world order: Traditional China's foreign relations* (pp. 1–10). Cambridge: Harvard University Press.

Feng, B. (2014). China to send its first infantry troops to U.N. Mission in South Sudan. *New York Times*, December 23. Retrieved January 6, 2015, from http://sinosphere.blogs.nytimes.com/2014/12/23/china-to-send-its-first-infantry-troops-to-u-n-mission-in-south-sudan/?_r=0

Feste, K. A. (1992). *Expanding the Frontiers: Superpower intervention in the cold war*. Westport, CT: Praeger.

Feste, K. A. (2003). *Intervention: Shaping the global order*. Westport, CT: Praeger.

Finnemore, M. (2003). *The purpose of intervention: Changing beliefs about the use of force*. Ithaca, NY: Cornell University Press.

Foot, S. (2001). Chinese power and the idea of a responsible state. *The China Journal, 45*, 1–19.

Foster, V., Butterfield, W., Chen, C., & Pushak, N. (2009). *Building bridges: China's growing role as infrastructure financier for sub-Saharan Africa* (Vol. 5). Washington, DC: The World Bank.

Francis, D. J. (2006). *Uniting Africa: Building regional peace and security systems*. Hampshire: Ashgate Publishing.

Francis, D. J. (2013). *The regional impact of the armed conflict and French intervention in Mali*. Norwegian Peacebuilding Resource Centre, Oslo. Retrieved July 13, 2016, from http://www.peacebuilding.no/var/ezflow_site/storage/original/application/f18726c3338e39049bd4d554d4a22c36.pdf

French, H. (2004). China in Africa: All trade, with no political baggage. *New York Times*, 8 August. Retrieved June 7, 2015, from http://www.nytimes.com/2004/08/08/international/asia/08china.html

Froman, M. B. (2014). The Strategic logic of trade: New rules of the road for the global market. *Foreign Affairs*, Vol. 93, No. 6.

Fukuyama, F. (2004). *State-building: Governance and world order in the 21st century*. Ithaca, NY: Cornell University Press.

Fung, C. J. (2015). What explains China's deployment to UN peacekeeping operations? *International Relations of the Asia-Pacific*. Retrieved May 16, 2016, from http://irap.oxfordjournals.org/content/early/2015/11/27/irap.lcv020.full.pdf+html

Gent, S. E. (2007). The strategic dynamics of major power military interventions. *The Journal of Politics, 69*(4), 1089–1102.

George, A. L. (1979). Case studies and theory development: The method of structured focused comparison. In P. G. Lauren (Ed.), *Diplomacy: New approaches in history, theory and policy* (pp. 43–68). New York: Free Press.

George, A. L., & Bennett, A. (2005). *Case studies and theory development in the social sciences*. Cambridge: MIT Press.

Gersovitz, M., & Kriger, N. (2013). What is a civil war? A critical review of its definition and (econometric) consequences. *The World Bank Research Observer, 28*(2), 159–190.

Gill, B., Huang, C., & Morrison, J. S. (2007). Assessing China's growing influence in Africa. *China Security, 3*(3), 3–21.

Givens, J. W. (2011). The Beijing consensus is neither: China as a non-ideological challenge to international norms. *St Antony's International Review, 6*(2), 10–26.

Goodman, P. S. (2004). China invests heavily in Sudan's oil industry; Beijing supplies arms used on villagers. *Washington Post*, 23 December. Retrieved February 7, 2016, from http://www.washingtonpost.com/wp-dyn/articles/A21143-2004Dec22.html

Goldstein, A. (1997). Great expectations: Interpreting China's arrival. *International Security, 22*(3), 36–73.

Goldstone, J. A. (2012). Protest and repression in democracies and autocracies: Europe, Iran, Thailand and the Middle East 2010–11. In S. Seferiades & H. Johnston (Eds.), *Violent protest, contentious politics, and the neoliberal state* (pp. 103–118). Surrey: Ashgate.

Gratius, S. (2008). *The international arena and emerging powers: Stabilising or destabilising forces?* Fundación para las Relaciones Internacionales y el Diálogo Exterior (FRIDE), Madrid. Retrieved September 21, 2014, from http://fride.org/download/COM_emerging_powers_ENG_abr08.pdf

Grbich, C. (2007). *Qualitative data analysis: An introduction.* Thousand Oaks, CA: Sage.

Gridneff, I. (2014). China halts arms sale to South Sudan after NORINCO shipment. *Bloomberg*, 30 September. Retrieved October 16, 2015, from http://www.bloomberg.com/news/articles/2014-09-29/china-halts-weapons-sales-to-south-sudan-after-norinco-shipment

Guelke, A. (1974). Force, intervention and internal conflict. In F. S. Northedge (Ed.), *The use of force in international relations* (pp. 99–123). London: Faber.

Haass, R. N. (2008). The age of nonpolarity: What will follow US dominance. *Foreign Affairs,* Vol. 87, No. 3, pp. 44–56.

Halper, S. (2012). *The Beijing consensus: Legitimizing authoritarianism in our time.* New York: Basic Books.

Hanauer, L., & Morris, L. J. (2014). *Chinese engagement in Africa: Drivers, reactions, and implications for U.S. policy.* California: RAND Corporation.

Handel, M. I. (1990). *Weak states in the international system.* London: Frank Cass.

Hart, A. F., & Jones, B. D. (2010). How do rising powers rise? *Survival, 52*(6), 63–88.

Heldt, B., & Wallensteen, P. (2007). *Peacekeeping operations: Global patterns of intervention and success, 1948–2004.* Stockholm: Folke Bernadotte Academy. Retrieved May 12, 2016, from http://papers.ssrn.com/sol3/papers.cfm?abstract_id=1899505

Hermann, M. G., & Hermann, C. F. (1989). Who makes foreign policy decisions and how: An empirical inquiry. *International Studies Quarterly, 33*(4), 361–387.

Hess, S., & Aidoo, R. (2010). Beyond the rhetoric: Noninterference in China's African policy. *African and Asian Studies, 9*(3), 356–383.

Hille, K. (2013). China commits combat troops to Mali. *Financial Times*, 27 June. Retrieved May 1, 2015, from http://www.ft.com/intl/cms/s/0/e46f3e42-defe-11e2-881f-00144feab7de.html#axzz48zjIGHJY

Hirono, M., & Lanteigne, M. (2012). Introduction: China and UN peacekeeping. In M. Lanteigne & M. Hirono (Eds.), *China's evolving approach to peacekeeping* (pp. 1–14). London: Routledge.

Hodzi, O. (2014). Political transition to democracy: The role of the security sector and regional economic communities in Zimbabwe and Cote d'Ivoire's democratic puzzle. *African Security Review, 23*(1), 1–12.

Hodzi, O., Hartwell, L., & De Jager, N. (2012). 'Unconditional aid': Assessing the impact of China's development assistance to Zimbabwe. *South African Journal of International Affairs, 19*(1), 79–103.

Hoge Jr, J. F. (2004). Global power shift in the making: Is the United States ready? *Foreign Affairs*, Vol. 83, No. 4, pp. 2–7.

Holmes, J. E. (1985). *The mood/interest theory of American foreign policy.* Kentucky: The University Press of Kentucky.

Holslag, J. (2009). China's new security strategy for Africa. *Parameters, 39*(2), 23–37.

Holsti, K. J. (1964). The concept of power in the study of international relations. *Background, 7*(4), 179–194.

Hough, P., & Malik, S. (2015). China: Security and threat perceptions. In P. Hough, S. Malik, A. Moran, & B. Pilbeam (Eds.), *International security studies: Theory and practice* (pp. 358–365). New York: Routledge.

Huang, C. (2012). Principles and praxis of China's peacekeeping. In M. Lanteigne & M. Hirono (Eds.), *China's evolving approach to peacekeeping* (pp. 15–28). London: Routledge.

Huntington, S. P. (1991). America's changing strategic interests. *Survival, 33*(1), 3–17.

Hurrell, A. (2006). Hegemony, liberalism and global order: What space for would-be great powers? *International Affairs, 82*(1), 1–19.

Huth, P. K., & Russett, B. (1984). What makes deterrence work? Cases from 1900 to 1980. *World Politics, 36*(4), 496–526.

Ikenberry, G. J. (2001). Review of saving strangers: Humanitarian intervention in international society, Wheeler, N.J. *Foreign Affairs*, Vol. 80, No. 6. Retrieved June 5, 2014, from http://www.foreignaffairs.com/articles/57287/g-john-ikenberry/saving-strangers-humanitarian-intervention-in-international-soci

Ikenberry, G. J. (2008). The rise of China and the future of the West: Can the liberal system survive? *Foreign Affairs*, Vol. 87, No. 1, pp. 23–37.

Ikenberry, G. J. (2010). The three faces of liberal internationalism. In A. S. Alexandroff & A. F. Cooper (Eds.), *Rising states, rising institutions: Challenges for global governance* (pp. 17–47). Washington, DC: Brookings Institution Press.

International Crisis Group. (2015). *South Sudan: Keeping faith with the IGAD peace process.* Africa Report No. 228, 27 July. Retrieved February 9, 2016, from http://www.crisisgroup.org/~/media/Files/africa/horn-of-africa/south%20sudan/228-south-sudan-keeping-faith-with-the-igad-peace-process.pdf

Ivanhoe, P. (2004). "Heaven's mandate" and the concept of war in early Confucianism. In S. H. Hashimi & S. P. Lee (Eds.), *Ethics and weapons of mass destruction: Religious and secular perspectives* (pp. 270–276). Cambridge: Cambridge University Press.

Jacobs, L. M., & Van Rossem, R. (2014). The BRIC phantom: A comparative analysis of the BRICs as a category of rising powers. *Journal of Policy Modeling, 36*, S47–S66.

Jakobson, L. (2009). China's diplomacy toward Africa: Drivers and constraints. *International Relations of the Asia-Pacific, 9*(3), 403–433.

Jiang, J., & Ding, C. (2014). *Update on overseas investments by China's national oil companies. Achievements and challenges since 2011.* IEA Partner Country Series, OECD Publishing, Paris. Retrieved June 10, 2015, from http://www.iea.org/publications/freepublications/publication/PartnerCountrySeriesUpdateonOverseasInvestmentsbyChinasNationalOilCompanies.pdf

Jiang, J., & Sinton, J. (2011). *Overseas investments by Chinese national oil companies.* IEA Energy Papers, no. 2011/03, OECD Publishing, Paris. Retrieved June 10, 2015, from http://www.oecd-ilibrary.org/docserver/download/5kgglrwdrvvd.pdf?expires=1456063139&id=id&accname=guest&checksum=EA84CD4E1E7E7AD5D92BCC1CF35BC439

Jorgic, D. (2014). China takes more assertive line in South Sudan diplomacy. *Reuters*, 5 June. Retrieved June 5, 2014, from http://uk.reuters.com/article/2014/06/05/uk-southsudan-china-insight-idUKKBN0EG01Z20140605

Kaarbo, J., Lantis, J. S., & Beasley, R. K. (2002). The analysis of foreign policy in comparative perspective. In R. K. Beasley, J. Kaarbo, J. S. Lantis, & M. T. Snarr (Eds.), *Foreign policy in comparative perspective: Domestic and international influences on state behaviour* (pp. 1–23). Washington, DC: CQ Press.

Kalyvas, N. S. (2007). Civil wars. In C. Boix & S. C. Stokes (Eds.), *The Oxford handbook of comparative politics* (pp. 416–434). Oxford: Oxford University Press.

Kambudzi, A. M. (2013). Africa and China's non-interference policy: Towards peace enhancement in Africa. In M. G. Berhe & H. Liu (Eds.), *China-Africa relations: Governance, peace and security* (pp. 29–45). Addis Ababa: Institute for Peace and Security Studies.

Kassim, Y. R. (2014). *The geopolitics of intervention: Asia and the responsibility to protect.* Singapore: Springer.

Kathman, J. D. (2010). Civil war contagion and neighbouring interventions. *International Studies Quarterly, 54*(4), 989–1012.

Kauffmann, M. (2008). *Building and using datasets on armed conflicts.* Amsterdam: IOS Press.

Kaufman, A. A. (2010). The "century of humiliation," then and now: Chinese perceptions of the international order. *Pacific Focus, 25*(1), 1–33.

Keene, E. (2002). *Beyond the anarchical society: Grotius, colonialism and order in world politics*. Cambridge: Cambridge University Press.

Kennedy, P. (1988). *The rise and fall of the great powers: Economic change and military power from 1500 to 2000*. London: Unwin Hyman.

Kennedy, P. (1987). *The rise and fall of the great powers: Economic change and military power from 1500 to 2000*. New York: Random House.

Keohane, R. O., & Nye, J. S. (2012). *Power and interdependence*. New York: Longman.

Khosla, D. (1999). Third world states as interveners in ethnic conflicts: Implications for regional and international security. *Third World Quarterly, 20*(6), 1143–1156.

Kitissou, M., McGarrah, J., & Kablan, P. G. (2010). Ethics in foreign-policy making: US and China's approach to the crisis in Darfur, Sudan. In M. Ndulo & M. Grieco (Eds.), *Failed and failing states: The challenges to African reconstruction* (pp. 39–58). Newcastle: Cambridge Scholars Publishing.

Kleine-Ahlbrandt, S. T. (2009). Beijing, global free-rider. *Foreign Policy*, 12 November. Retrieved September 3, from https://foreignpolicy.com/2009/11/12/beijing-global-free-rider/

Kleine-Ahlbrandt, S., & Small, A. (2008). China's new dictatorship diplomacy: Is Beijing parting with pariahs? *Foreign Affairs*, Vol. 87, No. 1, pp. 38–56.

Kline, J. (2010). *Ethics for international business: Decision-making in a global political economy*. London: Routledge.

Klingberg, F. L. (1996). *Positive expectations of America's world role: Historical cycles of realistic idealism*. Lanham: University Press of America.

Kornberg, J. F., & Faust, J. R. (2005). *China in world politics: Policies, processes, prospects*. Boulder: Lynne Rienner.

Krasner, S. D. (1978). *Defending the national interest: Raw materials investments and US foreign policy*. New Jersey: Princeton University Press.

Krasner, S. D. (1993). Power, polarity, and the challenge of disintegration. In H. Haftendorn & C. Tuschhoff (Eds.), *America and Europe in an era of change* (pp. 21–42). Boulder: Westview Press.

Kristof, N. D. (1993). The rise of China. *Foreign Affairs*, Vol. 72, No. 5, pp. 59–74.

Kupchan, C. A. (2012). The decline of the West: Why America must prepare for the end of dominance. *The Atlantic*, 20 March. Retrieved May 24, 2016, from http://www.theatlantic.com/international/archive/2012/03/the-decline-of-the-west-why-america-must-prepare-for-the-end-of-dominance/254779/

Kurlantzick, J. (2007). *Charm offensive: How China's soft power is transforming the world*. New Haven: Yale University Press.

Lai, H., & Lu, Y. (2012). *China's soft power and international relations*. London: Routledge.

Lam, T. B. (1968). Intervention versus tribute in Sino-Vietnamese relations, 1788–1790. In J. K. Fairbank (Ed.), *The Chinese world order: Traditional China's foreign relations.* Cambridge: Harvard University Press.

Lanteigne, M. (2014). *China's peacekeeping policies in Mali: New security thinking or balancing Europe?* NFG Working Paper No. 11/2014, Berlin. Retrieved April 12, 2016, from http://www.diss.fu-berlin.de/docs/servlets/MCRFileNodeServlet/FUDOCS_derivate_000000004251/wp1114-china-peacekeeping-policies-mali.pdf

Large, D. (2007). Arms, oil and Darfur: The evolution of relations between China and Sudan. *Small Arms Survey*, No. 7, pp. 1–12. Retrieved March 1, 2016, from http://www.smallarmssurveysudan.org/fileadmin/docs/issue-briefs/HSBA-IB-07-Arms.pdf

Large, D. (2008a). From non-interference to constructive engagement? China's evolving relations with Sudan. In C. Alden, D. Large, & R. S. De Oliveira (Eds.), *China returns to Africa: A rising power and a continent embrace* (pp. 275–294). London: Hurst.

Large, D. (2008b). China and the contradictions of 'non-interference' in Sudan. *Review of African Political Economy, 35*(115), 93–106.

Large, D. (2009). China's Sudan engagement: Changing northern and southern political trajectories in peace and war. *The China Quarterly, 199*, 610–626.

Large, D. (2011a). Southern Sudan and China: Enemies into friends? In D. Large & L. A. Patey (Eds.), *Sudan looks east: China, India and the politics of Asian alternatives* (pp. 157–175). New York: James Currey.

Large, D. (2011b). South Sudan looks east: Between the CPA and independence. *Association of Concerned Africa Scholars*, no. 86, pp. 54–58.

Large, D. (2012). *Between the CPA and Southern independence: China's post-conflict engagement in Sudan.* South African Institute of International Affairs, Occasional Paper No. 115. Retrieved July 9, 2015, from http://www.saiia.org.za/occasional-papers/33-between-the-cpa-and-southern-independence-china-s-post-conflict-engagement-in-sudan/file

Larkin, B. D. (1973). *China and Africa, 1949–1970: The foreign policy of the People's Republic of China.* California: University of California Press.

Layne, C. (1993). The unipolar illusion: Why new great powers will rise. *International Security, 17*(4), 5–51.

Layne, C. (2006). *The peace of illusions: American grand strategy from 1940 to the present.* Cambridge: Cambridge University Press.

Layne, C. (2008). China's challenge to US hegemony. *Current History, 107*(705), 13–18.

Lecocq, B. (2005). The Bellah question: Slave emancipation, race, and social categories in late twentieth-century Northern Mali. *Canadian Journal of African Studies/Revue canadienne des Ãctudes africaines, 39*(1), 42–68.

Lee, H. (2008). *Political disputes and investment: The effect of militarized interstate disputes on foreign direct investment.* PhD thesis, The University of Iowa.

Lee, P. K., Chan, G., & Chan, L. (2012). China in Darfur: Humanitarian rule-maker or rule-taker? *Review of International Studies, 38*(2), 423–444.

Legum, C. (1976). The Soviet Union, China and the West in Southern Africa. *Foreign Affairs*, Vol. 54, No. 4, pp. 745–762.

Lemke, D. (2003). African lessons for international relations research. *World Politics, 56*(01), 114–138.

Levy, J. (1983). *War in the modern great power system, 1495–1975*. Lexington: University Press of Kentucky.

Levy, J. S. (2008). Case studies: Types, designs, and logics of inference. *Conflict Management and Peace Science, 25*(1), 1–18.

Li, G. (2015). Xi's blue helmets: Chinese peacekeeping in context. *China Brief*, Vol. 15, No. 21. Retrieved May 18, 2016, from http://www.jamestown.org/programs/chinabrief/single/?tx_ttnews%5Btt_news%5D=44558&cHash=d348f26929a27218408abf17b59a157c#.Vzl39PlcSko

Lim, C. L. (2016). *Doing comparative politics: An introduction to approaches and issues*. Boulder: Lynne Rienner.

Little, R. (1975). *Intervention: External involvement in civil wars*. Lanham: Rowman & Littlefield Publishers.

Little, R. (1987). Revisiting intervention: A survey of recent developments. *Review of International Studies, 13*(01), 49–60.

Liu, S. (1995). Reflections on world peace through peace among religions—A Confucian perspective. *Journal of Chinese Philosophy, 22*, 193–213.

Lobell, S. E., Ripsman, N. M., & Taliaferro, J. W. (2009). *Neoclassical realism, the state, and foreign policy*. Cambridge: Cambridge University Press.

Lu, C. (2006). *Just and unjust interventions in world politics: Public and private*. New York: Palgrave Macmillan.

Luard, E. (1988). *Conflict and peace in the modern international system*. London: Macmillan.

Lucarelli, S. (2006). Introduction. In S. Lucarelli & I. Manners (Eds.), *Values and principles in European Union foreign policy* (pp. 1–18). New York: Routledge.

Macfarlane, R. (2012). Why has China been vilified by the west for its engagement in Darfur and to what extent is this justified? *Journal of Politics & International Studies, 8*(13, Winter), 161–202.

Mandelbaum, M. (1988). *The fate of nations: The search for national security in the nineteenth and twentieth centuries*. Cambridge: Cambridge University Press.

Mariani, B. (2015). China's role in UN peacekeeping operations. In C. P. Freeman (Ed.), *Handbook on China and developing countries* (pp. 252–271). Northampton: Elgar.

Mark, B. (2009). Hegemonic transition in East Asia? The dynamics of Chinese and American power. *Review of International Studies, 35*(1), 95–112.

Marks, S. (2006). China in Africa-the new imperialism? *Pambazuka News*, March 2. Retrieved April 29, 2015, from http://www.pambazuka.net/en/category/features/32432

Mastanduno, M. (1997). Preserving the unipolar moment: Realist theories and U.S. grand strategy after the Cold War. *International Security, 21*(4), 49–88.

Mastanduno, M., Lake, D. A., & Ikenberry, G. J. (1989). Toward a realist theory of state action. *International Studies Quarterly, 33*(4), 457–474.

Mayer, J., & Fajarnes, P. (2008). Tripling Africa's primary exports: What, how, where? *The Journal of Development Studies, 44*(1), 80–102.

Mearsheimer, J. (2001). *The tragedy of great power politics.* New York: W. W. Norton.

Mearsheimer, J. (2004). Why China's rise will not be peaceful. Retrieved September 1, 2018, from http://mearsheimer.uchicago.edu/pdfs/A0034b.pdf

Mearsheimer, J. (2005). The rise of China will not be peaceful at all. *The Australian,* 18 November. Retrieved August 21, 2015, from http://mearsheimer.uchicago.edu/pdfs/P0014.pdf

Medeiros, E. S., & Fravel, M. T. (2003). China's new diplomacy. *Foreign Affairs,* November/December Issue. Retrieved April 7, 2014, from https://www.foreignaffairs.com/articles/asia/2003-11-01/chinas-new-diplomacy

Miles, M. B., & Huberman, A. M. (1994). *Qualitative data analysis: An expanded sourcebook.* Thousand Oaks, CA: Sage.

Mohan, G., & Power, M. (2009). Africa, China and the 'new economic geography of development'. *Singapore Journal of Tropical Geography, 30*(1), 24–28.

Morgenthau, H. J. (1967). To intervene or not to intervene. *Foreign Affairs,* Vol. 45, No. 3, pp. 425–436.

Moyo, D. (2012). *Winner take all: China's race for resources and what it means for the world.* New York: Basic Books.

Mullenbach, M. J., & Matthews, G. P. (2008). Deciding to intervene: An analysis of international and domestic influences on United States interventions in intrastate disputes. *International Interactions, 34*(1), 25–52.

Muvawala, J., & Mugisha, F. (2014). South Sudan. *African Economic Outlook.* Retrieved September 9, 2014, from http://www.africaneconomicoutlook.org/fileadmin/uploads/aeo/2014/PDF/CN_Long_EN/SoudanDuSUd_ENG.pdf

Nadvi, K. (2014). Rising powers and labour and environmental standards. *Oxford Development Studies, 42*(2), 137–150.

Naidu, S., Corkin, L., & Herman, H. (2009a). Introduction. *Politikon, 36*(1), 1–4.

Naidu, S., Corkin, L., & Herman, H. (2009b). China's (re)-emerging relations with Africa: Forging a new consensus? *Politikon, 36*(1), 87–115.

Newman, E. (2014). *Understanding civil wars: Continuity and change in intrastate conflict.* London: Routledge.

Nolte, D. (2010). How to compare regional powers: Analytical concepts and research topics. *Review of International Studies, 36*(04), 881–901.

Nossal, K. M. (2001). Tales that textbooks tell: Ethnocentricity and diversity in American introductions to international relations. In M. A. R. Crawford & D. S. L. Jarvis (Eds.), *International relations – Still an American social science? : Toward diversity in international thought* (pp. 167–186). New York: State University of New York Press.

Ogunsanwo, A. (1974). *China's policy in Africa: 1958–71*. Cambridge: Cambridge University Press.

Okemuo, G. (2013). The EU or France? The CSDP mission in Mali the consistency of the EU Africa policy. *Liverpool Law Review, 34*(3), 217–240.

Organisation for Economic Co-operation and Development. (2007). *Glossary of statistical terms*. OECD. Retrieved April 6, 2014, from http://stats.oecd.org/glossary/detail.asp?ID=6181

Osondu, A. (2013). Off and on: China's principle of non-interference in Africa. *Mediterranean Journal of Social Sciences, 4*(3), 225–234.

Owen, D. S., & Strong, T. B. (2004). *The vocation lectures*. Cambridge: Hackett Publishing.

Pang, Z. (2005). China's changing attitude to UN peacekeeping. In M. Caballero-Anthony & A. Acharya (Eds.), *UN peace operations and Asian security* (pp. 73–87). London: Routledge.

Pang, Z. (2005). China's changing attitude to UN peacekeeping. *International Peacekeeping, 12*(1), 87–104.

Pang, Z. (2008). Playing by 'the rules'. Is China a partner or ward? *Spiegel*, 17 October. Retrieved May 18, 2016, from http://www.spiegel.de/international/world/playing-by-the-rules-is-china-a-partner-or-ward-a-584758.html

Pang, Z. (2009). China's non-intervention question. *Global Responsibility to Protect, 1*, 237–252.

Pang, Z. (2013). The non-interference dilemma: Adapting China's approach to the new context of African and international realities. In M. G. Berhe & H. Liu (Eds.), *China-Africa relations: Governance, peace and security* (pp. 46–54). Addis Ababa: Institute for Peace and Security Studies.

Panozzo, I. (2015). Asian players in Sudan: Social and economic impacts of 'new-old' actors. In B. Casciarri, A. M. Munzoul, & F. Ireton (Eds.), *Multidimensional change in Sudan (1989–2011): Reshaping livelihoods, conflicts and identities* (pp. 163–181). New York: Berghahn.

Patey, L. (2014). *The new kings of crude: China, India, and the global struggle for oil in Sudan and South Sudan*. London: Hurst.

Patrick, S. (2010). Irresponsible stakeholders? The difficulty of integrating rising powers. *Foreign Affairs*, Vol. 89, No. 6, pp. 44–53.

Pearson, F. S. (1974). Foreign military interventions and domestic disputes. *International Studies Quarterly, 18*(3), 259–290.

Perdue, P. C. (2015). The tenacious tributary system. *Journal of Contemporary China, 24*(96), 1002–1014.

Ping, J. (2014). The crisis in Mali. *Harvard International Review*, 22 March. Retrieved September 3, 2018, from http://hir.harvard.edu/article/?a=6033

Le Pere, G. (2008). The geo-strategic dimensions of the Sino-African relationship. In K. Ampiah & S. Naidu (Eds.), *Crouching tiger, hidden dragon? Africa and China* (pp. 20–39). Durban: University of KwaZulu Natal Press.

Poggo, S. S. (2009). *The first Sudanese civil war: Africans, Arabs, and Israelis in Southern Sudan, 1955–1972*. London: Palgrave Macmillan.

Pollins, B. M., & Schweller, R. L. (1999). Linking the levels: The long wave and shifts in US foreign policy, 1790–1993. *American Journal of Political Science, 43*(2), 431–464.

Qin, Y. (2003). Nation identity, strategic culture and security interests: Three hypotheses on the interaction between China and international society. *SIIS Journal*, No. 1.

Raghavan, S. (2012). South Sudan's president visits China during crisis. *The Washington Post*, 24 April. Retrieved March 1, 2016, from https://www.washingtonpost.com/world/africa/south-sudans-president-visits-china-during-crisis/2012/04/24/gIQAowXKfT_story.html

Raine, S. (2009). *China's African challenges*. London: Routledge.

Reczei, L. (1971). The political aims and experiences of the small socialist states. In A. Schou & A. O. Brundtland (Eds.), *Small states in international relations* (pp. 71–86). New York: Wiley-Interscience Division.

Regan, P. M. (1996). Conditions of successful third-party intervention in intra-state conflicts. *Journal of Conflict Resolution, 40*(2), 336–359.

Regan, P. M. (1998). Choosing to intervene: Outside interventions in internal conflicts. *The Journal of Politics, 60*(3), 754–779.

Regan, P. M. (2010). Interventions into civil wars: A retrospective survey with prospective ideas. *Civil Wars, 12*(4), 456–476.

Regilme Jr., S. S. F. (2014). The social science of human rights: The need for a 'second image reversed'? *Third World Quarterly, 35*(8), 1390–1405.

Reiter, D., & Stam, A. C. (2002). *Democracies at war*. New Jersey: Princeton University Press.

Reus-Smit, C. (2013). The concept of intervention. *Review of International Studies, 39*(5), 1057–1076.

Richardson, C. J. (2012). A responsible power? China and the UN peacekeeping regime. In M. Lanteigne & M. Hirono (Eds.), *China's evolving approach to peacekeeping* (pp. 44–56). London: Routledge.

Ritchie, J., & Spencer, L. (2002). Qualitative data analysis for applied policy research. In M. Huberman & M. B. Miles (Eds.), *The qualitative researcher's companion* (pp. 305–330). Thousand Oaks, CA: Sage.

Roberto, W. M., Closs, M. B., & Ronconi, G. B. A. (2013). The situation in Mali. *UFRGS Model United Nations Journal, 1*, 71–97.

Rose, G. (1998). Neoclassical realism and theories of foreign policy. *World Politics, 51*(1), 144–172.

Rose, A., & Chen, A. (2013). China to evacuate South Sudan oil workers to capital. *Reuters,* December 20. Retrieved December 20, 2013, from http://uk.reuters.com/article/2013/12/20/southsudan-unrest-china-idUKL3N0JZ24K20131220

Rosecrance, R. (2006). Power and international relations: The rise of China and its effects. *International Studies Perspectives, 7*(1), 31–35.

Rosenau, J. N. (1969). Intervention as a scientific concept. *Journal of Conflict Resolution, 13*(2), 149–171.

Roy, D. (2013). *Return of the dragon: Rising China and regional security.* New York: Columbia University Press.

Sarkees, M. R. (2014). Patterns of civil wars in the twenty-first century: The decline of civil war? In E. Newman & K. DeRouen Jr. (Eds.), *Routledge handbook of civil wars* (pp. 236–256). London: Routledge.

Schraeder, P. J. (1989). *Intervention in the 1980s: U.S. foreign policy in the third world.* Boulder: Lynne Rienner.

Schraeder, P. J. (1994). *United States foreign policy toward Africa: Incrementalism, crisis and change.* Cambridge: Cambridge University Press.

Schumann, P. (2010). International actors in Sudan: The politics of implementing comprehensive peace. In R. Furlong & B. Herrmann (Eds.), *Sudan – No easy ways ahead* (pp. 102–114). Berlin: Heinrich Böll Foundation.

Schwartz, B. I. (1968). The Chinese perception of the world order, past and present. In J. K. Fairbank (Ed.), *The Chinese world order: Traditional China's foreign relations* (pp. 276–288). Cambridge: Harvard University Press.

Schweller, R. L. (1999a). Realism and the present great power system: Growth and positional conflict over scarce resources. In E. B. Kapstein & M. Mastanduno (Eds.), *Unipolar politics: Realism and state strategies after the Cold War* (pp. 28–68). New York: Columbia University Press.

Schweller, R. L. (1999b). Managing the rise of great powers: History and theory. In A. I. Johnston & R. S. Ross (Eds.), *Engaging China: The management of an emerging power* (pp. 1–31). London: Routledge.

Schweller, R. L. (2011). Emerging powers in an age of disorder. *Global Governance, 17*(3), 285–297.

Scott, D. (2008). *China and the international system, 1840–1949: Power, presence, and perceptions in a century of humiliation.* New York: State University of New York Press.

Scott, P. (1985). The Sudan Peoples' liberation movement (SPLM) and liberation army (SPLA). *Review of African Political Economy, 33,* 69–82.

Seawright, J., & Gerring, J. (2008). Case selection techniques in case study research a menu of qualitative and quantitative options. *Political Research Quarterly, 61*(2), 294–308.

Shambaugh, D. (2000). China's military views the world: Ambivalent security. *International Security, 24*(3), 52–79.

Shambaugh, D. (2013). *China goes global: The partial power*. Oxford: Oxford University Press.

Shaw, S. (2013). Fallout in the Sahel: The geographic spread of conflict from Libya to Mali. *Canadian Foreign Policy Journal, 19*(2), 199–210.

Shichor, Y. (2009). Libya cautions China: Economics is no substitute to politics. *China Brief*, Vol. 9, No. 24, pp. 5–7. Retrieved May 7, 2015, from http://www.jamestown.org/programs/chinabrief/single/?tx_ttnews%5Btt_news%5D=35793#.VqCRr_l94dV

Shichor, Y. (2014). Respected and suspected: Middle Eastern perceptions of China's rise. In N. Horesh & E. Kavalski (Eds.), *Asian thought on China's changing international relations* (pp. 123–140). London: Palgrave Macmillan.

Shih, C., & Huang, C. (2014). *Harmonious intervention: China's quest for relational security*. Surrey: Ashgate Publishing, Ltd.

Shinn, D. H. (2006). The China factor in African ethics. *Policy Innovations, 21*, 1–6.

Shinn, D. (2013). China confronts terrorism in Africa. *China-US Focus*, 18 November. Retrieved September 3, 2018, from https://www.chinausfocus.com/peace-security/china-confronts-terrorism-in-africa

Shinn, D. H. (2013a). China's response to the Islamist threat in Mali. *China-US Focus*, 21 June. Retrieved February 3, 2016, from http://www.chinausfocus.com/peace-security/chinas-response-to-the-islamist-threat-in-mali/

Shinn, D. H. (2013b). China confronts terrorism in Africa. *China-US Focus*, 18 November. Retrieved February 3, 2016, from http://www.chinausfocus.com/peace-security/china-confronts-terrorism-in-africa/

Shinn, D. H. (2016). China's security policy in Africa and the Western Indian Ocean. *International Affairs Forum*. Retrieved May 16, 2016, from http://www.ia-forum.org/Content/ViewInternalDocument.cfm?ContentID=7925

Shinn, D. H., & Eisenman, J. (2012). *China and Africa: A century of engagement*. Philadelphia: University of Pennsylvania Press.

Simpfendorfer, B. (2015). The impact of the Arab revolutions on China's foreign policy. In K. Brown (Ed.), *The EU-China relationship: European perspectives* (pp. 201–212). London: Imperial College Press.

Smith-Hoehn, J. (2010). *Rebuilding the security sector in post-conflict societies: Perceptions from urban Liberia and Sierra Leone*. Muenster: LIT Verlag.

Snyder, R. S. (2005). Bridging the realist/constructivist divide: The case of the counterrevolution in Soviet foreign policy at the end of the Cold War. *Foreign Policy Analysis, 1*(1), 55–71.

Soto-Viruet, Y. (2012). The mineral industries of Mali and Niger. In *U.S geological survey yearbook 2010* (pp. 28.1–28.4). Retrieved September 3, from https://minerals.usgs.gov/minerals/pubs/country/2010/myb3-2010-ml-ng.pdf

St John, R. B. (2015). *Libya: Continuity and change*. London: Routledge.

Stein, J. G. (2010). From bipolar to unipolar order: System structure and conflict resolution. In U. Rabi (Ed.), *International intervention in local conflicts: Crisis management and conflict resolution since the Cold War* (pp. 3–18). London: IB Tauris.

Steiner, B. H. (2004). *Collective preventive diplomacy: A study in international conflict management.* New York: State University of New York Press.

Sterling-Folker, J. (1997). Realist environment, liberal process, and domestic-level variables. *International Studies Quarterly, 41*(1), 1–26.

Strange, S. (1975). What is economic power, and who has it? *International Journal, 30*(2), 207–224.

Strange, S. (1994). *States and markets.* London: Continuum.

Sun, Y. (2012). Syria: What China has learned from its Libya experience. *Asia Pacific Bulletin*, No. 12. Retrieved September 3, from https://www.eastwest-center.org/system/tdf/private/apb152_1.pdf?file=1&type=node&id=33315

Suzuki, C. (1968). China's relations with inner Asia: The Hsiung-nu, Tibet. In J. K. Fairbank (Ed.), *The Chinese world order: Traditional China's foreign relations* (pp. 180–197). Cambridge: Harvard University Press.

Suzuki, S. (2012). Why does China participate in intrusive peacekeeping? Understanding paternalistic Chinese discourse on development and intervention. In M. Lanteigne & M. Hirono (Eds.), *China's evolving approach to peacekeeping* (pp. 29 43) London: Routledge.

Swaine, M. D. (2015). Xi Jinping's address to the central conference on work relating to foreign affairs: Assessing and advancing major-power diplomacy with Chinese characteristics. *China Leadership Monitor, 46*(1), 1–19.

Taib, M. (2010). The mineral and oil industry of Libya. In *U.S geological survey, area reports – International – Africa and the Middle East: U.S geological survey minerals yearbook 2008* (Vol. III, pp. 25.1–25.6). U.S Government.

Taliaferro, J. W. (2004). *Balancing risks: Great power intervention in the periphery.* Ithaca, NY: Cornell University Press.

Taliaferro, J. W. (2006). State building for future wars: Neoclassical realism and the resource-extractive state. *Security Studies, 15*(3), 464–495.

Tardy, T., & Wyss, M. (2014). Introduction: Africa – The peacekeeping laboratory. In T. Tardy & M. Wyss (Eds.), *Peacekeeping in Africa: The evolving security architecture* (pp. 1–14). London: Routledge.

Taylor, I. (1998). China's foreign policy towards Africa in the 1990s. *The Journal of Modern African Studies, 36*(3), 443–460.

Taylor, I. (2000). The ambiguous commitment: The People's Republic of China and the anti-apartheid struggle in South Africa. *Journal of Contemporary African Studies, 18*(1), 91–106.

Taylor, I. (2007a). Governance in Africa and Sino-African relations: Contradictions or confluence? *Politics, 27*(3), 139–146.

Taylor, I. (2007b). *Unpacking China's resource diplomacy in Africa*. Working Paper, no. 18, Center on China's Transnational Relations, Hong Kong. Retrieved May 8, 2015, from http://www.cctr.ust.hk/materials/working_papers/WorkingPaper19_IanTaylor.pdf

Terhalle, M. (2015). *The transition of global order: Legitimacy and contestation*. London: Palgrave Macmillan.

Themnér, L. (2013). *UCDP/PRIO armed conflict dataset codebook*. Uppsala Conflict Data Program. Retrieved September 3, 2013, from http://www.pcr.uu.se/digitalAssets/124/124920_1codebook_ucdp_prio-armed-conflict-dataset-v4_2013.pdf

Thrall, L. (2015). *China's expanding African relations: Implications for US National Security*. RAND Corporation, California. Retrieved January 17, 2016, from http://www.rand.org/content/dam/rand/pubs/research_reports/RR900/RR905/RAND_RR905.pdf

Tillema, H. K. (1989). Foreign overt military intervention in the nuclear age. *Journal of Peace Research, 26*(2), 179–196.

UNCTAD. (2004). *The least developed countries report 2004*. Geneva: United Nations.

U.S. Energy Information Administration. (2015). *Country analysis brief: Libya*. U.S. Energy Information Administration, 19 November. Retrieved January 10, 2016, from https://www.eia.gov/beta/international/analysis_includes/countries_long/Libya/libya.pdf

Verba, S. (1971). Sequences and development. In L. Binder (Ed.), *Crises and sequences in political development*. New Jersey: Princeton University Press.

Verhoeven, H. (2014). Is Beijing's non-interference policy history? How Africa is changing China. *The Washington Quarterly, 37*(2), 55–70.

Virrall, M. (2012). Debunking the myth of China's soft power in China's use of foreign assistance from 1949 to the present. In H. Lai & Y. Lu (Eds.), *China's soft power and international relations* (pp. 138–189). London: Routledge.

Walker, B. (2012). China's uncomfortable diplomacy keeps South Sudan's oil flowing. *China Dialogue*, November 26. Retrieved May 25, 2015, from https://www.chinadialogue.net/article/show/single/en/5378-China-s-uncomfortable-diplomacy-keeps-South-Sudan-s-oil-flowing

Walt, S. M. (1985). Alliance formation and the balance of world power. *International Security, 9*(4), 3–43.

Walt, S. M. (1987). *The origins of alliance*. Ithaca, NY: Cornell University Press.

Walt, S. M. (1998). International relations: One world, many theories. *Foreign Policy*, (110), 29–46.

Waltz, K. N. (1979). *Theory of international politics*. New York: McGraw-Hill.

Waltz, K. N. (1986). Reflections on theory of international politics: A response to my critics. In R. Keohane (Ed.), *Neorealism and its critics* (pp. 322–345). New York: Columbia University Press.

Waltz, K. N. (1996). International politics is not foreign policy. *Security Studies, 6*(1), 54–57.

Wang, B. W. (2013). The Dragon brings peace? Why China became a major contributor to United Nations peacekeeping. *Stimson Center Spotlight*, 12 July. Retrieved July 24, 2015, from http://www.stimson.org/spotlight/the-dragon-bringspeace-why-china-became-a-major-contributor-to-united-nationspeacekeeping-/

Wang, H., & Rosenau, J. N. (2009). China and global governance. *Asian Perspective, 33*(3), 5–39.

Wang, X., & Lu, X. (2014). Investment in South Sudan: The opportunity and the challenge coexist. *People's Daily*, April 16. Retrieved July 24, 2015, from http://en.people.cn/102774/8599301.html

Wang, Y., & Yao, Y. (2003). Sources of China's economic. Growth 1952–1999: Incorporating human capital accumulation. *China Economic Review, 14*(1), 32–52.

Wang, Y. K. (2011). *Harmony and war: Confucian culture and Chinese power politics*. New York: Columbia University Press.

Weber, M., Owen, D. S., & Strong, T. B. (2004). *The vocation lectures*. Cambridge: Hackett Publishing.

Weiss, T. G. (2007). *Humanitarian intervention: Ideas in action*. Cambridge: Polity Press.

Wendt, A. (1992). Anarchy is what states make of it: The social construction of power politics. *International Organization, 46*(2), 391–425.

Wendt, A. (1999). *Social theory of international politics*. Cambridge: Cambridge University Press.

Whalley, J. (2011). *China's integration into the world economy*. New Jersey: World Scientific.

Wheeler, N. J. (2000). *Saving strangers: Humanitarian intervention in international society: Humanitarian intervention in international society*. Oxford: Oxford University Press.

Wickboldt, A., & Choucri, N. (2006). Profiles of states as fuzzy sets: Methodological refinement of lateral pressure theory. *International Interactions, 32*(2), 153–181.

Wicks, D. (2010). Deviant case analysis. In A. J. Mills, G. Durepos, & E. Wiebe (Eds.), *Encyclopedia of case study research* (pp. 289–291). California: Sage Publications.

Winfield, P. H. (1932). Intervention. In *Encyclopedia of the social sciences* (Vol. 8, pp. 236–238). New York: Macmillan.

Wing, S. D. (2016). French intervention in Mali: Strategic alliances, long-term regional presence? *Small Wars & Insurgencies, 27*(1), 59–80.

Wohlforth, W. C. (1993). *The elusive balance: Power and perceptions during the Cold War*. Ithaca, NY: Cornell University Press.

Wohlforth, W. C. (2009). Unipolarity, status competition, and great power war. *World Politics, 61*(01), 28–57.

Womack, B. (2006). *China and Vietnam: The politics of asymmetry*. Cambridge: Cambridge University Press.

Wu, X. (1998). China: Security practice for a modernizing and ascending power. In M. Alagappa (Ed.), *Asian security practice: Material and ideational influences* (pp. 115–156). Stanford: Stanford University Press.

Wu, Y. (2014). China's oil fears over South Sudan fighting. *BBC Chinese*, 8 January. Retrieved January 8, 2014, from http://www.bbc.co.uk/news/world-africa-25654155

Wuthnow, J. (2013). *Chinese diplomacy and the UN security council: Beyond the veto*. London: Routledge.

Yan, X. (2006). The rise of China and its power status. *The Chinese journal of international politics, 1*(1), 5–33.

Yang, J. (2009). The rise of China: Chinese perspectives. In K. J. Cooney & Y. Sato (Eds.), *The rise of China and international security: America and Asia respond* (pp. 13–37). London: Routledge.

Yao, F. (2011). War and Confucianism. *Asian Philosophy, 21*(2), 213–226.

Yin, R. K. (1994). *Case study research: Design and methods*. London: Sage Publication.

Yoon, M. Y. (1997). Explaining US intervention in third world internal wars, 1945–1989. *Journal of Conflict Resolution, 41*(4), 580–602.

Yu, G. T. (1977). China and the third world. *Asian Survey, 17*(11), 1036–1048.

Zafar, A. (2007). The growing relationship between China and sub-Saharan Africa: Macroeconomic, trade, investment, and aid links. *The World Bank Research Observer, 22*(1), 103–130.

Zakaria, F. (1992). Realism and domestic politics: A review essay. *International Security, 17*(1), 177–198.

Zakaria, F. (1998). *From wealth to power: The unusual origins of America's world role*. New Jersey: Princeton University Press.

Zakaria, F. (2008). *The post-American world*. New York: W.W. Norton.

Zan, S. Z. D. (2015). Economic impact of China's investments in Mali's construction sector on Mali. *Journal of International Relations and Foreign Policy, 3*(2), 27–33.

Zartman, W. I. (1976). Europe and Africa: Decolonization or dependency? *Foreign Affairs*, Vol. 54, No. 2, pp. 325–343.

Zeng, A. (2014). Strong foundations of friendship. *China Daily*, 7 May. Retrieved September 3, 2018, from http://usa.chinadaily.com.cn/opinion/2014-05/07/content_17489828_2.htm

Zhang, C. (2014). China-Zimbabwe relations: A model of China-Africa relations? *South African Institute of International Affairs*, Occasional Paper 205. Retrieved December 7, 2014, from http://www.saiia.org.za/occasional-papers/643-china-zimbabwe-relations-a-model-of-china-africa-relations/file

Zhang, J., & Wei, W. X. (2012). Managing political risks of Chinese contracted projects in Libya. *Project Management Journal, 43*(4), 42–51.

Zhang, Y., & Buzan, B. (2012). The tributary system as international society in theory and practice. *The Chinese Journal of International Politics, 5*, 3–36.

Zhao, S. (2015). Rethinking the Chinese world order: The imperial cycle and the rise of China. *Journal of Contemporary China, 24*(96), 961–982.

Zheng, B. (2005). China's "peaceful rise" to great-power status. *Foreign Affairs*, Vol. 84, No. 5, pp. 18–24.

Zhengyu, W., & Taylor, I. (2011). From refusal to engagement: Chinese contributions to peacekeeping in Africa. *Journal of Contemporary African Studies, 29*(2), 137–154.

Zhou, L. (2014). Chinese diplomats make exception to non-interference rule by meeting South Sudan opposition. *South China Morning Post*, 5 November. Retrieved November 5, 2014, from http://www.scmp.com/news/china/article/1632138/chinese-diplomats-make-exception-non-interference-rule-meeting-south

Zhu, X. (2012). Understanding China's growth: Past, present, and future. *Journal of Economic Perspectives, 26*(4), 103–124.

Zhu, Z. (2010). *China's new diplomacy: Rationale strategies and significance*. Surrey: Ashgate Publishing.

Zoellick, R. B. (2005). Whither China: From membership to responsibility? *NBR Analysis, 16*(4), 5.

Zoubir, Y. H., & White, G. (2015). *North African politics: Change and continuity*. London: Routledge.

Zweig, D. (2006). *Resource diplomacy' under hegemony: The sources of Sino-American competition in the 21st century?* Working Paper, no. 18, Center on China's Transnational Relations, Hong Kong. Retrieved May 8, 2015, from http://www.cctr.ust.hk/materials/working_papers/WorkingPaper18_DavidZweig.pdf

Index[1]

[1] Note: Page numbers followed by 'n' refer to notes.

O. Hodzi, *The End of China's Non-Intervention Policy in Africa*, Critical Studies of the Asia-Pacific,
https://doi.org/10.1007/978-3-319-97349-4

CPSIA information can be obtained
at www.ICGtesting.com
Printed in the USA
LVHW071646040420
652225LV00009B/73